A THEORY OF
PERCEPTION

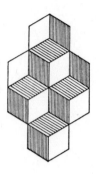

A THEORY OF

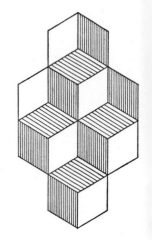

PRINCETON UNIVERSITY PRESS, 1971

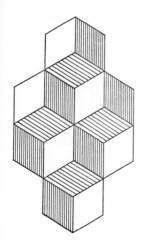

PERCEPTION

BY GEORGE PITCHER

Copyright © 1971 by Princeton University Press

ALL RIGHTS RESERVED

ISBN 0-691-97171-3

LC Card 73-120759

This book has been composed in Linotype Caledonia

Printed in the United States of America

by Princeton University Press

Princeton, New Jersey

I dedicate this book
to the memory of
my mother and father

Preface

I OFFER in these pages a philosophical theory of sense perception. Its fundamental idea is not new: for example, it lies at the heart also of D. M. Armstrong's philosophical theory and James G. Taylor's psychological one.[1] But I hope I have developed the idea along novel lines and defended the resulting theory in some new ways.

My debts to others, for a variety of benefits, are enormous. The first draft of the book was written during a year's leave from teaching, in 1965-1966, made possible by a grant from the John Simon Guggenheim Memorial Foundation and by generous support from Princeton University. My friends Edward Cone, Terry Penner, and Peter Strawson read all, or large portions, of the manuscript and made many helpful comments. The work has been improved immeasurably by the painstaking and acute criticism that Gilbert Harman and Richard Rorty lavished on it; I only wish there were more in the finished product that they could agree with. A lot of whatever is good in the following pages stems from discussions with my students in graduate seminars at Princeton and New York University. I do not exaggerate when I say that the book could not have been completed without the help of a certain la Bell, dame sans merci. Once again, I must acknowledge with thanks the superlative assistance of Mrs. Helen Wright who faultlessly typed the manuscript. Finally, to my colleagues at Princeton, I am grateful beyond the ability of words to say for their friendship and encouragement through the years.

G. P.

[1] D. M. Armstrong, *Perception and the Physical World* (London: Routledge & Kegan Paul; New York: The Humanities Press, 1961), 196 pp. See also the same author's more recent *A Materialist Theory of the Mind* (London: Routledge & Kegan Paul; New York: The Humanities Press, 1968), 372 pp. James G. Taylor, *The Behavioral Basis of Perception* (New Haven and London: Yale University Press, 1962), 379 pp.

Contents

Some Page References

A THEORY OF
PERCEPTION

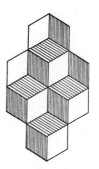

I

Sense-data and How to Avoid Them

I mean to present and defend a theory of sense perception—not, of course, a physiological theory or a psychological one, but a philosophical theory of sense perception. At the end of this opening chapter, I shall say something about what I take a theory of that kind to be. My remarks on this topic will be brief and dogmatic, for two reasons. First, an adequate discussion of it would embroil us in huge issues—for example, about the nature of philosophy: and I do not want to engage in metaphilosophical inquiries, but only in a philosophical one. And second, it should be fairly evident, from what I go on to do, what sort of thing I take a philosophical theory of perception to be. Nevertheless, so that the reader may know in a general way what he may expect, I shall set down my general position on the subject.

Partly in order to illustrate my metaphilosophical remarks, but mainly because I think this particular act of destruction is eminently worth doing, I shall devote the major part of this chapter to an attack on sense-datum theories. I take them to be seductive representatives of all those theories that stand in fundamental opposition to the direct realist theory that I shall be offering.

．．．．．

I would wish to argue that no matter what they may conceive themselves to be doing, most philosophers who write about sense perception actually present philosophical *theories* of perception. There can be little doubt that many of these philosophers do not think of themselves as propounding any sort of theory. Some sense-datum philosophers, for example, unquestioningly assume that we all simply *find*, or *come across*, sense-data whenever we perceive anything—that is, all the time. If called upon to justify their assumption, they would claim that the immediate objects of awareness in sense perception *obviously* have the (metaphysical) status of being sense-data. I consider this claim to be false. The type of error involved here is a common one; for what is in fact a debatable thesis or theory often becomes so deeply entrenched in a person's way of thinking, that he is not conscious of subscribing to it *as* a thesis or theory at all. It is one of his "absolute presuppositions," and either he is totally unaware of it, or, if it should come up for discussion, it strikes him as self-evident. In both cases, he looks at the world from its special point of view, and what he observes therefore naturally bears the stamp of its truth. Given that philosophy preeminently concerns itself with what are sometimes called "ultimate issues," one is not surprised to find that its practitioners are guilty of this familiar error more often and more evidently than most men are, despite the fact that they, more than others, ought really to be on their guard against it. The theory of sense-data has certainly been one of the most insidiously effective in finding its way quietly into the center of philosophers' "conceptual schemes." Hume's case, above all, attests eloquently to the extraordinary self-preservatory power of the sense-datum theory to lie silent and unobserved at the heart of even a great philosopher's view of things; because although Hume had an unsurpassed genius for uncovering his own absolute presuppositions, this one remained forever invisible to him. But there, nevertheless, it undeniably was, from the word 'go.' In the very first sentence of the *Treatise of Human Nature*, Hume informs us that "all the perceptions of the human mind resolve themselves into two distinct kinds, which I shall call *impressions* and *ideas*,"[1] and he adds at once that the only difference between them is that impressions are more forceful and lively than ideas. Impressions are what we are always and alone aware of in ordinary sense perception; they are "internal and perishing existences, *and appear as such*"[2] and are, it becomes perfectly clear, nothing more nor less than sense-data.[3] As the passage cited in the last sentence indicates, none of this presents itself to Hume in the aspect of a *theory*, nor as being in any way controversial; no argument is offered, for none is thought to be needed.[4] (Nothing that Hume does in the section "Of scepticism with regard to the senses" in the *Treatise* can be understood unless one realizes that this is so.) Hume confidently thinks of himself as being faced with what are ob-

---

[1] Hume, *A Treatise of Human Nature*, Bk. I, Part I, sect. 1, p. 1 of the Selby-Bigge edition.

[2] *Ibid.*, Bk. I, Part IV, sect. 2, p. 194 of the Selby-Bigge edition. My italics.

[3] Hume differs from most sense-datum theorists on one point: although he thinks that impressions exist only when they are being perceived, he thinks this is not a necessary, but only a contingent, truth. (See *A Treatise of Human Nature*, Bk. I, Part IV, sect. 2, pp. 206-11 of the Selby-Bigge edition.) Rather, it is *one* strain in Hume's thought; for, as John W. Cook has cogently argued, Hume also holds the conflicting—and orthodox—view that it is not a contingent, but a *necessary*, truth. (See Cook, "Hume's Scepticism with Regard to the Senses," *American Philosophical Quarterly*, 5 [1968], 1-17.)

[4] This is not quite accurate: for Hume does, in one or two perfunctory passages (e.g., in a short paragraph in *An Inquiry Concerning Human Understanding*, sect. XII, Part I), allude to philosophical arguments which show that

> nothing can ever be present to the mind but an image or perception, and that the senses are only the inlets through which these images are conveyed, without being able to produce any immediate intercourse between the mind and the object. (*Ibid.*)

But these arguments are clearly regarded by Hume as superfluous props to a truth that does not need any such support.

viously sense-data whenever he uses his senses: he does
not think of doubting that he just *finds* them, or, as he
might have put it, that he just *stumbles* over them, in all his
sense-experience.

What seems painfully evident to me, on the contrary, is
that sense-data do not have the status that Hume accords
them; I do not believe that the (direct) objects of awareness in all sense perception simply *present* themselves to us
in the shape of sense-data. Hume acknowledges that "almost all mankind, and even philosophers themselves, for
the greatest part of their lives . . . suppose, that the very
being, which is intimately present to the mind, is the real
body or material existence."[5] However, just *because* he
takes it as obvious that it is only impressions (i.e., sense-
data) that we are ever directly presented with in sense
perception, Hume naturally cannot see this belief of "almost all mankind" right side up—that is, as the belief that
in normal sense perception what are "intimately present to
the mind" are independently existing physical things
(such as matchboxes, clouds, and whatnot). Instead, he
sees it upside down, that is, as the belief that one's impressions (sense-data)—which everyone, according to
Hume, recognizes as "internal and perishing existences"—
are identical with physical things, that is, with things that
everyone thinks have both a continued existence (i.e., an
existence that goes on even when one is not perceiving
them) and an existence that is "distinct from the mind and
perception."[6] So construed, the common belief is, of course,
incoherent, and thus calls not for analysis, much less justification, but for causal explanation. And this is exactly what
Hume proceeds to give it. But surely Hume *is* wearing inverting spectacles: surely, "almost all mankind, and even
philosophers themselves, for the greatest part of their lives"
are not confused in the way Hume makes out. They simply
think that they perceive (and directly, too, if that adds
anything) things and events in the physical world; and

[5] *Treatise*, Bk. I, Part IV, sect. 2, p. 206 of the Selby-Bigge edition.
[6] *Ibid.*, p. 188 of the Selby-Bigge edition.

they quite definitely do not think that they are always being confronted with something else, namely, with sense-data. Sense-data, in short, are theoretical entities (or states of awareness of sense-data are theoretical states) posited by certain philosophers; they are not what everyone must recognize to be observables.

There are, or have been, other sense-datum philosophers who avoid the error of the first group (to which Hume belongs), but fall instead into another. These theorists realize that the things we are immediately aware of in sense experience do not carry the unmistakable stamp of being sense-data on their faces. They hold, rather, that the existence of sense-data is something that has to be argued for —and in this they are surely correct; but then they go on to assert, falsely in my opinion, that the existence of sense-data is subject to deductive proof. These philosophers, of whom Berkeley is a good example, are only slightly more emancipated from the relevant "absolute presupposition" than the members of the first group. They argue in the following way: starting with the existence of a certain perceptual phenomenon or perceptual fact, they try to show that this phenomenon or fact *entails* the existence of sense-data. But I am bound to view this sort of attempt as doomed to failure. I shall try to show later that these arguments, construed as deductive demonstrations, are one and all invalid. What these philosophers are actually doing in their arguments is positing sense-data as theoretical entities (or the awareness of sense-data as theoretical states of the perceiver), and thus, in effect, claiming that the sense-datum theory offers the best account of the particular phenomenon or fact in question. They mistake what is actually an inference to the (alleged) best theory[7] for a purely deductive inference, and they do this because no alternative to their sense-datum theory presents itself to them as even a possibility.

So both groups of sense-datum philosophers are, in a

[7] See G. Harman, "The Inference to the Best Explanation," *The Philosophical Review*, 74 (1965), 88-95.

way, partially blinded by their central notion—only they
are blinded at different levels. The first group, who are
under the illusion that they simply find sense-data labeled
as such, so to speak, on the phenomenal surface of things,
are unable to see any alternative to viewing what they are
aware of in sense perception (or at any rate *directly*
aware of in sense perception) as being sense-data. The second group, on the other hand, realize that in order to explain the facts of perception, theoretical entities (states, or
whatever) must be posited. But they are unable to see any
alternative to attributing certain specific features to what
is thus posited—just those features, namely, that sense-
data (awareness of sense-data, or whatever) are thought to
have. This group of sense-datum philosophers find sense-
data not, as it were, on the surface of things (as the first
group do) but in the theoretical depths. It is now, however, generally recognized, even by sense-datum philosophers themselves, that any account of perception in terms
of sense-data is really a philosophical *theory* of perception
and can only be one among a number of competitors for
the job.

A caveat before proceeding. I have been talking as if (a)
the distinction between theoretical terms (e.g., the names
of theoretical states or entities) and observational terms is
clear and clear-cut, and as if (b) the term 'sense-datum' is
(clearly) one of the former. Proposition (a) is notoriously
false, and I hereby repudiate it, but I do subscribe to (b),
especially if the word 'clearly' is deleted. I undertake no
proof of (b), and I am not absolutely sure that I could provide one if I tried. Nevertheless, along with all modern
sense-datum philosophers known to me, I shall continue
to speak of sense-datum *theories*, as if (b) were true, because it will be very convenient to do so. For our purposes,
no serious consequences will ensue from this practice should
(b) turn out to be false, as long as it is granted—and I
think it must be granted—that one has the viable option
of *not* employing the concept of a sense-datum in his account of the nature of sense perception. There will be no

such consequences because among the many reasons for rejecting sense-datum *theories* of perception there are some formidable ones that count equally against views of perception in which the term 'sense-datum' figures as an observational, rather than as a theoretical, term. So in the end it doesn't really matter whether sense-data are treated as theoretical entities (or the awareness of sense-data are treated as theoretical states of perceivers)—as I shall treat them—or whether they are treated as observables.[8]

I want now to state and then criticize the most important of the traditional, allegedly deductive, proofs for the existence of sense-data. I regard this as worth doing because I consider sense-datum theories, despite the fact that they are currently out of fashion, to be extremely plausible, psychologically persuasive, and therefore formidable alternatives to the theory I wish to defend. Since the traditional arguments for the existence of sense-data are the primary sources of strength for these theories, it would be foolish to ignore them; for then the forces that make these arguments, and hence sense-datum theories attractive might well continue to work on our thinking, clouding our vision and preventing us from seeing things aright.

First, let us ask: what sorts of things are sense-data alleged to be? In answering this question, I shall be satisfied to give merely a rough sketch of them, rather than a detailed portrait. This will be enough for my purposes, and will, I hope, involve no unfairness to sense-data, since my discussion of them will deal only with their highly generic characteristics.

Whatever disagreements there may be amongst different sense-datum philosophers as to the nature or status of

---

[8] An additional reason for thinking that it is a mistake to regard sense-data as observables is that, as sense-datum philosophers themselves usually insist, we can be said to observe things like tables and chair, not things like sense-data: on the contrary, we are said to *have* sense-data. On the general problems connected with the distinction between theoretical and observational terms, see the lucid discussion in Peter Achinstein's *Concepts of Science: a Philosophical Analysis* (Baltimore: The Johns Hopkins Press, 1968), esp. Chapters 5 and 6.

sense-data, most of them would, I think, be willing to assert some form or other of the following unclear principle: that the term 'sense-datum' refers to what is "immediately" or "directly" given or presented to someone's consciousness in all sense experience; that is, to what is immediately and directly before one's consciousness in sense perception (whether "veridical" or not) when the work of the mind or the imagination, which usually and automatically performs an act of interpretation (or inference, or "taking for granted") is stripped away. Practically all sense-datum theorists hold that the awareness of a sense-datum (or of sense-data), although an essential element, is not the only element in normal perceptual consciousness; but they disagree about what else is involved.[9] I shall ignore these internal disputes, since they are not relevant to my concerns.

This first point of general agreement among sense-datum philosophers (granted that we understand it) may be harmless enough; but there is a second, and far more important, one that is certainly the source of whatever evil the notion of sense-data has inflicted on the philosophical world. This is the idea that sense-data are ontologically distinct from physical objects, and even from the surfaces of physical objects, where 'physical object' is construed in the realists' sense, namely, as designating an extended object whose existence is not dependent on its being perceived. Since only some physical existents are objects and only some have surfaces, however, the claim might better be generalized as follows: no sense-datum is identical with anything in the physical world.[10] I consider this non-identity thesis

[9] There is a group of philosophers who dispute the claim of sense-datum theorists that awareness of a sense-datum is a distinguishable component of ordinary perceptual consciousness, and who insist, instead, that what is directly presented in ordinary sense perception are ostensible physical objects, or percepts. (See R. Firth, "Sense-Data and the Percept Theory," *Mind*, 58 [1949], 434-465, and 59 [1950], 35-56.) For my stance towards percepts, as contrasted with sense-data, see p. 11f. below.

[10] I mean to exclude the identity only of the "contents" of a sense-datum with that which it purports to be a sense-datum *of* (e.g., the identity of a sense-datum of a green square with any real green

to be absolutely essential to any view that can properly be called a sense-datum theory: it is, at any rate, essential to any sense-datum theory that I should ever wish to quarrel with.[11]

Thirdly, there is also a consensus among sense-datum theorists that each sense-datum is "private" to the individual who has, or experiences, it, in that it exists only when, and for as long as, the perceiver is aware of it—its *esse* is *percipi*[12]—and in that no two persons could possibly experience the same (i.e., numerically the same) sense-datum. It is the conception of a sense-datum embodied in the foregoing three theses that I shall be concerned to criticize.

Before proceeding, I want to make it quite clear that although I shall be explicitly impugning sense-datum theories only, my real target is actually a wider range of theories. I shall attack sense-datum theories only because they are outstanding examples of a more general type of theory that I consider to be disastrously mistaken—I mean any theory maintaining that, in ordinary sense perception, the immediate or direct object of awareness is always something other than the physical object (event, state of affairs,

---

square). Thus I am not excluding the identity of a sense-datum (or of the having of a sense-datum) with a brain state of the perceiver.

[11] G. E. Moore was the most famous admitted sense-datum theorist to insist that certain sense-data might conceivably be identical with the surfaces of physical objects; he was even "strongly inclined to believe" that some of them are. But he was equally strongly inclined to think, along with practically all other sense-datum theorists, that no sense-datum could possible be identical with the surface of any physical object. (See *The Philosophy of G. E. Moore*, ed. by P. A. Schilpp [New York: Tudor Publishing Company, 1942; second edition, 1952], pp. 653-60.) In one of his last statements, in fact, Moore candidly confessed that he thought he was mistaken in thinking that a visual sense-datum of an opaque object might possibly be identical with part of the object's surface. ("Visual Sense-Data," in C. A. Mace [ed.], *British Philosophy in the Mid-Century* [London: George Allen and Unwin Ltd., 1957], p. 210.)

[12] Again, there are dissenting sense-datum theorists: Bertrand Russell once held that *possible* sense-data, at least, exist without being perceived. See his "The Relation of Sense-Data to Physics" in *Mysticism and Logic and Other Essays* (New York, Bombay, Calcutta, Madras: Longmans, Green & Co., 1918).

or whatever) that is perceived. I shall focus my criticism of sense-datum theories on just those elements of them that they share with percept theories, theories that employ the notion of "sensory appearances," and the like. My real enemy, in short, is not sense-datum theories *per se*, but any theory at all that stands in opposition to direct realism.

One more preliminary matter: there is a well-known view about sense-data that I want to place safely aside. I mean the view, once defended by Professor Ayer, that it is a mistake to think there is any such thing as a sense-datum *theory*—i.e., a body of doctrine that makes claims about the way things are, that makes claims to truth—since the fact is that there is only a recommended sense-datum *terminology*, or sense-datum *language*, in which one can allegedly express, in a philosophically advantageous way, all the perceptual propositions that can be expressed in ordinary language.[13] Thus, for example, instead of saying that a person sees an apple which appears to him to be purple, one can describe the very same fact by saying that the person is sensing a sense-datum which really is purple and which belongs to the apple.[14] Since my main concern in this chapter is to oppose a conception of sense-data that is an integral part of a substantive *theory* of perception, I shall not take time to discuss Ayer's quite different conception at any length. (The fact that if Ayer's view is correct, then the target of my criticism does not really exist, is of minor importance. Most sense-datum philosophers have certainly thought of themselves as championing the notion of a sense-datum that I am gunning for; and even if Ayer were right, it still remains true that in philosophy, mere spectres that are widely believed in are often the creatures that most need to be destroyed). But suppose Ayer were right. Then I would contend, although I will not try here to justify the contention, that it is both unnecessary and dangerous to introduce this technical terminology (the 'sense-datum' ter-

[13] See A. J. Ayer, *The Foundations of Empirical Knowledge* (London: Macmillan & Co. Ltd., 1953), especially Chapter 1.
[14] See *ibid.*, p. 58.

minology): unnecessary, because it is admitted that, for the purpose of discussing perception philosophically, we can already describe in ordinary language all the perceptual facts we need to be able to describe;[15] and dangerous, because despite the alleged metaphysical and epistemological neutrality of the sense-datum language, the introduction of the noun 'sense-datum' inevitably seduces the philosopher into thinking that the term refers to a special kind of object of direct awareness—into thinking of sense-data, that is, in accordance with the conception of them that I shall presently be attacking.[16] That Ayer himself fell into this trap, and indeed into the even worse one of thinking that *only* sense-data really exist (as far as the "material world" goes, at least), is persuasively argued by J. L. Austin in *Sense and Sensibilia*.[17]

I move now to the arguments that have been thought to prove—deductively—that sense-data must exist, and that they are indeed the sole objects of direct awareness in all sense perception. There are several such arguments, but I shall consider only four that I take to be the most important ones. I have arranged them in an order of increasing persuasiveness.

A. THE ARGUMENT FROM HALLUCINATIONS

The argument:

(a) When a person has a hallucination, he is directly aware of some "sensuous manifold," for it seems to him as if he were perceiving something.

(b) But what he is thus aware of is not objective, i.e., is not in the physical world.[18]

---

[15] See *ibid.*, p. 25f.

[16] For a cogent critique of the "alternative language thesis," see R. J. Hirst, *The Problems of Perception* (London: George Allen and Unwin Ltd.; New York: The Macmillan Company, 1959), pp. 111-21.

[17] Oxford, at the Clarendon Press, 1962. See esp. p. 106f.

[18] Here, and throughout this chapter, I allow the propounders of the arguments to equate the objective with the physical (or spatial). This ignores the possibility that there may be objective existents (i.e., existents whose existence is independent of any mind) that are non-

(c) Therefore, what he is directly aware of must be nothing but a sense-datum.

(d) But what one is directly aware of in normal sense experience is qualitatively indistinguishable from what one is directly aware of in hallucinatory experiences.

Conclusion: therefore, even in normal sense experience one must always be directly aware of nothing but sense-data.

Lest the conclusion of the argument seem too outrageous to be believed, I hasten to say that the sense-datum theorist does not mean to imply by it that one cannot *also* be said to be aware of (to see, hear, etc.) things in the physical world in sense experience. He insists only that this is true in a different sense of 'aware' (and of 'see,' 'hear,' etc.). He insists that we are *directly* aware of (we *directly* see, hear, etc.) nothing but sense-data, and that we are only *indirectly* aware of (we *indirectly* see, hear, etc.) things in the physical world, presumably as the result of making an inference from the "directly presented" sense-data, or as the result of "interpreting" them, or something of the sort.[19]

In order to evaluate the argument from hallucinations, we need to know what is involved in having a hallucination. Despite the fact that some philosophers have lumped them all together, it is reasonably obvious that hallucinations are altogether different from delusions, which are not essentially perceptual phenomena at all,[20] and from illu-

---

spatial: some philosophers, for example, hold that sounds have this special sort of being. Ignoring such possibilities renders all four arguments of the present chapter strictly invalid; but I shall not press the point since (a) I regard these "third possibilities" as implausible, (b) they are irrelevant to the particular criticisms I want to make of the arguments, and (c) it greatly simplifies the discussion to quietly ignore them.

[19] For a criticism of the sense-datum theorists' use of the distinction between direct and indirect perception, see Austin, *Sense and Sensibilia*, pp. 14-19; and for an annihilating attack on their alleged distinction between two senses of perceptual verbs, see *ibid.*, Chap. IX.

[20] See *ibid.*, p. 23.

sions, such as the Mueller-Lyer illusion and the moon illusion.[21] There are certain kinds of aberrant experiences that everyone would agree are hallucinatory: for example, Macbeth's "seeing" a dagger, the drunk's "seeing" pink rats, and a psychotic's "hearing" voices revile him in obscene terms. Many of the things "seen" or "heard" by people who are senile or who have certain kinds of brain tumors or lesions, and by epileptics when suffering seizures, are also clearly classifiable as hallucinations. Let us call these the *central cases* of hallucinations. They seem to be characterized by the following: (i) the experience is idiosyncratic, unlike illusions; (ii) the person's powers of judgment or discrimination are, at least temporarily, more or less seriously deficient; and (iii) there is nothing in the environment answering to what he claims to see (hear, feel, etc.), or, in case he knows that he is suffering a hallucination, to what he claims to "see" ("hear," "feel," etc.).

The central cases form a reasonably homogeneous group; but the tidiness of this situation is marred by the existence of certain phenomena which one is strongly tempted to call hallucinatory, and which have been widely so called, but which lack one or more of the three characteristic features of the central cases. I am thinking especially of two things: first, the effects on perception of such drugs as mescal, lysergic acid, and adrenochrome, and second, the effects on perception of radical sensory deprivation. If a person is injected with a sufficient amount of adrenochrome, for example, things look quite startlingly different to him: a portrait looks plastic, alive, three-dimensional; familiar buildings look sharp and unfamiliar. In addition, visual patterns are seen with the eyes closed.[22] Similarly, after prolonged periods (e.g., six days) of isolation, with sensory deprivation, subjects find the room to be undulating and

[21] See *ibid.*, p. 23f. I shall discuss illusions in the third argument, below.

[22] See A. Hoffer, H. Osmond, and J. Smythies, "Some Psychological Effects of Adrenochrome," reprinted in D. C. Beardslee and M. Wertheimer (eds.), *Readings in Perception* (Princeton: D. van Nostrand Company, Inc., 1958), pp. 37-42.

swirling, other people appear to grow tall and then short, straight edges look curved, objects seem to glitter (due to exaggerated color and brightness contrast).[23] In many of these experiences, then, the subject sees real objects, so that feature (iii) of the central cases (above) seems to be missing. It is not clear to me whether one ought to say that since feature (iii) is missing, the experiences are not hallucinations at all, but rather merely illusions;[24] or whether to say that despite the fact that feature (iii) is missing, the experiences are still classifiable as hallucinations (with an appeal, perhaps, to the notion of family resemblance); or whether to say, finally, that feature (iii) *is* present—since although the drugged subject sees real enough objects, the qualities and movements that he claims to see (or "see") do not exist—and therefore the experiences in question are straightforwardly hallucinatory.

The phenomena associated with drugs such as mescal and with sensory deprivation also give rise to some doubts about feature (ii) of the central cases—namely, that the subject's powers of judgment or discrimination are more or less seriously deficient. There is, to be sure, adequate evidence that in certain instances the subject's powers of judgment and general mental competencies are fairly seriously impaired; but where mescal has been administered, there is room for dispute.[25]

For our purposes, fortunately, there seems to be no pressing need to settle these issues: for the argument from hallucinations does not in the least have to base itself on the *whole* class of hallucinations. It can perfectly well confine itself to what I have dubbed the central cases of hallucinations, without losing whatever cogency it has. So let us allow it to do this, and let us see, now, how great this cogency actually is.

[23] W. Heron, B. K. Doane, and T. H. Scott, "Visual Disturbances after Prolonged Perceptual Isolation," in Beardslee and Wertheimer (eds.), *op. cit.*, pp. 328-34.

[24] Hirst takes this line. See his *The Problems of Perception*, p. 43.

[25] See J. R. Smythies, "A Note on Mr. Hirst's Recent Paper," *Mind*, 63 (1954), 388-89, and R. J. Hirst, *The Problems of Perception*, p. 43f.

In thinking about hallucinations, we can be drawn in opposite directions. We might suppose that the (visually) hallucinated person *must* see something, for otherwise he would not act and speak as he does; and yet since there is nothing like what he describes to be seen where he is looking, we think he *cannot* see anything there. The difficulty is easily resolved, apparently: we say that he "sees" or that he *is seeing* something (for example, pink rats), but that he does not see any pink rats or that he sees nothing. But is it necessarily true, as premiss (a) suggests, that a visually hallucinated man must at least be seeing or "see" something? Well, that depends, naturally, on what it means to say that someone is seeing, or "sees," something. If it means merely that the hallucinator *thinks* he sees something (in those cases where he is "taken in" by the hallucination), or that he has some inclination to think that he sees something although he knows full well that it really is not there to be seen (in those cases where he isn't "taken in")—let us call this sense 1 of 'to be seeing' or 'to "see"'— then it can hardly be denied that a hallucinator always "sees" something. But this cannot be the sense of 'to be seeing' or 'to "see"' intended in the argument, for if it were, the argument would collapse. The reason for this is that a person's "seeing" something in sense 1 is perfectly compatible with his seeing nothing but what is really there to be seen and (to consider just the case where he is "taken in") mistakenly thinking, in his drunken stupor, or whatever, that it is pink rats. He might, for example, see the (real) pattern on the coverlet or the wallpaper and, since his powers of discrimination are not up to snuff, erroneously take it to be a multitude of rats. But then premiss (b) becomes false, and the door through which sense-data were supposed to enter is thus blocked.

So a defender of the argument from hallucinations must spurn sense 1 of 'to be seeing' or 'to "see"'. No doubt he would argue that the beliefs, or inclinations to believe, of sense 1 need some further explanation. "Why," he might ask, "does the hallucinator have his strange beliefs about

pink rats?" And he is ready with an answer: because the
drunkard has, spread out before his consciousness, a private pink-rats-ish visual presentation—i.e., a pink-rats-ish
visual sense-datum.

This account of hallucinatory experience is entirely plausible, so let us accept it. Let us, in fact, grant all three premisses (a)-(c). What has to be noted now is that even after
all of this is conceded, it is still possible to hold that sense-
data are not involved in *normal* sense perception. The hallucinator's awareness of sense-data could plausibly be
viewed as a pathological condition brought about by the
morbid state of his central nervous system—and therefore
as one that doubtless does not obtain when the central nervous system is normal, as in standard cases of sense perception.

Enter now premiss (d). I think this proposition is extremely dubious. There is literally no reason to think that
all, or even many, objects of hallucinatory experiences
are "qualitatively indistinguishable" from the objects of
ordinary sense experience. The fact that hallucinators are
sometimes terrified by the pink rats or snakes that they
"see" proves nothing, for in those cases, the person's
powers of judgment are seriously deficient: he might mistake almost anything for rats or snakes. And where the hallucinator's mental faculties are not grossly impaired, he is
well aware that what he "sees" is quite different from the
sort of thing he usually sees.

But actually it is not important whether premiss (d) is
true or false; for even if it be granted, along with premisses
(a)-(c), the conclusion of the argument does not follow.
Even if the objects "seen" in hallucinations were "qualitatively indistinguishable" from the objects seen in ordinary
sense experience, and even if in hallucinations one were
always aware of nothing but sense-data, it might still be
the case that in ordinary sense experience one is aware
(directly, too) not of sense-data, but of real things and
events. To be sure, if there were some characteristic that
sense-data wore on their faces marking them unmistakably

for what they are, as Hume evidently thought, then the argument would indeed be valid; for then, in virtue of premisses (c) and (d), what we are directly aware of in normal sense experience must have this patent characteristic and hence be sense-data—for otherwise it presumably would not be "qualitatively indistinguishable" from what we are directly aware of in hallucinatory experiences, namely, by premiss (c), sense-data. But then the argument, although valid, would be entirely otiose; the truth of its conclusion would be obvious and would stand in no need of proof.

The argument is not, however, in this way trivially valid, since sense-data do not happen to have any such self-identifying characteristic as Hume envisaged. But then it ought to be at least possible for the relation of being "qualitatively indistinguishable" to hold between the experience of having a hallucination, which we may grant consists of nothing but the awareness of sense-data, and the experience of being directly aware of things and events in the real world—and normal sense experience might very well be of this kind. Thus even if we grant all the premisses of the argument, it is still an open possibility that in ordinary sense experience one is directly confronted not by sense-data, but by things in the physical world.[26] And so the argument is simply invalid.[27] (To be sure, if another premiss were added to the effect that the only way of telling whether one is having a hallucination or having normal sense experiences is by noticing the "quality" of what one is aware of, then it would follow that one could never tell whether he was aware of sense-data or whether he was perhaps aware of something altogether different, since he could never tell whether he was having a hallucination [in which case he would be directly aware of sense-data] or whether he was having a normal sense experience [in which case he might be directly aware of physical

[26] See Austin, *Sense and Sensibilia*, p. 52.

[27] For a further comment on the argument, see footnote 46, p. 57 below.

things]. But that is another, and complicated, matter over which we fortunately need not linger; for we are concerned only with arguments that try to prove that in normal sense experience, we *must* be directly aware of sense-data.)

B.   The Argument from Differential Certainty[28]

The argument:

(We are to imagine that the speaker in the argument, a "normal percipient," is seated in a well-lighted room before a table on which there is nothing but a ripe red tomato. He has no knowledge of what sort of thing is on the table other than what he can get from looking at it.)

(a) It is not certain that I see, or that I am, in a visual mode, directly aware of, a (real) tomato, for I could be having a hallucination, I might be the victim of an illusion, someone could have placed a wax object there to deceive me, or any number of other possibilities that exclude my seeing a (real) tomato might be actualized.

(b) It is certain that I am, in a visual mode, directly aware of something red and with a tomato-ish shape.

(c) Therefore, the red tomato-shaped somewhat that I certainly am, in a visual mode, directly aware of cannot be identical with a tomato (if, indeed, there is one). It must be a sense-datum.[29]

Conclusion:

Since the same sort of argument can be applied in any visual situation, I must always, in visual sense perception, be directly aware of nothing but sense-data. (Parallel arguments can be constructed for the senses other than vision.)

.   .   .   .   .

In this argument, another, and tremendously important,

[28] This title is borrowed from Hirst, *The Problems of Perception*, p. 32.

[29] I here assume that the field of visual sense-data can have, and normally does have, three spatial dimensions. Sense-datum theorists who dispute that assumption can easily construct a slightly different version of this same argument.

role of sense-data emerges. Here they are being posited not to explain perceptual phenomena such as illusions or hallucinations, but rather to provide nothing less than solid foundations for the theoretical edifice of human empirical knowledge. They do this by being the (alleged) objects of infallible knowledge. I said that sense-data have been characterized as the objects of direct awareness and that the special way that we perceive sense-data has been characterized as *direct* perception. But these notions are scarcely intelligible apart from the idea of incorrigibility; and many sense-datum theorists have doubtless thought of sense-data, and of our mode of awareness of them, primarily in terms of incorrigibility, rather than in terms of directness.[30]

We need spend no time at all criticizing the principles implicit in steps (a) and (b) of the argument, for the job has already been done by numerous others, perhaps most forcefully by J. L. Austin in *Sense and Sensibilia*, pp. 110-15, and in the section called "Sureness and Certainty" in his article "Other Minds."[31] The most important principle lying behind the two premisses is this: empirical statements can be divided into the two classes of those which are certain and those which are not certain, *simply by examining them*, as it were—i.e., simply by understanding what sort of claim they make about the way things are. Into the "intrinsically not certain"-pile go such statements as scientific hypotheses, generalizations, and, what is more relevant here, even simple categorical statements about things in front of one's nose (e.g., "There is a tomato on the table" or "The tomato is red"). There is no universal agreement

[30] See, for example, Ayer, *The Foundations of Empirical Knowledge*, p. 23.

[31] Reprinted in A. Flew (ed.), *Logic and Language* (Oxford: Basil Blackwell, 1955), pp. 123-58. The cited section is found in pp. 135-42. See also sect. III of Anthony Quinton's article, "The Problem of Perception," *Mind*, 64 (1955), 39-45. C. S. Peirce and John Dewey, of course, argued long ago that there is no such thing as an incorrigible empirical judgment, not even excepting reports of "immediate experience."

among sense-datum theorists about the proper form an empirical statement really should have in order to be unquestionably in the "intrinsically certain"-pile. Some liberals might allow statements that ascribe "observable properties" to something, otherwise unspecified, currently to be found in the speaker's perceptual field—for example, the statement "I am directly aware of something red and (roughly) tomato-shaped" of premiss (b). But the majority, conservatives at heart, would insist on some one or another of a set of more stringent formulas, such as "I apparently see something that looks such-and-such" or "It seems to me now exactly as though I were seeing something such-and-such."

Since, as I said, the wrecker's job has already been well done on this principle by other philosophers, there is nothing left for me to do but simply assert what I take Austin and the others to have demonstrated—namely, that the class of empirical statements cannot be divided, by the proposed method of inspection, into those that are intrinsically certain and those that are not.[32] It *might* be true that for the speaker in our argument from differential certainty, the statement "I see a tomato," in the conditions specified, is less certain than statements such as "I am directly aware of something red and with a tomato-ish shape" or "It seems to me now as though I were seeing something red and tomato-shaped." But even if this should be so—and it is by no means obvious that it is— there is still no good reason for thinking that the last two

[32] Some philosophers dispute Austin's claim. For example, Richard Rorty has argued eloquently (in his article "Intuition" in P. Edwards [ed.], *The Encyclopedia of Philosophy* [New York: The Macmillan Company and The Free Press, 1967], Vol. 4, pp. 204-12) that certain sentences are specifically designed to express incorrigible empirical propositions—and presumably 'It seems to me now exactly as though I were seeing ————' would represent one such class of sentences. He adds, however, that this incorrigibility is, to put it crudely, a matter of convention. But if so, then Rorty's doctrine will be cold comfort to sense-datum theorists, for it would mean that the existence of sense-data is a matter of convention, so far as this particular argument for their existence is concerned.

statements are absolutely incorrigible; and this means that the argument cannot possibly establish the presence, in all sense perception, of a special kind of "object of direct awareness" which is distinct from physical things and about which incorrigible knowledge is to be had.

The *soundness* of the argument certainly depends on the truth of premisses (a) and (b); and I have been alluding to reasons that have been offered for viewing them with grave suspicion. But the *validity* of the argument is another matter. And it is quite easy to see that it is not valid. Even if premisses (a) and (b) were impeccable, step (c) is not implied by them, and hence neither is the conclusion. From the fact that what I see (or am directly aware of) is certainly red and tomato-ish shaped, but not certainly a tomato, it by no means follows that the red tomato-ish shaped thing is not identical with a tomato, any more than it follows from Descartes's certainty that he (his self) exists and his lack of certainty that his body exists, that he (his self) must be entirely distinct from his body.[33] Or, to choose a humbler example: even if it were absolutely certain that what you see before you is a child in a mask asking for tricks or treats, and not at all certain that what you see before you is young Jimmy Quackenbush, it by no means follows that the child in the mask is not Jimmy Quackenbush. This invalid form of argument has been exposed enough times to make unnecessary any further hostile remarks about it on my part.[34]

Before (c) is left behind, one should notice that it rests on a time-honored, although mistaken, assumption—namely, that propositions having different degrees of certainty must be about ontologically different kinds of things. Thus Plato, in his middle period at least, thought that propositions possessing certainty (those that are capable of being *known*) are exclusively about the eternal and immutable Forms, while propositions lacking certainty (those

[33] See N. Malcolm, "Descartes's Proof That His Essence Is Thinking," *The Philosophical Review*, 74 (1965), 328-31.
[34] See, for example, Hirst, *The Problems of Perception*, p. 34.

that are capable merely of being *believed*) are exclusively
about things that are subject to change (*Republic*, end of
Book V). The assumption underlying step (c), then, is no
doubt graced with advanced years; but as Lady Bracknell
rightly remarked, nowadays that is no guarantee of either
respectability or character.

The argument from differential certainty exemplifies a
general tendency on the part of sense-datum theorists to
misconstrue the various kinds of perceptual reports one can
make. Consider the following pairs of sentences:

A	B
1. I see a tomato.	1. I see something red and (roughly) tomato-shaped.
2. I see a tomato.	2. I see what seems to be a tomato.
3. I see a tomato.	3. It looks to me now exactly as if I were seeing a tomato.

Sense-datum theorists are apt to regard statements made
by using the B-sentences as being intrinsically more certain
than those made by using the A-sentence, and to suppose
that the B-statements are about things (viz., sense-data)
that are ontologically distinct from what the A-statements
are about (viz., a physical object). But it seems obvious to
me that sentences B1 and B2 are normally used to say something about a perfectly good physical object—a tomato,
most likely. The contrast between A1 and B1 is not that envisaged by some sense-datum theorists: rather, in uttering
A1, a person is (normally) classifying what he sees (i.e.,
telling what kind of thing it is), while in uttering B1, he is
(normally) describing *the very same thing*. In uttering B2,
a speaker is (normally) making a guarded classification of
what he sees; but what he claims to see need not be, and
usually is not, anything but an ordinary physical object. A
person who utters B3—probably a philosopher—(normally)
makes a statement about his present "visual experience";
but there is no reason whatever to suppose that the "object"
of that experience cannot be a physical object, or anyway
something straightforwardly physical, for it might well be

a red ball, a trompe l'oeil tomato, or even a ripe tomato. So the assumption that the corresponding A- and B-sentences must be used to make statements about ontologically distinct kinds of things (physical objects and sense-data, respectively) is wholly unwarranted.

Some sense-datum theorists lay great stress on certain special cases where two statements can be made about what a person sees on a given occasion, where each statement contains a different description of what is seen, and where it seems impossible to maintain that the two descriptions apply to the very same object (or state of affairs). And if they do not in fact apply to the very same object, it seems reasonable to suppose that although one of them no doubt refers to something in the physical world, the other must refer to something non-physical—to a sense-datum. Here is one familiar example of such a case. A man standing on a high mountain sees his white house many miles away on the horizon. He can say both

A	B
4. I see my house, and	4. I see a tiny white dot on the horizon.

The natural impulse of a philosopher who opposes sense-data is to urge that the tiny white dot on the horizon *is* the speaker's house—and, indeed, this particular identity statement (for that is what it appears to be) sounds perfectly all right. But, if it were actually true, then all the non-intensional predicates that apply to the tiny white dot must apply as well to the speaker's house, and vice versa. There seem to be predicates, however, that mar the identity: for instance, the speaker's house is over 100 feet high, Victorian, and made of brick, but the tiny white dot, it seems, is none of these. Again, the speaker lives in that house, but he does not live in a tiny white dot. Sense-datum philosophers take comfort in these disparities and happily conclude that while the house of (A4) is a respectable physical object all right, the tiny white dot of (B4) must be a sense-datum.

It is not difficult, however, to explain away the examples that seem to disrupt the identity. A tiny white dot is a fairly definite sort of physical "thing"; it is a small area of white such as one finds all over some polka dot ties, or such as can be made with a piece of chalk on a blackboard. My dictionary defines 'dot' as "1. A small point made with a pointed instrument. 2. A speck; also, a small, usually round, figure. . . . 4. *Music*. a. A point placed after a note or rest to indicate increase in its length, by one half if one, or by three quarters if two. b. A point placed over a note to indicate staccato." (B4), then, is false, if construed literally: no one could possibly see a tiny white dot on the horizon —certainly not with the naked eye. And when we stop to think about it, (B4) would naturally be understood as asserting not that the speaker sees what is *in fact* a tiny white dot on the horizon, but rather that he sees on the horizon something that *looks like* a tiny white dot—i.e., it looks the way a real white dot looks from, say, arm's length away. And now all the predicates that apply to the object mentioned in (A4) (viz., the house) *do* apply to the object that is referred to in (B4), namely, the object that looks like a tiny white dot. For the house is over 100 feet high, Victorian, and made of brick, and so is the object that looks like a white dot; and the speaker lives in both, too. So these cases are no more favorable to sense-datum theories than any of the earlier ones.

A Sense-datum theorist might object to my interpretation of (B4): he might argue that the speaker cannot be asserting the existence of something that merely *looks like* a tiny white dot, but must rather be asserting the existence of an actual tiny white dot—for there is, after all, a tiny white dot before his (visual) consciousness. To this objection, I would reply as follows. I take it that the words 'a tiny white dot is before his (visual) consciousness' cannot mean more than

(a) It looks to him as if he were seeing a tiny white dot. The objector holds that anyone entitled to assert (a) is ipso facto entitled to assert

(b) There exists a tiny white dot—namely, the one he is now (visually) aware of.

If (b) is interpreted in such a way that the dot it refers to is a real physical one, then the inference from (a) to (b) would clearly be invalid: it does not follow from the fact that it looks to someone as if he were seeing an x (an elephant, say) that he *is* seeing an x (an elephant). But if (b) is interpreted instead in such a way that the dot it refers to is a phenomenal dot—that is, a sense-datum dot—then (b), and hence also (B4), simply presuppose the truth of the sense-datum theory, in which case the (A4)-(B4) example can provide no grounds whatever for accepting that theory. If the evidence is interpreted in a way that presupposes the truth of the very theory for which it is meant to *be* evidence, it gives up its claim to be evidence.

I have been talking about an assumption shared by Plato and many sense-datum theorists—namely, that propositions having different degrees of certainty must be about ontologically different kinds of things. This jointly held conviction is connected with another one: both Plato and the sense-datum theorist maintain that the ontologically distinct kinds of things that they think correspond to the different degrees of certainty are each apprehended by different human faculties. For Plato, the Forms are grasped by the "faculty of knowledge," while it is the business of the "faculty of belief" to deal with changing things, such as are found in space and time. For the sense-datum theorist, our various physical senses latch directly on to sense-data, but it is by virtue of the work of some other faculty or faculties that physical objects are dragged before our consciousness. Most sense-datum theorists, I think, whether they be phenomenalists or representational realists, would say, with Kant, that it is the combined efforts of the imagination and the understanding (i.e., what is more usually called the faculty of reason) that accomplish this useful task—although the phenomenalist would be more likely to stress the importance of the imagination, and the representational realist, that of reason. This splitting up of perception into fragments, this parcelling out of perceptual jobs and distributing them among separate faculties, seems to me to be yet another misguided feature of sense-datum theories, and I shall have some further unkind things to say about it later.

C. The Argument from Perceptual Relativity

This is a slightly more general version of an argument that has traditionally been called the argument from illusion.[35]

The argument:

   (a) Under certain non-standard conditions, things look different from the way they actually are. For example, from a distance, green hills look purple; to people suffering from certain kinds of color-blindness, red (or green) things look grey; a straight stick half submerged in water looks bent.

   (b) In all these cases, *something* has the apparent qualities. Take the example of the distant hills looking purple: *something* must be purple, for the perceiver certainly has a purple expanse before his consciousness. Something purple is definitely perceived.

   (c) But this something is not, *ex hypothesi*, identical with the physical thing that is being looked at: for example, it is not the distant hills that are purple, for we are supposing that they are really green.[36]

---

[35] So called in one of its forms, at least. Roderick Firth, in his article "Austin and the Argument from Illusion" (*Philosophical Review*, 73 [1964], 372-81), claims that the term 'argument from illusion' has been applied to two quite different arguments: first, to an argument used by Berkeley and others to refute naive realism, and second, to what is really an "attempt to identify sense experience by appealing to cases of abnormal perception" (p. 373). The argument I am here concerned with is a generalization of the first kind of argument only.

[36] I take it that almost everyone who would admit that the qualities of things—e.g., their colors and shapes—are not "mere subjective appearances" would agree that whatever the metaphysical status of "physical objects" may be, a uniformly colored object of determinate shape has just that particular color, and that particular shape, and no other. I mention this because some theories—notably Whitehead's

(d) Therefore the perceiver must be (directly) aware of a (non-physical) representation of the physical thing he is looking at, and the perceived quality must inhere in this representation. Such a non-physical representation is a sense-datum. (Similar arguments can be constructed for all the other visually perceived qualities as well).

(e) It cannot be maintained that although in non-standard conditions, one is directly aware of the qualities of sense-data, nevertheless in standard conditions, one is directly aware of the qualities of the (physical) thing itself; for non-standard conditions shade imperceptibly into standard ones, and it would be absurd to claim that at some arbitrary point, one stops being directly presented with the qualities of sense-data and starts being directly presented with the qualities of the physical thing itself. For example, if one approaches the distant hills and they gradually stop looking purple and begin to look green, it would be ridiculous to claim that at some point, one stopped sensing the color of a sense-datum and began to perceive the color inhering in the hills themselves directly.

Conclusion:

Therefore, all the qualities we are ever directly presented with in visual sense perception, even in standard conditions, belong only to sense-data, and so we must always, in visual sense perception, be directly presented with nothing but (visual) sense-data. (Parallel arguments can be constructed for the senses other than vision.)

. . . . .

Once again we find the theoretical status of sense-data coming to the fore: they are introduced here to explain

---

Objective Relativism and Russell's early Selective Realism—while insisting that colors and shapes really do inhere in objects, deny at the same time that any given uniformly colored expanse or object of determinate shape has only one real color and only one real shape. Such theories would therefore reject premiss (c) and so the whole argument from perceptual relativity.

the (alleged) fact that under varying conditions objects appear to have a vast range of different colors, shapes, sizes, and whatnot, although we conceive of them as *really* having, usually, only one color (or pattern of colors, at any rate), one shape, one size, and so on. This is pathetic, in a way, because sense-data, like young cuckoos (in England) or cowbirds, tend to take over any place where they find a home. We need sense-data, it is thought, to be the objects of direct awareness under certain non-standard or unusual conditions. But then, when it is noticed that one's "visual experiences" under standard conditions are remarkably similar to—and indeed often indistinguishable from— one's "visual experiences" under these non-standard conditions, the idea obtrudes itself that one must be directly aware of nothing but sense-data under standard conditions as well. So before we know it, sense-data are all we are ever directly aware of. And then comes the unkindest cut of all: despite the fact that, at least as far as the present argument is concerned, sense-data were invited into our world-view primarily to preserve inviolate the ontological primacy and uniqueness of the one color, the one shape, the one size, and so on, that we were convinced any given object has at one particular time, we find to our horror, once sense-data have multiplied to fill, alarmingly, our entire perceptual field, either that (a) objects are transformed into "families" of sense-data, and are thus endowed with a bewildering array of different colors, shapes, sizes, and so on, all equally real, even if not all equally important (as in phenomenalism when carried to its logical conclusion), or else that (b) they are transformed into unknowable things-in-themselves, and thus are endowed, as far as we are able to tell for certain, with absolutely no color, shape, size, and so on, whatever (as in representational realism when carried to its logical conclusion). The thing to do, obviously, is to bar the door to sense-data right from the beginning, if this can possibly be done.

Before criticizing the argument from perceptual relativity, however, I want to answer an objection to the way I

have formulated the argument. The objection, which at-
tacks my use of premiss (c), is found in R. J. Hirst's book
The Problems of Perception (p. 47) and may be expressed
as follows. "You should not use premiss (c), which says
that the hills are really green, because then the problem
arises of explaining how one can come to know that this
is their real color. Presumably, the knowledge can only be
gained by direct observation of the hills themselves, and
then it is admitted that on at least some occasions, people
are directly aware not of sense-data, but of things in the
(physical) world, contrary to the alleged conclusion of the
argument." It seems to me that this objection misconceives
the nature of the argument. As I see it, the argument is
designed to overthrow the common-sense assumption that
in sense perception we are directly confronted, at least normally, by things in the physical world. It begins by supposing for the time being that the assumption is true, and
that we know, for example, that a certain range of hills
is green. Then it points out that whatever may be the case
under standard conditions, under certain *non*-standard conditions, at any rate, one must be directly confronted not
with anything in the physical world but rather with a
sense-datum. Then it tries to persuade us that we are always, in sense perception, directly confronted with nothing but sense-data, thus showing that the original common-
sense assumption is false. The argument may thus be
viewed as a *reductio*: from the assumption that in sense
perception we are at least sometimes directly confronted
with things in the physical world, it purports to derive,
with the help of certain other premisses, the contradictory
of that assumption.

This argument, whose most illustrious champion in the
history of philosophy was doubtless Bishop Berkeley, can
seem, and has seemed to many philosophers, very compelling indeed. One almost irresistible version of it involves
the phenomenon of double vision. If you press one of your
eyeballs in a certain way, while holding a pencil before
you, the pencil will appear to double. There are then surely

two *somethings* before your consciousness; but since there is only one pencil, whatever there are two of cannot be identical with it. They must be sense-data. Hume was so impressed by the implications of double vision that he cited it as his first and primary example of an experience that shows "that our sensible perceptions are not possest of any distinct or independent existence,"[37] which was the only way he had of saying that in sense perception we are immediately aware not of physical things but of sense-data. I shall return later to the case of double vision, but first I want to consider the argument in its more general form.

It is clear from premises (a) and (b) that the whole argument rests on the assumption (let us call it Assumption A) that if something, x, looks F to someone (to speak just of vision for the moment), then where x is not in fact F, something else, y, different from x really *is* F and is being seen by that person (or the person, at any rate, is aware, in a visual mode, of y). Moore goes so far as to maintain that to say the one is just another way of saying the other; "to say that, e.g. if I am wearing blue spectacles, a wall which is white but *not* bluish-white 'looks' bluish-white to me, is merely another way of saying that I am directly seeing an expanse which really is of a bluish-white colour. . . ."[38] But without going as far as Moore, we may ask whether, when something looks F to someone, but is not so, we are required to suppose that something else really *is* F.

If we are required to do this in the case of vision (and 'looks'), then presumably the same would be true for the other senses as well. But in the case of touch (and 'feels'), at least, it is difficult, if not altogether impossible, to think of a single example where the required supposition is even plausible, much less actually true. Snakes are sometimes said to feel slimy, although usually they are not actually

[37] *Treatise of Human Nature*, Bk. I, Part IV, sect. 2, p. 211 of the Selby-Bigge edition.
[38] Moore, "Visual Sense-data," in C. A. Mace (ed.), *British Philosophy in the Mid-Century*, p. 208.

so; must we conclude that something else really *is* slimy? And what would that be—the person's sense-datum? But what can be made of the notion of a slimy sense-datum? My dictionary tells me that to be slimy is to be "of the consistence of slime; covered or smeared with or full of slime; slippery, hard to hold." Certainly the sense-datum theorist has a degree of freedom in specifying the nature of sense-data, since they are, after all, theoretical entities that he himself has introduced. But I cannot think he would want, nor be able, to conceive of them in such a way that any of them could possibly be said to be "covered or smeared with or full of slime." There is no apparent difficulty connected with the notion of a sense-datum *of* something slimy; but that is not the same thing as the notion of a sense-datum that *is* slimy—and it is just this latter that the argument from perceptual relativity seems to require.

It will not do for the sense-datum theorist to object as follows: "We just don't happen to have a word for the relevant quality of the tactual sense-datum in this example. Our words, after all, are designed to meet practical needs, and so it is not surprising that in general we have words only for qualities that inhere in physical objects—for example, 'slimy.' But there is a quality F' of the tactual sense-datum answering to the sliminess of slimy objects—we just don't have a word for it in English." This won't do, because Assumption A requires the sense-datum to be *slimy*—not to have some quality that merely "answers to" sliminess. (In a moment, however, I shall discuss something very like this rejoinder more thoroughly.)

Very few, if any, of the qualities that we apprehend by touching things—warmth, roughness, bristliness, softness, stickiness, and so on—seem intelligible to attribute to sense-data. The move, then, from the fact that something feels F, but is not, to the conclusion that something else, a sense-datum, must really *be* F, is not only unwarranted; it is in most, or perhaps even all, cases unintelligible.

Moreover, it is not difficult to find examples of corresponding moves for the other standard senses—viz., hearing, smelling, taste, and vision—that are equally illegitimate. Thus, when something tastes salty, but is not so, we are surely not entitled to infer that something else—and a sense-datum at that—really *is* salty. And consider size in connection with visual sense-data: how should one go about determining whether an after-image of a green circle[39] is two inches, two feet, two thousand miles, or any particular distance across? It would seem that (absolute) size cannot literally be ascribed to a visual sense-datum. These examples must cause us to regard with suspicion what Assumption *A* presupposes—namely, that it makes sense to ascribe "publicly observable" properties to items (sense-data) that are alleged to be necessarily private. This presupposition is certainly false for some properties, as we have seen: and if Wittgenstein's attack on the notion of a private language is sound, it may be universally false.

Suppose someone objects to this criticism as follows: "Look here, you are simply assuming, along with the direct realist and perhaps also the ordinary man, that real physical objects (in their sense) exist, and that predicates like 'slimy' and 'salty' can only be applied literally to such objects. But surely phenomenalism is a logical possibility, and if it happened to be true, predicates like 'slimy' and 'salty' would have to be literally predicable of sense-data. So your criticism rests on a dubious assumption—moreover, on one that is explicitly rejected by one group of philosophers (namely, the phenomenalists) that you are trying to defeat."

In reply to this charge, I would say that in the system of phenomenalism, 'slimy' and 'salty' would still presumably be applicable, in their literal sense, only to things like wet walls and soups—that is, only to *families* of sense-data, not to individual sense-data, as the argument from perceptual relativity requires. Surely the argument cannot be construed, anyway, as assuming the truth of phenomenalism, for then it would be assuming what it sets out to prove.

[39] After-images are held up, by some sense-datum theorists, as being paradigm cases of sense-data.

It may be equally unfair to construe the argument as starting out from the direct realist's or ordinary man's point of view—although I think that is the most natural, and perhaps the only possible, way to read it—but however it is construed, the argument categorically demands that there be *some* kind of important distinction between, on the one hand, things like walls and bowls of soup (whatever their metaphysical nature may be) and, on the other, individual sense-data. My criticism does, indeed, rest on the assumption—and it rests *only* on it—that predicates like 'slimy' and 'salty' can be attributed, in their literal sense, only to the former kinds of things: but I do not see how anyone can deny this assumption.

I take it that enough has been said to indicate that there is something conceptually "fishy" about Assumption A. Notice, by the way, that I have confined my objections, as much as I could, to properties that are plausible candidates for being "directly perceivable" ones. It would have been all too easy to make Assumption A look even more ridiculous if one—unfairly—brought in "inferred" properties: if, for example, one insisted that according to Assumption A, whenever anything, x, looks broken (or highly polished, or dead) to someone, something else, y, must really *be* broken (highly polished, dead). The notion of a broken (highly polished, dead) sense-datum is an absurdity if anything is. So Assumption A must be construed as being confined to "directly perceivable" properties, and as not applying also to "inferred" ones. (This is an additional difficulty with it, since the distinction between a "directly perceivable" and an "inferred" property is notoriously neither a clear nor a sharp one. But I do not press this difficulty now.) I have tried to argue that even when Assumption A is thus restricted, at least some substitution instances of it are not conceptually sound.

It is pretty evident that if the argument from perceptual relativity is to have any hope of being what sense-datum theorists clearly want it to be, namely, a *general* argument—that is, an argument that can be applied to all "directly perceivable" properties of all the senses—it cannot be made to rest, as it does now, on Assumption A. The argument will have to be reformulated so as to rest on some modification of Assumption A—let us call it Assumption A'. But I doubt that any such reformulation will work: for in stating Assumption A', what could come after the words 'If something, x, that is not F, looks F to someone'? The only possibilities that come to my mind are the following:

"then something else, y, that is different from x and of which that person is directly aware, must have a property F' analogous to F"

and

"then something else, y, that is different from x and of which that person is directly aware, must be *as of F*."

Neither of these Assumption A''s, however, has so much as the appearance of self-evidence (as the original Assumption A may have had, or at least purported to have). It is not even clear that we know how to construe them: for we do not yet know how, precisely, F' is supposed to be analogous to F (first version of A') or what it means to say that something is *as of F* (second version of A'). So these versions of Assumption A' need some support, and they need it in two ways: first, we want to know how they are to be understood, and then we want to know why we should accept one or the other (or both) of them.

On the first point: I can think of no other way to interpret either version of A' than to suppose that the y is in fact a sense-datum. Consider the first version. The only way I can understand "y has a property F' that is analogous to F" is to think of y on the model of something like an after-image: property F' is analogous to F in the way that the greenness or the circularity of an after-image is analogous to the greenness or circularity of real physical objects. So the y which allegedly has property F' must be essentially like an after-image—i.e., it must be a sense-datum. Similarly, the only way I can understand "*y* is *as of F*" in the second version of *A'* is to think of *y* as a sense-datum of something that is *F*.

But now we ask, turning to the second point: What reason is there for accepting Assumption *A'* understood in this way—that is, understood in such a way that the *y* referred to in *A'* is a sense-datum? And the answer, I think, is clearly that there is none—none, at any rate, provided by the present argument from perceptual relativity. For the first part of this argument now reduces to the following: whenever something looks to someone to have a (directly perceivable) property *F* that it does not really have, we must suppose that he is not directly aware of that thing, but is instead directly aware of a sense-datum that has a property *F'* analogous to that (physical) property. But the words 'we must suppose,' here, can only have the force of 'the best explanation of this phenomenon is.' The argument, however, offers not the slightest reason for accepting this claim. The so-called "argument," in fact, is now reduced to the brute *assertion* that the sense-datum theory is the best one to explain the relevant phenomenon. The sense-datum theory may in fact *be* the best one, but the argument from perceptual relativity, when it includes Assumption *A'* in place of *A*, provides no grounds whatever for thinking so; it is not, in short, an *argument* at all.

Indeed, even if we revert to Assumption *A*, limiting the argument from perceptual relativity now to just those cases where Assumption *A* has not been shown to be conceptually unsound, we will find that the argument still really amounts to nothing more than bare assertion. For suppose we allow—what is after all quite possible—that certain special substitution instances of Assumption *A* are conceptually sound; suppose we grant, for instance, that it is perfectly all right to ascribe color and shape to visual sense-data. Do we have to accept such substitution instances as true? By no means. A direct realist would maintain that when a person sees something, *x*, that looks, say, green to him, but is not really green, there is no call whatever to suppose that some other object, *y*, different from *x*, actually is green and is being seen by that person. Something, if you like, is green in such cases—namely, the way *x* looks to the perceiver. But it is a mistake, the direct realist would hold, to reify the way *x* looks. The perceiver, when he sees *x*, is in a perceptual state that is similar, in at least one respect, to the state he is in when he is looking at grass, leaves, or other green things under normal conditions of observation. His aberrant perceptual state can be explained by reference to whatever is non-standard in the total situation in the relevant respect—for example, perhaps he is wearing green goggles, or the illumination is green. There is no need to appeal to a metaphysically private green object, that is, to a green sense-datum: for there is no difficulty whatever in the supposition that the perceiver is (directly) aware of the (non-green) object *x* itself, but that because of some non-standard condition(s), the thing happens to look green to him.

We see that the direct realist is able to give a perfectly coherent account of situations in which something looks *F* to a perceiver when it is not really *F*. So once again, what the sense-datum theorist puts forward as a deductive proof is revealed as something quite different—it turns out to be little more than the bare unjustified assertion that the positing of sense-data is the best explanation of such situations.

There are some sense-datum theorists who would object to my criticisms in the following way. They would say that I have been assuming an incorrect "act-object" analysis of the awareness of sense-data, and that I should adopt the correct "adverbial" view of such awareness. That is, I have been treating sense-data, unfairly, as though they were a kind of object, and therefore as though it made sense to attribute certain properties directly to them; but actually, for a variety of reasons, it is far better to think of sense-data as being merely features or aspects of certain kinds of states of persons (or animals), and hence as not being eligible to have any properties ascribed directly to them. So we ought not to construe "John has a red circular sense-datum," for example, as though it were of the form "There are an x and a y such that x is a person, y is a sense-datum, x has y, and y is red and circular." Rather, we are to construe it as of the form "There is an x such that x is a person, and x is in state S (where S is the state of 'having a sense-datum of the red-circle-ish sort')."[40] Another familiar way of putting the same point is to say: "John has a red circular sense-datum" does not assert "John has a y, and y is red and circular," but rather "John senses (or perceives) red-circle-ly." On this view of sense-data, the red circle that John is aware of is no kind of object, but rather the subjective "sense-contents" of John's state of sensuous awareness, no more separable from the state of awareness itself than a somersault is separable from the act of turning it, or than a jig is from the act of dancing it.

Of course, if what this objection maintains is correct, then my criticisms of the argument from perceptual relativity fall to the ground; but so, again, does the whole argument itself, for this objection completely undermines the crucial Assumption A. My quarrel throughout has been only with the notion of a sense-datum viewed as a kind of private object of awareness, and therefore as something to which it *seems*, at least, to make sense to directly ascribe various properties; and the argument from perceptual relativity purports to show only that we must posit sense-data *as so viewed*.

Can an altered version of the argument from perceptual relativity be constructed to prove the existence of sense-data when these are viewed adverbially? I do not think that a sound one can. For how would the argument have to go? The original premiss (a) (p. 28) can stand as it is. But premiss (b) must give way to something like this:

[40] This way of putting the point is adapted from a passage in Thomas Nagel's article "Physicalism," *The Philosophical Review*, 74 (1965), 342. He is discussing sensations there, but sense-datum theorists clearly think of sense-data as being essentially like sensations in a way that is relevant here.

(b′) In all these cases, the qualities that the perceiver is aware of—the color purple, the color grey, the shape of being bent—are such that their names must go in the underlined position of such sentences as the following which are true of the perceiver:

(i) The perceiver perceives (or sees) <u>purple-hills-ly</u>,

(ii) The perceiver perceives (or sees) <u>grey-ly</u>,

(iii) The perceiver perceives (or sees) <u>bent-stick-ly</u>.

We may tentatively accept premiss (b′), suppressing a raised eyebrow reaction to its bizarre way of putting things, until we see what comes next.

What must come next is not premiss (c) of the original argument, but something along these lines:

(c′) What the perceiver is directly aware of in these cases cannot be identical with the physical thing that is being looked at: for example, it cannot be the distant green hills, the red (or green) thing, the straight stick.

At this point, however, the proposed new argument simply breaks down; because no reason has been given for accepting (c′). A direct realist can perfectly well concede premisses (a) and (b′), and yet deny (c′), insisting that what the perceiver is directly aware of in each cited instance is the actual physical thing itself, not some alleged subjective "sense-contents." So the direct realist would interpret the unfamiliar expressions of (b′) objectivistically. For example, he would construe the sentence (b′)(i) as saying that the person's perceptual state is like that of someone who sees, under normal conditions, purple hills; and he would insist that on this interpretation, it is an open possibility that what the person is (directly) aware of is something perfectly objective—some hills, perhaps. I cannot see why the direct realist should not be allowed to construe the odd expressions of (b′) in this way, and hence why he should not be free to reject (c′). The sense-datum theorist, in offering (c′), is in effect simply asserting, without attempting to justify the assertion, that the peculiar expressions of (b′) *must* be construed in accordance with his doctrines— for example, that the sentence (b′) (i) must be understood as claiming that the perceiver is aware of a certain kind of subjective "sense-contents," namely, a purple-hills-y one. But then we need to know why those expressions must be so understood. The reason why, so a sense-datum theorist would presumably say, is this: if something looks to a perceiver different from the way it actually is, he cannot be directly aware of that thing. But the simple reply to this is: Why not? And I do not know how a sense-datum theorist can answer this query.

I conclude that the argument from perceptual relativity, when viewed as a deductive one, fails to establish the existence of sense-data, whether these are regarded in accordance with the act-object analysis of the awareness of sense-data, or whether they are regarded instead in accordance with the adverbial analysis.

Before leaving the argument from perceptual relativity, I want to say a word or two about the phenomenon of double vision, since it seems to have hypnotized many philosophers; they have seen no way of accounting for it other than positing sense-data as the immediate objects of awareness. (Cf. p. 31f.). But we are not in the least forced to posit these entities; a direct realist need not be even slightly embarrassed by the fact of double vision. Luigi Dallapiccola once remarked that Vivaldi did not write 400 concertos; he wrote one concerto 400 times. A direct realist could quite properly say, similarly, that in double vision a person does not see two somethings (e.g., two pencilish sense-data); he sees one thing (e.g., a pencil) twice, once with the left eye and once with the right eye.

At this point, the sense-datum theorist might retort to the direct realist: "Look here, in normal vision, too, you are committed to saying that the perceiver sees the pencil once with his left eye and once with his right eye. But then how is double vision to be distinguished from normal vision, on your account? You certainly haven't explained double vision when all you have done is appeal to something that, on your view, happens in every case of normal vision as well!" In reply to this, the direct realist could say that the difference between normal and double vision is simply this: in double vision it looks to the perceiver as if there are two pencils.

Sense-datum theorists regard cases of double vision in the following way. They argue that since it looks to the perceiver as though he were perceiving two of something (e.g., two pencils), he must be directly aware of two somethings. These somethings must be private to the perceiver, since there really are not two somethings of the required kind in his physical surroundings. The two somethings must be sense-data. (So the sense-datum theorists appeal here to a version of Assumption *A*, in which it deals now with numbers rather than with qualities.)

But plausible as this view of double vision may be, it is by no means forced on us. The problem in these cases is just to account somehow for the duality that is unquestionably present in the perceiver's visual field. This duality is satisfactorily accounted for in a direct realist theory by saying that the object (e.g., the pencil) as seen by one eye looks to the perceiver to be displaced from the (very same) object as seen by the other eye, thus making it look to him as though there were two pencils. This is duality enough for any man, and yet the account does not require that the perceiver be directly aware of anything but perfectly good physical objects. Therefore, as an alleged demonstration that sense-data *must* exist, the argument from double vision fares no better than its parent, the argument from perceptual relativity.

I turn now to the last, and by far the most impressive, of the major arguments designed to demonstrate the existence of sense-data. It is

D. The Argument from the Physiology (or the Causation) of Sense Perception

The argument:

(a) Science gives us an account of how we see. Roughly, this is what happens. Light rays are emitted, or reflected, from an object and enter the eye of the perceiver, where an (inverted) image of the object is formed on the retina. The rods and cones of the retina, being thus stimulated, originate electro-chemical impulses that proceed via the optic nerve and thalamus to the occipital lobes of the brain. The perceiver does not see the object until the impulses reach the brain.

(b) It is the stimulation of certain portions of his brain, then, that is the final stage in the purely physical process that causes a person to see things. This brain state either is (i.e., is identical with), or directly causes, a mental act or state—an act or state of (sensuous or perceptual—in particular, *visual*) awareness.

(c) Part, at least, of this act or state consists in the perceiver's being aware of a sensuous manifold of various colors, lines, and shapes. Since this awareness either is, or is the direct effect of, nothing but the stimulation of certain brain cells, which are of course far removed from the object at the other end of the causal chain, what can it be but the awareness of a mere representation, or image, of the object? But such representations or images can of course only be sense-data.

Conclusion:

Therefore, in visual sense perception one is always directly aware of nothing but sense-data. (Parallel arguments can be constructed for the senses other than vision.)

. . . . . .

The idea that seeing, hearing, and so on, are acts, states, or processes that occur at the end of a causal chain has a very long history. Its main effect seems to have been to disturb philosophers by giving them a dim view of the senses as purveyors of knowledge of the "external world." Some, mainly rationalists, have looked upon sense perception as tainted by the very fact that bodily processes are involved in it at all: if our bodies were constructed differently, they have argued, the sensuous manifold presented to consciousness in sense perception would be quite different. The body is thus a kind of non-eliminable distorting medium, and the sensuous manifold of sense perception represents the nature of this medium at least as much as it does the nature of the external object perceived.[41]

Many philosophers have thought ill of sense perception, not because bodily events, in particular, are links in the causal chain that produces its sensuous manifold, but rather because the manifold is generated at all, by *any* sort of causal process. Since the manifold occurs only at the end of a causal chain originating in the object, they have reasoned, there is no ground for thinking that it resembles, or accurately represents, the object—for why should an effect, and especially if it is separated from its cause by numerous intermediate steps, resemble its cause? It is as reasonable to think that the feeling of warmth caused in us by the fire resembles some feature of the fire itself, as it is to think that the stomach-ache caused by eating a bad oyster resembles some feature of the oyster.[42]

Our main concern here, however, is not with the traditional idea that the causation involved in sense perception entails its inaccuracy,[43] but with the more fundamental idea, underlying the present argument, that since the awareness we have in sense perception comes at the end of a causal chain, the objects we are thus aware of cannot be identical with whatever it is in the "external world" that figures in an early stage of that causal chain. This more fundamental idea has struck many philoso-

[41] See Spinoza, *Ethics*, Book II, Prop. XVI.

[42] See Locke, *An Essay Concerning Human Understanding*, Book II, Chapter 8, sect. 16.

[43] I discuss this issue in Chapter IV.

phers as unassailably true, and especially so when they consider the fact that light energy and electro-chemical nerve impulses travel at only a finite speed. For example, it takes the light emitted by most stars a huge number of years to reach our eyes, and so it cannot be the stars themselves that are directly presented to us when we look at them; they may even have gone out of existence sometime during the vast stretch of time it takes their light to reach us. And this time-lag is only shorter, not non-existent, when we perceive things that are closer to us than stars. It is always at least logically possible that between the time light rays bounce off an object—no matter how close at hand it may be—and the time those rays produce the necessary brain stimulation in a perceiver, the object may lapse, instantaneously, into non-existence. Since the perceiver would have the very same visual presentation whether this miracle happens or not, it cannot be the object itself that he is directly aware of in either case. He must, rather, be aware of a mere representation of the object—that is, he must be aware of a sense-datum. (Let us call this the *time-lag argument.*)

The matter seems to be settled beyond dispute, moreover, when it is pointed out that the optic nerve, say, can (at least conceivably) be stimulated in such a way that the effect on the brain, and the sensuous manifold that the person is aware of, are indistinguishable from what they would have been if they had been caused in the normal way—viz., by light rays proceeding from something in the "external world." If the optic nerve were so stimulated, it would certainly be false to say that the resulting sensuous manifold of which the person was aware contained items existing in the "external world," for doubtless there are no items there answering to that particular sensuous manifold, and if there were, that would merely be a matter of chance. But since, as we are supposing, the sensuous manifold and the brain state that either is, or is the direct cause of, the person's awareness of it, are exactly the same as they would have been had they been produced in the

normal way (by light rays, etc.), then when they *are* produced in the normal way, it cannot be true then, either,
that the person is directly aware of things in the "external
world." In both cases, he must be directly aware merely
of *representations* (or seeming-representations) of such
things; that is, he must be directly aware merely of sense-
data. (Let us call this the *argument from the short causal
chain*.)

This battery of arguments and considerations has an im-
posing force at first blush; but I think they do not in fact
compel one to accept the sense-datum theory of perception. The crucial consideration in the argument from the
physiology, or causation, of sense perception, is that the ultimate brain stimulation in the visual perceiver occurs at
some distance from the object that he sees and that figures
in an early stage of the causal chain leading to that brain
stimulation. It is this consideration alone that is supposed
to force us to admit that the perceiver must be directly
aware of a sense-datum, and to deny that he can be directly
aware of the light-emitting, or light-reflecting, object itself. But clearly there is a link missing in the argument:
for we need to know what the connection is between (a)
the fact that event x (the brain stimulation in the observer)
occurs at some distance from event y (the object's emitting or reflecting light rays toward the observer) and (b)
the (alleged) facts that event x cannot be, or immediately
give rise to, a direct awareness of the object, and that
event x must be, or immediately give rise to, a direct awareness of nothing but a sense-datum. Why should (a) be
thought to imply (b)?

I think that anyone who believes that (a) implies (b)
must reason along something like the following lines. He
starts with the necessary truth that any event occurs at
just the spatial position it does occur at, and the natural
assumption that if one event immediately causes another,
the latter must occur at a place contiguous to the former.
Applying these principles to the event x (the observer's
brain stimulation), he imagines that since x either actually

is, or else immediately causes, the occurrence of some object of awareness O, O must either occupy the same spatial position that x does or else a contiguous one. But only a sense-datum is close enough to x to be able to fulfill the requirements placed on O: the object that figures in event y (the emitting or reflecting of light rays toward the observer) is too far away.

But this picture is obviously full of confusion. Imagining that x either is, or immediately causes, *the occurrence of some object of awareness O*, makes it look as though x either is, or directly causes, some *thing*, some *object*, which then must be (at least) quite close to x. Well, even if one were to grant the legitimacy of this way of putting things, it would still be false, or senseless rather, to say that a sense-datum satisfies the requirements placed on O—because a sense-datum occupies no position in (real physical) space and hence is not at, or quite close to, or yet any distance from, the spatial position occupied by x. But in fact we cannot allow this way of putting things: for x is not either identical with, or the direct cause of, *the occurrence of some object of awareness O*, but is rather either identical with, or the direct cause of, *the observer's state (or act) of awareness of something, O*. And as soon as we put the matter in this correct way, we see that there is no evident reason to think that O *cannot* be (identical with) the physical object from which light rays are being emitted or reflected. It is no whit easier to understand how x might be, or cause, the (direct) awareness of a sense-datum than it is to understand how it might be, or cause, the (direct) awareness of a physical object. So a direct realist need have no qualms about admitting all the physiological, and other physical, facts involved in the causation of sense perception. He can perfectly well insist that what happens as a result of the light rays, neural impulses, and brain stimulation is that the (physical) things before the perceiver's eyes are (directly) revealed to him, just as they are in themselves. There is no reason to think that just because the brain stimulation occurs at some distance from the objects perceived, it must therefore be, or give rise to, the (direct) awareness of a mere copy of the objects themselves. It is perfectly possible to look upon the light rays, neural impulses, and brain stimulation as being the physical preconditions of the perceiver's ability to apprehend, directly, certain objects in his environment.

So far, we have taken up only the basic argument—the argument from the physiology, or causation, of sense perception. I take it that we have now quelled any antagonism that that argument might have engendered against the possibility that a causal theory of perception might at the same time be a direct realist one. But now we must see if the other arguments can be as easily dealt with.

A direct realist does not have much to fear from the time-lag argument. He can simply insist that the finite speed of light does not entail that we do not directly see things and states of affairs in the "external world," but only that we must see them *as they were some time ago*. We see real physical things, properties, and events, all right, but we see them late, that is all. According to a direct realist, it is a mere prejudice of common sense—and one on which the time-lag argument trades—that the events, and the states of objects, that we see must be simultaneous with our (act of) seeing them. If light waves travelled as slowly as sound waves, he would say, common sense would never have made that erroneous assumption. When one is watching a baseball game from some distance away, the sound of the bat hitting the ball reaches us a few seconds after it is actually made, but that fact does not, and should not, lead one to suppose that he is (directly) aware only of an auditory sense-datum, and not of the crack of the bat actually hitting the ball. He *is* (directly) aware of the real physical sound made by the bat hitting the ball, but he simply hears it a few seconds late. It is a scientific discovery that the same sort of thing must be said, *mutatis mutandis*, about our seeing of things and events. But that discovery need not have the slightest tendency to make a direct realist abandon his theory in favor of a sense-datum theory.

Notice that the time-lag argument is virtually the same as the main argument (from the physiology, or causation, of sense perception): the only difference is that where the latter involves space, the former involves time. The causal chain that originates with light rays being emitted, or reflected, from the object (call it event y) and ends with the stimulation of the perceiver's brain (call it event x), not only creates a spatial gap between event y and event x— it also creates a temporal gap between the two. The picture underlying the argument from the physiology of sense perception demanded, as we saw, that the object of awareness that allegedly either is, or is directly caused by, event x, occupy the same place as x, or a contiguous one. Similarly, the picture that seems to underlie the present time-lag argument is that the object of awareness that either is, or is directly caused by, event x must occur (i.e., come into existence) at the same time as x, or immediately thereafter. But this picture is as confused as the earlier one and in the same way. What event x either is, or directly causes, is not the occurrence of an object of awareness, but the perceiver's state (or act) of awareness of something, O. And just as O might very well be at some distance from event x, so the state of O that the perceiver sees might very well occur (or have occurred) at some time before event x. This possibility *sounds* odd, of course, because it appears to attribute to all of us a supernatural power to "see into the past." But the ability to see into the past is fantastic only when it is *contrasted* with ordinary seeing, which is commonly supposed to be "seeing into the present," that is, seeing things as they now are. A direct realist, however, since he denies just this contrast—because he asserts that ordinary seeing *is* seeing things as they were some time ago (usually, an extremely short time ago)— cannot be charged with attributing to us all a supernatural power. (A direct realist can, of course, assent to the statement "in visual perception, we see things as they are at the present moment," but he would construe this as being true merely for most practical purposes, for it is not true when we are dealing with, say, stars. And if the statement "In visual perception, we can see into the past" is supposed to mean that we are able literally to see such things as yesterday's baseball game or last week's automobile accident, without the aid of television sets and the like, then the direct realist would reject it along with almost everyone else.)

I conclude that although the considerations cited in the time-lag argument, like those cited in the main argument from the physiology of sense perception, are consistent with sense-datum theories, they are also consistent with direct realisms. If this is so, then those arguments cannot possibly be conclusive demonstrations that sense-datum theories are true.[44]

Let us turn next to the argument from the short causal chain. This argument is psychologically persuasive, without a doubt. It is easily conceivable that an experimenter with his electric probes should be able to produce a sensuous state of consciousness S that is not the awareness of an objective state of affairs:[45] how can the mere fact that light rays bounce off an object and, via the perceiver's eyes and optic nerves, produce an identical state of consciousness S magically transform S into a direct awareness of that object?

But persuasive as this line of reasoning may seem, it is nevertheless invalid, as I shall now try to show. There are two possibilities open to the sense-datum theorist: he may hold that a certain brain event *is* (identical with) the direct awareness of a sense-datum, or he may say that the brain event *causes* the direct awareness of a sense-datum.

---

[44] For an excellent recent discussion of the time-lag argument, see W. A. Suchting, "Perception and the Time-gap Argument," *The Philosophical Quarterly*, 19 (1969), 46-56.

[45] I mean: if this state of consciousness S is just like one a person would have if, under normal conditions, he were seeing, say, a red circle, then it cannot count as being an awareness *of a* (real, physical) *red circle*. But I should not wish to deny that this S might, in certain circumstances, count as an awareness *of the experimenter's probes*, or whatever.

I shall consider these two possibilities in turn, starting with the former.

Imagine that we have a description of a brain event in purely physiological terms—as the firing, let us say, of certain brain cells in a certain order and pattern. Call this brain event, as so described, event x. We suppose, in accordance with the former of the two possibilities just mentioned, that the sense-datum theorist holds that event x is (identical with) the direct awareness of a visual sense-datum—of a red triangular one, let us say. It can be shown that if this identity of the brain event x and the direct awareness of a visual sense-datum is presupposed, the argument from the short causal chain rests on an illegitimate assumption.

In the argument, the sense-datum theorist is clearly assuming that if a certain brain event x is identical with the direct awareness of a visual sense-datum, then every other numerically different brain event y that is qualitatively the same, physically, as x must also be identical with the direct awareness of a visual sense-datum. (Call this Assumption B.) To say that "brain event x is identical with the direct awareness of a visual sense-datum," I take it, is to say that the predicate '_____ is the direct awareness of a visual sense-datum' applies to, or is true of, x. I also assume that to claim that "y is qualitatively the same, physically, as x" is to claim that there is some description couched in some kind of fundamental physicalistic terms (in this case, in terms of the firing of certain specific brain cells in a certain specific order and pattern, or something similar) that completely and accurately describes both x and y.

But Assumption B, so understood, gets whatever plausibility it may have solely by being an instance of a more general principle. This principle—call it Principle P—may be stated as follows: if two different events or states of affairs, E_1 and E_2, both have exactly the same description D (except that their spatial and/or temporal co-ordinates are of course different, since they are numerically distinct events or states of affairs), where D satisfies the following two conditions,

1. It is a complete description, and
2. It is couched entirely in basic physicalistic terms,

then any additional predicate, expressed in terms other than those specified in condition 2, that either E_1 or E_2 has, the other must have also. If one can manage to ignore the terrible unclarity and vagueness in this formulation, Principle P has a certain prima facie appeal. For example, suppose that D_1 describes, in the required way, the breaking of a certain kind of fragile physical object, and that D_1 applies to two such breakings, E_3 and E_4. Then if E_3 is the breaking of a beautiful vase, so must E_4 be, and vice versa. But, as stated, principle P is manifestly false for ever so many cases: for instance, it is obviously false that if E_3 is the breaking of *Aunt Emma's* vase, then E_4 must also be the breaking of Aunt Emma's vase. And it is false that if E_3 is the breaking of a window *in a living room*, then E_4 must also have that same predicate.

These examples show that if Principle P is to be acceptable, it must at least be reformulated so as to rule out such cases. Let us grant that this can be done: for it appears that whatever is wrong with Assumption B does *not* derive from this particular kind of weakness in Principle P. I want to attack P at a point of weakness that does get transmitted to Assumption B and vitiates it. So consider *causal* predicates, such as '——— is caused by C_1' and '——— is caused by C_2.' If Assumption B, and hence Principle P, are to support the argument from the short causal chain, the possibility must of course be left open that E_1 and E_2, though they have the same complete physicalistic description D, nevertheless have *different* causes: thus if E_1 and E_2 are brain events of a certain kind, E_1 might be caused by light rays being reflected from an object (cause C_1) while E_2 might be caused by direct electrical stimulation of the person's optic nerves or brain (cause C_2). In that case, '——— is caused by C_1' would be a predicate that applies to E_1

and not to E_2, while '_____ is caused by C_2' would be one that applies to E_2 but not to E_1. But then Principle P is in trouble again: for neither of the statements "E_1 is caused by C_1," and "E_2 is caused by C_2," can be included in D (since all the statements in D must apply to *both* E_1 and E_2), and this means that E_1 and E_2 each have an "additional predicate" not shared by the other, contrary to what Principle P asserts.

Let us, however, try once more to be as generous towards P as we possibly can: let us assume that the principle can again be reformulated so as to deal satisfactorily with this kind of causal predicate. Our generosity is short-lived, however; our patience with P, at least in so far as it is supposed to lend credence to Assumption B, must perforce give out at once. The reason it must is that there are any number of "additional predicates" of an event or state of affairs that make a tacit reference to its causes, so that even though two events E_1 and E_2 otherwise satisfy the conditions laid down in Principle P, they might each have one or more of these special "backward-looking" predicates not shared by the other whenever they have a different type of causal history. Moreover, it is quite possible that this is precisely the situation that obtains in the kind of case envisaged in Assumption B.

Let me explain all this. First, I shall give a simple example that illustrates my complaint. Consider two events, E_5 and E_6, each of which consists of a certain kind of red car smashing into a certain kind of black car in exactly the same way, resulting in the death, in both cases, of the black car's driver. And suppose a causal antecedent of E_5 is that the red car's driver deliberately steered his car towards the black one with the intention of killing its driver, while a causal antecedent of E_6 is that the red car's driver accidentally lost control of his steering. Then the additional predicate '_____ is the carrying out of a murder' will doubtless apply to E_5 and not to E_6, contrary to P. The predicate '_____ is the carrying out of a murder' makes tacit reference to a certain kind of causal antecedent of the events to which it applies; E_5 has the requisite kind of causal history, and E_6, we may suppose, does not.

Let us apply this lesson to Assumption *B*. It should now be reasonably clear that we are under no intellectual obligation whatever to accept *B*. A direct realist can easily just categorically deny it. He can urge that if a brain event x is caused by electric impulses from an experimenter's probes, then it does, indeed, satisfy some such further description as '_____ is the direct awareness of a red triangular sense-datum (image, or whatever),' but that this does not in the least entail that when another brain event y that is "qualitatively the same, physically, as x" is caused instead by light rays being emitted, or reflected, from a physical object O (e.g., from a real red triangle), it then must also satisfy that same additional sense-datum description. On the contrary, he would say, y would satisfy the quite different further description '_____ is the direct awareness of a (real) red triangle'—and it cannot simultaneously satisfy both this description and the incompatible description '_____ is the direct awareness of a red triangular sense-datum.' The direct realist can very plausibly, and in my opinion, rightly, hold that the predicate '_____ is the direct awareness of a (real) red triangle' is one of those that make tacit reference to a certain kind of causal antecedent (involving, for example, light rays) of the brain events to which they truly apply: since this causal history is lacking in the case of the event x that is produced by the experimenter's probes, that event x cannot satisfy this further description.

So if the sense-datum theorist is to make the argument from the short causal chain stick, he must *show*, in opposition to the direct realist, that Assumption *B* *is* valid. He must make a case for it. But clearly this would require that he bring in some additional support—support that is totally lacking in the original argument (from the short causal chain) itself. In other words, that argument is not a demonstrative proof of its conclusion.

I turn now to the second of the two possibilities open to

the sense-datum theorist—that is, to the view not that certain brain events *are* (identical with), but rather that they *cause*, the direct awareness of sense-data. This alternative seems at first blush to give the argument from the short causal chain a better chance of going through. If an experimenter, using his electric probes, causes a brain event *x* in some subject, it must be allowed that *x* causes, according to the present alternative, the subject's direct awareness of a red triangular sense-datum. But then when an exactly similar brain event *x* is caused in the normal way, by light rays being reflected from a real red triangle, how can it be denied that *x* must again cause the subject's direct awareness of a red triangular sense-datum, since like causes must have like effects?

But a direct realist has a plausible and, I think, entirely valid, rejoinder to this. He can charge that the sense-datum philosopher stacks the cards unfairly in his own favor when he describes the effect caused by event *x*, in the "experimenter's probes"-case, as being the subject's direct awareness of a red triangular sense-datum. To be sure, this description may be granted to have genuine application in that case, but by presenting it as the *only*, or at any rate the basic, relevant description of the effect, the sense-datum philosopher proceeds unfairly. This may be seen as follows. The description 'the subject's direct awareness of a red triangular sense-datum' makes tacit reference to a certain kind of causal antecedent—or perhaps it might be better to say that its application presupposes the *lack* of a certain kind of causal antecedent. Anyway, the reason one is willing to concede that the description in fact applies in the "experimenter's probes"-situation is that one knows that brain event *x* is not caused in the usual way, i.e., by light rays being reflected from a real red triangle. Therefore it is unfair to offer that description as the basic one; because in the other, normal case, the case about which one is supposed to infer something on the basis of what one says about the "experimenter's probes"-case, the very causal history of brain event *x* whose absence allows the sense-datum description to apply to the "experimenter's probes"-case is *present*—for in the second, normal situation, brain event *x* *is* caused by light rays being reflected from a real red triangle. The only valid way to proceed in the argument, then, so the direct realist would (rightly) continue, is to provide a neutral, non-question-begging description for the effect caused by brain event *x* in the "experimenter's probes"-case: perhaps the description 'the subject's direct awareness of a red triangular manifold' or 'the person's state of its looking to him exactly as if he were seeing a red triangle' will do as well as any. Once this has been done, one can readily agree that the original sense-datum description *also* applies to that same effect. But what follows from this about the contrasting, normal case of vision? The neutral description may be allowed to apply to the effect caused by brain event *x* in this normal situation, but what reason has anyone to suppose that the sense-datum description also applies to it? The only ground for such a judgment would seem to be a principle along the lines of Principle *P*—but the weakness of *P* indicates that the sense-datum theorist can expect no help from that quarter. Nothing in the argument prevents the direct realist from denying that the sense-datum description applies in the normal case: nothing prevents him from asserting that, on the contrary, in the normal case it is the incompatible additional description 'the subject's direct awareness of a (real) red triangle' that properly applies. Indeed, one might even expect that this additional description probably *does* then apply; for a necessary condition for its applicability is surely that the perceptual state referred to is caused in a certain way by a (real) red triangle—and that condition is fulfilled in the normal case.

In offering this second version of the argument from the short causal chain, then, the sense-datum theorist has made a use of the principle "Like causes have like effects" that stands in need of justification. This principle, although it may be true for every cause-and-effect pair, is not true for them *under every description*. Consider the following example: light is reflected from Sarah Jones and ultimately produces a certain brain event, w, in a visual perceiver, Q. Imagine that w is described in purely physiological terms. It may well be true that w has the following effect in this case: Q sees Sarah Jones. Now imagine that Sarah Jones' place is taken by her identical twin, Mary, who is dressed and made up just as Sarah was, and is standing in exactly the same way that Sarah was, down to the smallest detail. Light rays are reflected from Mary Jones and produce in Q a "qualitatively identical" brain event w as before. But this time, we cannot say that w has the effect that Q sees Sarah Jones, for he sees Mary Jones. To be sure, like causes have like effects, and under another description, w does indeed produce the same effect this time that it did before; for in both cases it has the effect that Q sees a woman dressed in such-and-such a way, standing in such-and-such a manner, and looking thus-and-so. The principle "Like causes have like effects," then, must be used with caution: if it is not, bad arguments may result. The present version of the argument from the short causal chain blandly assumes that its invoking of the principle is a legitimate one. But as we have seen from the direct realist's rejoinder, this assumption badly needs support—support that is altogether lacking in the argument itself. And this means that the argument as it stands is just not valid.

We must conclude that both versions of the argument from the short causal chain are invalid; the argument does not in the least force one to embrace the sense-datum theory of perception. A direct realist is able to accommodate all the facts cited in that argument.[46]

---

[46] The earlier argument from hallucinations may be viewed as appealing to the following assumption: If one of two "qualitatively indistinguishable" visual experiences is the direct awareness of a (visual) sense-datum (as it is in the case of a visual hallucination), then the other experience (which is caused, perhaps, by light rays being reflected from an object, as in normal sense perception) must also be the direct awareness of a (visual) sense-datum. This assumption is clearly based on a kind of mentalistic version of Principle P—a version that is no better than the original P.

This concludes my discussion of what I take to be the four most weighty arguments for the existence of sense-data. What I have tried to show is that when these arguments are viewed, as they often are by their defenders, as deductive arguments—i.e., as demonstrative proofs that it is only sense-data that we are ever directly confronted with in sense perception—they are simply invalid. All the facts cited in the premises of the arguments can be readily accommodated within a direct realist view of sense perception.

In launching the foregoing attack, I certainly intended to undermine one's faith in the existence of sense-data, but I do not regard the assault as having been absolutely fatal. Those who favor sense-data still have the very live option of retreating to the following line of defense—one that seems to me, moreover, to be the only proper line of defense for them: to concede that the four arguments we have considered are not deductively sound, and to claim, rather, that the sense-datum theory is the best philosophical theory of sense perception, and offers better accounts than its competitors do of various (and, it is hoped, *all*) perceptual phenomena and of other philosophically relevant facts about sense perception. The four arguments could easily be recast to accord with this new view of the matter: they would then take the form not of deductive proofs but rather of non-deductive "inferences to the best theory." The argument from hallucinations, for example, would urge that the best explanation for the striking similarity between the experience of having a hallucination of pink rats and that of seeing real pink rats is provided by supposing that in both cases the person is directly confronted with a qualitatively identical item—namely, a pink-rats-ish sense-datum. And so on.

I believe that this way of regarding the doctrine of sense-data is the only legitimate one, because it reveals the true colors of the doctrine: it shows that we are really dealing with a philosophical *theory* of sense perception, one that posits sense-data as theoretical entities (or the awareness of sense-data as theoretical states of perceivers, if you prefer), and one to which there are conceivable alternatives. My objection to the doctrine as so viewed is that the sense-datum theory is an incredibly bad theory of perception.

E. SOME GENERAL REMARKS ABOUT THEORIES OF PERCEPTION

When I pass this harsh judgment, I am presumably appealing to one or more criteria of what constitutes a good philosophical theory of perception. I shall take this opportunity to indicate, very briefly and dogmatically, what I take these criteria to be, so that the reader will know both what the basis of my condemnation of the sense-datum theory is and what virtues I shall be seeking to embody in the theory of perception that I offer.

I begin with some remarks on what I understand by a philosophical theory of perception. Such a theory must include two major features: first and foremost, a characterization, in its own basic theoretical terms, of the various kinds of perceptual and quasi-perceptual states of perceivers, and second, a statement of necessary and sufficient conditions for a perceiver to perceive something in the different sense modalities (e.g., to see something). I should suppose that characterizations of perceptual states and lists of the conditions just indicated could be formulated in any number of different ways, not all of which would yield what we would happily call *philosophical* theories of perception. The philosopher's peculiar interest in perception has always been mainly epistemological and metaphysical. He has wanted answers to such questions as: How reliable are our perceptual states? To what extent is the nature of the physical world accurately revealed to us in perception? What is the metaphysical status of the objects of perception, and of our perceptual states? Now I suggest that what primarily distinguishes philosophical theories of perception from others (e.g., from psychological or physiological ones) is just that they reflect these traditional epistemological and metaphysical interests, and so are designed

specifically to provide direct answers to such questions.
(Or perhaps I should say that this is what marks off what
I, along with most philosophers in the Western tradition,
take seriously as philosophical theories of perception. Since
philosophy is not just "one thing," however, there may well
be philosophical theories of perception that reflect quite
different interests.)

A large part of the philosopher's epistemological and
metaphysical interest in sense perception is aroused by
doubts and worries that afflict him when he thinks about
certain perceptual phenomena and various facts concerning perception—e.g., when he thinks about hallucinations, illusions, the physiology of perception, and so on.
And a philosophical theory of perception must of course
be able to accommodate all these facts and phenomena:
for example, it must provide a way of characterizing hallucinatory states that takes account of the fact that they
are quite similar, in some ways, to "veridical" perceptual
states; it must assert nothing that is inconsistent with well-
established facts about the causation of perception, and so
on.

From these considerations, I conclude that there are two
major criteria for the goodness of a philosophical theory of
perception. First: that it takes account more satisfactorily
than its competitors do of all perceptual phenomena and
established facts about perception—for example, the results of psychological experiments in perception. This criterion is rather obscure as I have stated it, but I shall have
to leave it that way for the present; I return to it, and say
a lot more about it, in Chapter III. The second, and more
important, criterion of excellence is that the theory provides
more satisfactory answers than its competitors do to the
relevant epistemological and metaphysical questions. The
degree of satisfactoriness of answers is measured here, I
suppose, by the number and difficulty of the philosophical
problems raised by the different theories—the fewer and
easier, the better. To put the same point in another way:
one theory of perception is better than others if it has more

nearly satisfactory consequences in the areas of metaphysics and epistemology than its rivals. What a philosopher will count as "satisfactory consequences" will depend, naturally enough, on his general philosophical position. In fairness to my readers, I shall set down here what I would consider to be *un*satisfactory consequences of any theory of perception in the two relevant areas. As for metaphysics: being a materialist and behaviorist (of sorts), I would consider it a grave disadvantage of any theory of perception if it relied on non-physical states, events, processes, entities, or whatever; I believe that the problems such theories are faced with—for example, that of giving a coherent account of the metaphysical connection between the non-physical items and the perceiver's body—are insuperable. So I regard it as a prime virtue of the theory I shall be presenting that it is physicalistic; thus according to this theory, it would be entirely possible that a robot should see (hear, feel, and so on).

I am therefore bound to regard certain versions of the sense-datum theory as unsatisfactory on this score. Consider first those theories that analyze the awareness of sense-data adverbially. In this view, having a sense-datum is a way, or manner, of being aware (conscious) in a sensuous dimension; in short, it is a way of sensing. For example, to have a green circular sense-datum is to sense green-circle-ly. If a philosopher analyzes sense-data in this way, and, in addition, holds that such states of awareness must be attributed to separate mental entities (e.g., to Cartesian immaterial substances), then he has the mind-body problem squarely on his hands and his theory to that extent labors under what I consider to be a crippling weight. If, however, he regards those states of awareness as attributable to certain kinds of purely physical bodies, then his theory is not thus handicapped.

I would make the same comments, *mutatis mutandis*, about theories that embody an act-object analysis of the awareness of sense-data. But there is an additional disadvantage that all sense-datum theories of this second kind suffer from: they posit the existence of entities (viz., sense-data) whose metaphysical nature is extremely baffling. They are wholly distinct from objects (events, states of affairs) in the physical world; presumably, then, either they are neutral (neither physical nor mental) or they are mental in character. But in either case, they raise a storm of questions. Can they exist without being sensed by anyone? If so, it would seem that a whole new metaphysical realm has to be set aside to house them. The standard view is rather that they cannot exist unsensed. But then we shall need an explanation of why these objects have the amazing property of springing into existence, and lapsing into non-existence, as perceivers sense, and cease sensing, them. Do they have any causal efficacy? Can more than one person sense the (numerically) same sense-datum at any given time? The usual answer is that this is not possible, that a sense-datum is private to the individual who has it. But this is an extraordinary characteristic for any kind of object to have, and we require some account that will make the doctrine intelligible to us. No sense-datum theorist, to my knowledge, even tries to offer satisfaction on these and other related points. Typically, he simply lists the characteristics he takes sense-data to have. In a way, this is all right; because sense-data are theoretical entities and so we must just accept the word of the theorist as to their nature—his word, after all, must be law. But when we discover, from the list of characteristics that is usually submitted, that sense-data are entities of a very puzzling kind, no one can blame us for regarding them with suspicion or for assigning low marks to theories of perception that resort to them.

Turning now to the area of epistemology: I would view with dismay any theory that had sceptical consequences, that ruled out the possibility of our having any justified perceptual knowledge of the furniture of the world. Thus I regard it as another virtue of the theory I offer in these pages that it is a version of direct realism. I shall have more to say about this aspect of the theory in the fourth, and final, chapter.

It is just here that the most serious and notorious deficiencies of sense-datum theories are encountered. If the sense-datum theorist maintains the existence of physical objects (states of affairs, and so on), as ordinarily conceived, then his claim that sense-data are metaphysically distinct from anything in the physical world commits him to a version of representational realism. The enormous epistemological difficulties faced by theories of this kind are well known, and so I shall not say anything about them, except that I regard them as insuperable and would go—indeed, I have gone—to great lengths to seek an alternative theory of perception that is free from them. If, on the other hand, the sense-datum theorist abjures the existence of physical objects (states of affairs, and so on), as ordinarily conceived, he commits himself pretty inevitably to some form of phenomenalism;[47] these theories may avoid the sceptical consequences of representational realisms, but they run afoul of numerous well-known ills of their own that are quite as hard to bear.

My aim in this book is to present a philosophical theory of perception that satisfies the criteria outlined in the last few pages. It is time now to set to work on this formidable task.

[47] Critical realisms provide additional options for sense-datum theorists; but I ignore those theories because I understand them only imperfectly.

II

The Evolution of the Theory

A. CRUDE APPROXIMATIONS

It does not seem possible to deny that the physiologist's causal account of perception, as far as it goes and in its main lines, is correct. It cannot be denied that in the case of vision, for example, light rays reflected or emitted from objects enter the eyes of the perceiver and form images on his retinas, that electro-chemical signals are sent along the nerve fibres making up his optic nerves, and that the visual centers in his brain are thus stimulated. There is, of course, a tremendous amount that we do not yet know about what goes on in the eye, the optic nerve, and especially in the brain, when a person sees something; but the broad outlines of the story are surely beyond dispute. In the preceding chapter, it was, I hope, shown that there is no reason whatever to suppose and good reason not to suppose, that the stimulation of the visual centers in the brain gives rise to visual sense-data, or to the awareness of visual sense-data. What are we to say *does* happen, then, as a result of the brain stimulation? One right answer might be: The person sees the object(s) from which the light was reflected or emitted. This is true but not helpful, since what we as philosophers are after is precisely an account of what it *is* to see something.

One traditional answer is: The person then acquires some knowledge about the object(s) from which the light was reflected or emitted. But since knowledge can presumably be analyzed in terms of true belief (plus, of course, some other notions), it might be better to phrase this traditional answer as follows: The person acquires certain true beliefs about the object(s) from which the light was reflected or emitted. From this, the following rudimentary theory of perception could be derived: sense perception is the acquiring of true beliefs concerning particular facts about one's environment, by means of or by the use of, one's sense organs. Thus, for example, to see something is just to acquire certain true beliefs about it by the use of one's eyes. If this analysis—or rather this first rough approximation of an analysis—could be modified and elaborated so as to meet several more or less obvious objections, it would be, I think, a highly tempting one.

Suppose there is an insect crawling across a white piece of paper which is lying in front of someone on his desk. If he sees that the insect is crawling across the piece of paper, almost everyone would agree that this necessarily involves his acquiring, by the use of his eyes, the belief that the insect is crawling across the paper. But to see *that such-and-such is the case* is to see something in what some philosophers have called the propositional sense of 'see'; and it might be maintained that this kind of seeing is entirely dependent on a more basic kind—viz., on seeing in the non-propositional sense of the term—and that to see something in this more basic sense does not necessarily involve the acquiring of any beliefs. Thus, in our present example, in order for the person to see that the insect is crawling across the paper, he must see the insect and he must see the piece of paper; and—so the claim would go—neither of these "acts" of (non-propositional) seeing can plausibly be said to be constituted by the acquiring of any beliefs about the insect or the paper. But is this contention correct?

There can be no doubt that one's first reaction to the thesis that seeing something consists of nothing but acquiring certain true beliefs about it by using one's eyes is to dismiss it as obviously false. But I think, on the contrary, that one can go a long way towards defending the thesis; it is not nearly so outrageous as it appears to be at first glance. If, for example, our man with the insect on his paper comes, as the result of using his eyes in a certain way—I mean, by looking at the insect and the paper—to believe, truly, and in fact to know, such things as that there is a piece of paper lying before him, that it is white and rectangular, approximately so big, and that there is an insect crawling over it that is grey, is about half an inch long, has several legs, is now near the upper right hand corner of the piece of paper, and so on—then is this not enough to constitute his actually seeing the insect and the piece of paper? What more could possibly be required? It will doubtless be objected that what is left out of this account is the very essence of seeing—namely, the sensuous visual presentation or manifold. But the answer to this might well be that to be aware of, or to have, that visual presentation or manifold just *is* to know, by means of using one's eyes, that there is a piece of paper lying before one, that it is white and rectangular, and so on. And this reply could be dismissed out of hand as being obviously inadequate only if the having of beliefs and knowledge were to be construed —wrongly—as necessarily involving the making of judgments, or the conscious entertaining of thoughts. So there is something to be said for the thesis.

Indeed, I think the thesis is very nearly correct. At least this much, anyway, seems to me to be true: an adequate theory of sense perception can be formulated which employs as its central notion that of acquiring certain kinds of beliefs. In this chapter I propose to present and defend just such a theory; but first it would be well to attend to a preliminary matter.

Many will be put off at the outset by the very idea of a theory of sense perception that is couched in terms of acquiring beliefs. "It seems wholly unnatural," they might object, "to suppose that we all go around, for most of our waking life, acquiring *beliefs* about things in our environment. If the circumstances are perfectly ordinary, then when the man in your earlier example looks down and just happens to see an insect crawling across a piece of paper, are we really supposed to imagine that he thereby acquires a new set of *beliefs?* Surely the whole idea sounds very fishy indeed." This objection speaks out not only against the *identification* of perception with the acquiring of (true) beliefs, but also against the far weaker thesis that in normal, everyday cases of perception, one regularly acquires beliefs as an adjunct of, or as the *result* of, seeing something, hearing something, or whatever. It objects, in short, to any sort of intimate connection between the concepts of sense perception and belief.

The objection does not, nor does it pretend to, take the form of an argument; rather, it merely voices an intuitive feeling of dissatisfaction with the idea that the acquiring of beliefs has anything very essential to do with sense perception. Whatever psychological force this feeling may have derives, I think, solely from the fact that one does not usually *speak* of the acquisition of beliefs in connection with seeing, hearing, and the rest. We would not, for example, ordinarily say of someone who sees an insect crawling across a piece of paper that he thereby acquires the belief that there is an insect before him, that it is crawling on a piece of white paper, and so on; it is far easier and more natural, if we bother to take note of the fact at all, to say simply that he sees an insect crawling across a piece of paper. By using the 'see'-locution, we can efficiently sum up the relevant information acquired by the perceiver and indicate, moreover, the means by which he acquired it. But precisely *because* of these facts, it is positively to be expected that when one tries to give a philosophical theory of sense perception, i.e., to say what it *is*, he will be forced to bring in notions that "sound odd" in just the way pointed out by the objection. Therefore, if one is to indulge in philosophical theories of perception at all, he must be prepared to treat lightly such objections as the one now under discussion. I realize that the issue between me and the propounder of the objection could only be settled, if at all, by a full scale discussion of such matters as the nature and point of certain kinds of philosophical theories and the importance of ordinary language in philosophy. But there is here no possibility of going into those matters in the necessary detail, and so I must content myself with the bare assertion that since I am determined to offer something that I take to be a philosophical theory of sense perception, I cannot and do not consider the objection to be of much weight.

It might, however, look unduly brash to leave it at that. Therefore, I shall venture a few more words in an effort to allay the possible misgivings of readers who feel the psychological force of the objection. I want to urge that although we do not always, or even ordinarily, speak of beliefs in connection with sense perception, nevertheless we sometimes do, and furthermore we always might or could so speak, without excessive oddity. Thus, leaving aside for the moment the precise nature of the connection between perception and belief, I want to argue that it is entirely reasonable to think that in perceptual situations somethings that can aptly be called beliefs enter in in an important way.

Let us consider one or two examples. Suppose that someone, spying a chair in the corner, walks across the room with the intention of sitting down in it, but that when he does so, the thing dissolves at the first touch, to his utter consternation, into fragments—for it is made of very thin, very fragile glass and painted to look like an ordinary chair. How can it be denied that before he attempted to sit down in the object he had the belief that the thing was a chair, and that it was sturdy enough to support his weight? Certainly as he sits or lies there dumbfounded among the debris, it would be correct to say of him that he had thought (assumed, believed) that the thing was a chair and was substantial enough to carry his weight. And this way of speaking would be entirely unexceptionable even if his misinformation had been gleaned solely from his own perceptual sources.

The foregoing example was perhaps a bit spectacular, but it is easy to think of innumerable humdrum ones. If I see a teapot and some cups on a table in a house I am visiting, then although I should no doubt be puzzled if someone were to ask me whether I thought, or believed, there was a teapot on the table, whether I thought, or believed, there were some cups on the table, whether I thought, or believed, the teapot and cups were white (they were!), and so on, then I should have to confess that yes, I did believe those things, despite the fact that those thoughts had not entered my head before the questions were raised. My believing those things, what is more, stems pretty directly from my seeing the teapot and the cups.

Whether or not, then, we go on to *identify* perception with the acquiring of beliefs, there seems to be no persuasive reason to deny that one always, or nearly always, acquires certain beliefs at least as the *result* of seeing something, hearing something, and so on. The concepts of perception and belief, in other words, are not nearly so alien to one another as the objection we have been considering claims they are.

Indeed, I think we can go further: I think reasons can be given for *identifying* certain perceptual states of a person—e.g., the state of x's looking F (or $F\text{-}er$) to him—with his being in a certain kind of belief-state. Consider, for example, the moon illusion: the moon standardly looks larger when it is near the horizon than it does when near the zenith. The best explanation we have of this phenomenon at present seems to be this. When the moon is near the horizon, it looks farther away, because of the intervening terrain over which it is seen; and since the angle it subtends in our visual field is the same near the zenith and near the horizon, it looks larger near the horizon—for normally if two objects, x and y, subtend the same visual angle, but we know, or think, that x is farther away than y, x will look larger to us than y.[1]

The question I now want to raise is: What can the moon's looking larger to us when it is near the horizon than when it is near the zenith *consist in*? What is the nature of that perceptual state? It cannot consist in the moon's subtending a larger angle in our visual field, because it demonstrably doesn't. The only answer that I can think of is that it consists in our automatically *believing*, or assuming, or having an immediate impulse or inclination to believe, as we look at the moon near the horizon, that it really *is* larger than it normally is—i.e., when it is higher in the sky. If this is in fact the nature of that perceptual state—and I cannot think of anything else that it might be—then there is reason for thinking that perceiving and believing may be very intimately bound up with one another in all cases.

I shall call any belief like those concerning the teapot and cups—any belief, namely, that is acquired by using one's sense organs in standard ways—a *perceptual belief*. This is not the time to attempt a full-scale account of the nature of belief; but I want to indicate very briefly what general sort of view I hold about the nature of perceptual beliefs, so that the reader will know what thesis it is that I shall be defending in these pages.

Philosophers have sometimes distinguished two main kinds of beliefs: conscious and nonconscious. A conscious belief, it is held, is one that the believer is currently aware of having, in that he is actually entertaining a certain proposition and assenting to it, either overtly or covertly. There can be little doubt that the having of any belief entails much more than just entertaining and assenting to a proposition; but anyway if a conscious belief is one that requires at least the performance of those two acts, perceptual beliefs are not conscious beliefs. I shall not be defending the absurd thesis that sense perception consists, either wholly

[1] See L. Kaufman and I. Rock, "The Moon Illusion," *Scientific American*, Vol. 207, No. 1 (July 1962), 120-130.

or in part, of entertaining propositions and assenting to them, of making (conscious) judgments, or anything of that sort.

A nonconscious belief is one that the believer is not at the moment consciously considering. The usual view is that to have a belief of this kind is to have a complex disposition to act (or behave) in certain ways under certain specifiable conditions. I shall hold that perceptual beliefs are one and all nonconscious. Furthermore, I would wish to defend the usual—i.e., dispositional—view as to the nature of such beliefs. There are well-known formidable-looking objections to the dispositional view of belief (e.g., Chisholm's) but I think, and in any case shall here simply have to assume, that they can be met.

I said earlier that I thought one could go quite a long way towards defending the view that sense perception is nothing but the acquiring of certain true beliefs by means of using one's sense organs—that to see something, for example, is nothing but to acquire certain true beliefs about it by using one's eyes. Let us see precisely how far one can go in this direction. The view sounds sufficiently implausible to attract a host of objections; let us see how many of them it can meet before having to be modified or abandoned.

There is, first of all, one quite obvious way in which the thesis, as stated, needs to be modified. It is not always the case that when one sees something, he thereby *acquires* or *gains* a (new) belief. For example, there is a dogwood tree just outside my study window. I quite often look outside and see this nice tree; but each time I do so, I do not *acquire* the belief that a dogwood tree is there, for I was already aware of that fact. Again, if someone looks more or less steadily at an object for a few minutes, then after the first moment he still sees the thing, but he does not acquire, at each instant, the (new) beliefs that it is there, that it has such-and-such characteristics, and so on, for he presumably had those beliefs from the first moment.

I think that some cases of the kind just mentioned can

be handled without changing the original formulation of
our thesis. This becomes evident when we realize that on
our thesis as properly understood a given (act or state
of) perception is seldom or never the acquiring of just a
single perceptual belief; it is rather the acquiring of a
more or less large *set* of such beliefs. This point needs to
be stressed; if it is ignored, our thesis will appear to be even
more implausible than it already does, since it will then
seem to have no chance whatever of capturing the great
richness of perceptual consciousness. Consider now the example of the dogwood tree. We must, I think, concede
that the single belief expressible by the words "There is
a dogwood tree outside the study window" is certainly not
acquired when, after all these years, I glance out the window and catch sight of it once again. But normally, I do
acquire a host of other, new beliefs when I see that old,
familiar object—such beliefs as that it is now roughly so
many feet away from me, that its branches are moving in
a certain way (or are not moving), that its leaves (if
any) are of a certain color, and many more besides. Our
thesis, then, evidently does not need any reformulating
to accommodate the dogwood-tree-type of case; for since
it can plausibly be construed as maintaining that sense perception is the acquiring, by means of using the senses, of a
large *set* of perceptual beliefs, it need not be embarrassed
by the fact that certain members of the set may be old beliefs.

Still, I am not quite happy with this defense of the
original formulation of our thesis. First, the old belief that
there is a dogwood tree outside my window, a belief that
I certainly do have as I sit gazing at it, is one that seems
to constitute an integral part of my perceptual consciousness; and full justice is not accorded to this status by saying
merely that the belief is a member of a new *set* of perceptual beliefs. Second, there are certain rarified cases of perception where the contention that the perceiver acquires
any relevant new beliefs at all has little or no plausibility.
Suppose, for example, that someone's visual field consists of

nothing but a grey circle against a white background. After a few seconds, at most, of gazing at this circle, the perceiver will have acquired all the perceptual beliefs about it that he is likely ever to acquire—and yet he can undoubtedly go on seeing it.

These considerations show that the concept of *acquiring* perceptual beliefs is not the one we want, since it contains the undesirable suggestion that the perceiver did not have the relevant beliefs before. The suggestion can be eliminated if we say of the person not that he *acquires* his perceptual beliefs, but that he is *caused* to have them in a certain way. This gets rid of the unwanted implication: thus even though I already have the belief that there is a dogwood tree outside my window, nevertheless when I now look at it again, the tree (once again) causes that (perceptual) belief. It is *a* (present) cause of my belief, along with its other (past) causes. The same goes for the example of looking at the grey circle: the circle keeps causing the perceiver to believe that there is a grey circle before him as long as he looks at it: it keeps being *a* cause of his believing that. The fact that in these cases there are also other (previous) causes of the beliefs does not impugn this point in the least.[2] Our (crude) thesis, then, may be reformulated as follows: a person's perceiving something is nothing but his being caused, via his sense organs, to have certain true beliefs. But the expression 'being caused to have a belief' is cumbersome. To enable myself to construct somewhat less contorted sentences, I shall sometimes use the technical locution 'causally-receives'[3]: 'Person Q causally-receives a (perceptual) belief' is to mean exactly the same as 'Q is caused to have a (perceptual) belief' does. So a new way of expressing our thesis is as follows: a person's perceiving something is nothing but his causally-receiving, via (or by using) his appropriate sense organ(s), certain

[2] I am indebted here to Alvin I. Goldman's "A Causal Theory of Knowing," *Journal of Philosophy*, 64 (1967), 362, n. 7.

[3] I shall also occasionally use the corresponding noun expression 'causal-reception.'

true beliefs. A person's seeing something, for example, is nothing but his causally-receiving, via (or by using) his eyes, certain true beliefs. (Note: Since the expression 'causally-receiving a belief' means nothing significantly different from 'acquiring a belief,' except that it lacks the unwanted suggestion indicated earlier, I shall, for the sake of verbal variety, often use the latter expression when its unwanted implication does no harm.)

Let us see now whether our thesis, as modified, is able to counter the more powerful-seeming objections that might be arrayed against it. Surely one of the most formidable looking among them is this: that the view seems to leave out the very heart of perception. If we confine ourselves for the moment to the sense of sight, what it leaves out, according to this objection, is the visual manifold, the visual presentation, that which is before one's consciousness when he sees something. In place of the rich concrete complexity of the visually given, we are offered a mere battery of beliefs. To be sure, the thesis, as presented, denies that the beliefs it claims to be essential to sense perception are conscious judgments; but in so far as it substitutes a thin cognitive abstraction for the full-bodied sensuous reality, it is no better than the old rationalist view that sense perception is just a low-grade kind of thinking.

Although it cannot be denied that this objection carries quite a bit of psychological force, and indeed that it crowds in upon one almost as soon as our thesis is enunciated, nevertheless it is not entirely clear precisely what it amounts to. If by 'visual presentation' it means a manifold of sense-data, then, as the argument of the last chapter has shown, one must count it as a point in favor of the thesis that it "leaves out" the visual presentation. But if it is not sense-data that the objection claims are left out, what does it think the thesis omits? Not the perceiver's (act or state of) seeing whatever it is he sees, for that is just what the thesis purports to give an account of. Not *what* is seen, for what is seen, normally, are things like tables, chairs, shadows, clouds, and so on—and it does not leave *them* out! It appears that the objection cannot make good its charge that our thesis leaves something out of account.

But once the charge that the thesis leaves out the essence of seeing is dropped, the objection reduces to the claim that the thesis does not offer a satisfactory or adequate account of the nature of seeing. But this is nothing more than an assertion which stands in need of some backing; it is a mere expression of dissent without the slightest indication of a reason.

The objection was not intended, of course, to point out faults of detail in our thesis. It does not, for example, assert that there are certain perceptual phenomena that escape its explanatory or descriptive net, or that there are certain disadvantages involved in accepting it. Rather, it labels the entire thesis as misconceived in principle from the start. What it says, in effect, is that the thesis cannot be considered as a competitor for the title of the correct, or even a respectable, account of perception. "The nature of beliefs," the objection seems to suggest, "is such that their being caused in a person could not possibly constitute the essence of his (act or state of) perception. Beliefs are the wrong kind of thing; so your offered thesis is just not in the running." But this is mere a priori prejudice. I hope I have shown that the concept of belief is not *totally* or *wildly* unrelated to that of perception; and therefore, until some actual arguments or considerations are raised against our account, it must be allowed to stand and be judged.

If someone still cannot rid himself of the disturbing idea that there must be some virtue in the objection, this may be because he is thinking along the following lines: "Look here, I know perfectly well what it is to have one of your nonconscious beliefs; I have literally hundreds of them at this very moment—about my age, my weight, my profession, who is President of the United States, and so on and on. But the having of such beliefs is nothing whatever like the experience of seeing or hearing something. Indeed, just because they are *non*conscious, having them is not an *experience* at all. And precisely here lies the ab-

surdity of your thesis: for it tries to analyze one form of
consciousness—perceptual consciousness—in terms, if I
may put it so, of a form of nonconsciousness." This line of
thought, I suspect, is what gives the objection its psychological force. But it is entirely without merit. First, the perceptual beliefs of our thesis, although nonconscious, are
far "richer" than the kind of nonconscious beliefs mentioned in the objection. A person's belief about what his
age is, for example, consists almost exclusively of a disposition to act in a rather limited variety of purely linguistic
ways—i.e., to do such things as say "sixty" when asked
what his age is (to put it far too crudely). Even the simplest
sort of perceptual belief, on the other hand, consists of
a highly complex disposition to act, or behave, in a wide
variety of ways, among which linguistic behavior figures
only peripherally if at all.

Second and more important, although it is true that our
thesis analyzes sense perception in terms of nonconscious
beliefs, it does not identify it with the *having* of such beliefs. That would indeed be to identify a form of consciousness with a form of nonconsciousness. Rather, it identifies
seeing and the other kinds of sense perception with nonconscious beliefs' being *caused* in one, and caused, furthermore, in a special way—namely, via the use of one's sense
organs, that is, by the stimulation of one's sense organs.
It is by no means self-evident that the causal-reception of
such beliefs in that way cannot be a "conscious experience,"
that it cannot in fact be exactly what is meant by perceptual
consciousness. I would even go further than this. If, just
by looking at, say, a vase of flowers, you were able, if
called upon, to indicate with confidence roughly how far
away it is, in what direction from you it is, what the colors
of the flowers are, how the leaves and stems are disposed,
and so on for a great multitude of further details—that is,
if you causally-received, by using your eyes, certain true,
but probably nonconscious, beliefs about the vase of flowers—then I would say that you certainly saw the vase of
flowers, that you were (visually) conscious of it. So it seems

to me that there is no a priori reason whatsoever for thinking that the causal-receptions of nonconscious beliefs in
certain ways cannot be "conscious experiences"; on the
contrary, there is reason to think that they are, at least
in the case of sense perception. Therefore, although some
may find the objection we have been considering to be
psychologically persuasive, we, who are of course free from
all prejudice, should not find it so, for there is no rational
virtue in it.

Having saved our thesis from premature a priori destruction and perhaps having even removed its initial air of
implausibility, we must turn now to some objections that
are more legitimate. We shall not have to consider very
many, for, as we shall see, the thesis as now formulated will
give way soon enough.

The first of these objections might be put as follows:
"Your thesis that seeing is the causal-reception of true
beliefs by using one's eyes cannot be correct, for the devas-
tating reason that a person can see something and yet acquire *false* beliefs about it. If, for example, a man is artfully
camouflaged, by the use of skin dyes and painted clothing,
to look exactly like a small tree, then someone might see
the man but causally-receive the false belief that he is
looking at a small tree. Again, anyone who is taken in by
the standard optical illusions may see the lines or figures
perfectly clearly, and yet he acquires false beliefs about
them—e.g., that the lines are curved when they are really
straight, that one line is longer than another when the
two are of the same length, and so on."

The objection shows that our thesis needs to be slightly
modified: although it does not explicitly say so, the thesis
suggests that in order to perceive (e.g., see) something, one
must causally-receive nothing but true beliefs. And this is
surely wrong: for as the examples indicate, a person can
see something even when he acquires some false beliefs
about it. But it is important to realize that if a person should
causally-receive *nothing but* false beliefs about something,
or even, I should think, *too many* false beliefs about it,

then he could not be said to perceive it. The right thing to
say, then, is that perceiving something requires the causal-
reception of *some* true beliefs about it via, or by using,
one's appropriate sense organ(s). And in the examples of
the objection, the perceivers presumably do acquire some
true beliefs about the perceived objects by using their eyes.
The person who is deceived by the camouflaged man, for
instance, no doubt acquires the beliefs that something is
there before him, that it is approximately so high, that it
is predominantly brownish in color, that it is not moving,
and so on. Our thesis may now be stated as follows: a person's perceiving (e.g., seeing) something is nothing but
his causally-receiving, via (or by using) his appropriate
sense organ(s) (e.g., his eyes), certain beliefs, some of
which, at least, are true. There is a big question, to be
sure, of just what sorts of true beliefs, and (roughly) how
many, our thesis requires a person to causally-receive if
he is really to perceive something. But there is little point
in discussing the question in that form at the present
time (although we shall return later to what is essentially
the same question); for the next objection will cause us
to modify our thesis radically. Lest the reader be tempted
to abandon this book upon hearing that announcement, I
urge him not to despair; all will not be lost, and in fact
the heart of our thesis will turn out to be salvageable.

Before proceeding to the fateful objection, however, I
should like to discuss briefly a further question that arises
in connection with such cases as that of the camouflaged
man. To change the example, suppose that a pheasant hen
is sitting motionless on her nest among dry brown twigs
and grasses so that she blends perfectly into her surroundings. Imagine a hunter approaching quite close and looking
directly at her, but failing to distinguish her from the general background of sticks and grasses. Which of the following are we to say of this perceptual state of affairs?

(a) (i) The hunter acquires some (true) perceptual
        beliefs about the pheasant by means of using his eyes.

(a) (ii) The hunter acquires no (true) perceptual beliefs about the pheasant.

(b) (i) The hunter sees the pheasant.

(b) (ii) The hunter does not see the pheasant.

A case can, I think, be made for each of these assertions. It is obvious how (a) (ii) and (b) (ii) might be defended. And if instead of construing the expression '*p* is a belief about *y*' stringently, as we do in (a) (ii), we treat it liberally, then (a) (i) can be held to be true on the ground that the hunter certainly acquires some true perceptual beliefs about various brownish surfaces that are *in fact* (although the hunter does not realize it) parts of the surface of the pheasant. Similarly, if 'sees' is conceived liberally, (b) (i) is true, for the hunter is looking directly at, and sees, something that is in fact the pheasant, even though he mistakenly takes it to be nothing but brown grass and twigs.

In a great many, and perhaps most, cases, I suppose, 'see' is treated stringently; for if someone says "Jones saw a(n) *F*" (e.g., "Jones saw a pheasant"), there is usually an implication that Jones recognized what he saw as a(n) *F* (e.g., as a pheasant). But 'see' is quite often used liberally as well. It is easy to imagine circumstances in which it would be true and not misleading to say "Jones saw a pheasant" where Jones did not recognize the thing as a pheasant. In practically all of these cases, the perceiver does recognize the pheasant as something-or-other—as a big bird, some kind of flying thing, a big brown animal, or whatever. But it is, I think, just possible to allow our example of the hunter and the pheasant, where the perceiver does not recognize the bird even as a distinct object, to count as a (perhaps degenerate) case of seeing it.

One may well be led astray if he ignores these distinctions (between the liberal and stringent readings of 'see' and 'belief about') or is careless with them. For example, if, in dealing with the case of the hunter and the protectively colored pheasant, one were to construe 'belief about' liberally (so that (a) (i) is rendered true) and at the same time construed 'see' stringently (so that (b) (ii) is rendered true), then it would look as though our thesis were overthrown—for the hunter would then acquire some true beliefs about something in the required way, and yet fail to see it, contrary to what our thesis maintains. The same unhappy consequences would appear to ensue, of course, if 'belief about' were to be construed stringently (making (a) (ii) true) and 'see' liberally (making (b) (i) true). But our thesis is not in fact seriously threatened in these ways, since there is no reason whatever why anyone *must* ever adopt the damaging "mixed" readings of 'see' and 'belief about': on the contrary, one may very well choose—and I do so choose—either to interpret both terms liberally or to interpret both stringently, and then the hunter-pheasant case poses no embarrassment to our thesis.

There is no need for us to make a sweeping decision ahead of time either for the joint liberal reading of the terms 'belief about' and 'see' or for their joint stringent reading. There is certainly no need to do this for absolutely all cases, nor even, I think, a need to do so for any given case. I would suppose that the special circumstances of an individual situation, as well as one's interests (concerns, attitudes, points of view, or whatever) in describing it, would determine whether one chooses the joint liberal reading or the joint stringent reading for that particular case. Consider once again our example of the hunter and the protectively colored pheasant: if we were to view this situation from the practical point of view of a hunter, we should most likely deny that the hunter saw the pheasant, thus interpreting 'see,' and hence also 'belief about,' stringently. But the liberal sense of 'see' and hence also of 'belief about' might be more appropriate if we adopted a less practical point of view. Then we could argue that the hunter's eyes were opened and functioning properly, that they were aimed directly at the pheasant, and that he most certainly saw *something* in the volume of space that was in fact occupied by the pheasant. So he must have seen the pheasant, although it would no doubt be misleading to say so without qualification.

In the hunter-pheasant example, then, 'see' and 'belief about' can be treated either stringently or liberally. Other cases do not seem to lend themselves so readily to the stringent interpretations. For example: imagine that Smith looks at a huge blow-up picture of several horses, but owing to special circumstances he does not realize that it is a *picture* he is looking at—he thinks he is viewing some real horses.[4] Here it seems difficult to deny that Smith sees the picture, and thus difficult to treat 'see' stringently. Perhaps the relevant difference in the two cases is that Smith is not "out to get" pictures, is not looking for or hunting pictures, whereas the hunter was "out to get" (looking for, hunting) pheasants. So in the Smith-picture case, 'see' is naturally treated liberally. It may be a trifle less natural to treat 'belief about' liberally here—to hold, in other words, that Smith acquires some (perceptual) beliefs about what is *in fact* the picture, despite his not knowing that it is a picture. Nevertheless, we can so treat it. The slight difference in the relative degrees of naturalness of treating 'see' and 'belief about' liberally reflects a difference in the concepts of seeing and believing. Since Smith indubitably sees something, it must be the picture that he sees, for nothing else is there to be seen. But the objects of belief, on the other hand, do not have to exist; and so one must concede that Smith acquires perceptual beliefs about some (nonexistent) horses. But I insist that this concession by no means rules out the possibility that Smith at the same time acquires some beliefs about (what is in fact) the picture, where 'belief about' is thus construed liberally.

Because it looks as though any "seeing"-situation can lend itself to the liberal interpretations of 'see' and 'belief about,' whereas this does not seem to be so for the stringent interpretations, and because it is easier to do so, I shall deal almost exclusively with the liberal interpretations in what follows.

---

[4] For this example, I am indebted to William Kalke.

The liberal reading of 'see' is anyway more fundamental than the stringent one in the sense that the latter includes the former but contains an additional element besides. Thus, for example, 'He sees (stringent reading) the pheasant' can be analyzed into (i) 'He sees (liberal reading) the pheasant' and (ii) 'He recognizes it as a pheasant' (or perhaps 'He causally-receives the belief that it is a pheasant').

On both the stringent and liberal readings of 'see,' any object that a person sees must actually be there to be seen; hence both are what Miss Anscombe calls "material uses" of the verb, to be distinguished from its "intentional use."[5] When 'see' is used intentionally, what is seen is an intentional object, which need not "be there to be seen"; so on this use, a person sees rays shooting out from a light when he screws up his eyes (p. 169), or, in our example of Smith and the picture of horses, Smith sees some horses. I shall steadfastly ignore the intentional use of perceptual verbs (e.g., 'see'), because I am wary of intentional objects. This will not really be a deficiency in my account, however, for it would not be difficult to show that the cases where the intentional use of perceptual verbs comes naturally can all be perfectly adequately characterized by using such phrases as 'looks as though,' 'what sounds like a so-and-so,' etc.—which means that my theory will be able to handle the intentional cases, since it will provide analyses of these phrases.

We come now to the damaging objection mentioned earlier. It is this: "Seeing something cannot possibly consist of nothing but the causal-reception of certain (true) beliefs about it by the use of one's eyes, because there are cases of seeing something in which the person causally-receives no beliefs whatever about it, true or false. Suppose, for example, that a man is stumbling across the desert when suddenly there looms before him what he takes to be a mi-

[5] See G.E.M. Anscombe, "The Intentionality of Sensation: A Grammatical Feature," in R. J. Butler (ed.), *Analytical Philosophy*, 2nd ser. (Oxford: Basil Blackwell, 1965), pp. 158-180.

rage, or better yet, a hallucinatory vision, of an oasis. He is absolutely sure that his senses are deceiving him, or that his mind is, because that has been the case on the forty-three very recent occasions when he thought he saw an oasis. This time, however, the oasis is genuine. Surely it cannot be denied that the desert traveller sees the oasis. And yet he has not acquired a single belief about the oasis, for he is positively convinced that there isn't any. He does not even believe that there is something or other there in the desert before him that *looks* like an oasis; he thinks the whole thing is generated internally by the unhealthy state of his nervous system. I conclude that your thesis, which implies that this combination of circumstances is impossible, must be rejected."

There can be no doubt that this is a damaging objection; so damaging, I think, that our thesis in its present form is unable to survive it. The example of the man in the desert presents us with the following situation: it looks to him as though there is an oasis before him, but because of his beliefs about the state of his nervous system or the state of his mind or whatever, he refuses to believe that there is any such oasis. I argued earlier that our thesis makes provision for the so-called "visual presentation"; this contention may be interpreted as making the claim that our thesis gives an account of what it is for something to *look* so-and-so to someone, or of what it is for it to *look as though* so-and-so were the case to someone, or of what it is for something to have a certain *look*. However, the account that our thesis gives of these things is in terms of the perceiver's causally-receiving certain relevant beliefs, and it presupposes that the perceiver does causally-receive some of them; and the case of the desert traveller is embarrassing precisely because it is one in which although it looks to the perceiver as though there were something (an oasis) before him, he nevertheless causally-receives none of the relevant beliefs. Hence, our thesis is unable to cope with it.[6]

[6] One might try to cope with this example by saying that the desert traveller *does* causally-receive a suitable perceptual belief—the belief

This example would be enough by itself to upset our thesis as now formulated; but it is by no means a rare or isolated counterexample. There are lots of others. For instance, consider a person who looks at a straight stick that is lying before him on his desk, in perfectly ordinary circumstances. According to our thesis, he causally-receives, by means of using his eyes, the belief, among others, that there is a straight stick before him. But suppose that he then immerses half the stick in a bucket of water; although it now looks bent, our knowledgeable perceiver still causally-receives the same belief that there is a straight stick before him. The stick first looks to be what it is, namely, straight, and then it looks bent; since it can account for the way things look only in terms of the beliefs that the perceiver actually causally-receives, our thesis has no way of distinguishing between the two different ways the stick looks to our perceiver.

The examples of the desert traveller and of the stick half submerged in water are typical of two broad classes of cases. The first, illustrated by the desert traveller, is the class of situations in which things look to be exactly (or almost exactly) what they are, but the perceiver, for some reason or other, thinks they do not. The second, illustrated by the stick half submerged in water, is the class of situations in which things look different from what they are, and the perceiver, for some reason or other, thinks, or knows, that this is the case. These two classes obviously include a great many different kinds of situations, some of them more common than others. And our present thesis, since it cannot give any account of them, must either be modified or totally abandoned.

---

that it looks to him as though he were seeing an oasis up ahead, or perhaps the belief that he is aware, in a quasi-visual way, of an oval expanse surrounded by palm-tree-shaped expanses. But for various reasons—hinging on the fact that the suggested beliefs include, either explicitly or implicitly, the very notion (viz., "looking as though . . .") that we are trying to give an account of—I spurn this attempted defense of our thesis.

B. Looking

What is needed in order to deal with these cases, obviously, is an account of what it is for things to look so-and-so to a perceiver that does not demand that he actually causally-receive a certain set of relevant beliefs. I shall try now to develop such an account that will remain true to the spirit of our original thesis, even if the final result may be that the thesis has to be rather drastically modified. To begin, it would be well to indicate clearly exactly which locution(s) containing the verb 'looks' are going to be dealt with. There are, of course, very many such locutions. It might seem as though a natural one to start with would be

I. A thing, x, looks F to someone, Q.

In fact, however, statements of this form are fairly complicated; because in order for something, x, to look a certain way (F) to someone, he must actually *see* x. (This is awkward if one wants, as I shall, to analyze 'see' in terms of 'looks'!) So sentence schema I entails the conjunction of (1) Q sees x, and (2) It looks to Q as though x is F. I think that it would be wiser to concentrate our attention on locutions of the general type

II. It looks to someone, Q, as though p,

and, in particular, on the following species of that general type

IIA. It looks to someone, Q, as though there is an x at place u.

It must be confessed that this type of 'looks'-locution is probably the easiest of all for our theory. I think it will be fairly clear, however, that one will be able to provide similar, albeit more complicated, analyses for the more difficult locutions. I shall make no attempt to do that, for I think there is little to be gained thereby: the major objections to the kind of account I shall be presenting will find their points of application just as well in the account of type IIA locutions as in the more complicated accounts that would be required for other kinds of 'looks'-locutions. So I shall treat our analysis of the IIA locutions as a sample for the whole class of 'looks'-locutions and take it for granted that analyses in the same spirit (i.e., using the same theoretical notions) can be provided for all other members of the class.

There are many sentences of type IIA that are normally used in describing situations that have nothing very directly to do with sense perception—e.g., 'It looks to the President as though there is a potential threat to our security in Cuba.' Let us ignore sentences of this sort, and deal rather only with those sentences of type IIA that are most appropriately used with what I shall call a *phenomenal* sense of 'looks'—i.e., the sense of 'looks' involved when it can be said of a person who is looking, under perfectly normal conditions, at a pencil lying on his desk, "It looks to him as though there is a pencil lying on his desk."[7]

The perceptual situations in which it would be true to say of a perceiver, Q, that it looks (in our phenomenal sense) to him as though there is an x at place u may be arranged in a (rough) series according to the beliefs Q causally-receives, by using his eyes, about the existence of an x at place u. At one end of the series are the cases in which Q causally-receives in that way the belief, which he does not question, that there is, indeed, an x at place u. This kind of case is probably the most common of those we are now considering; it is, I suppose, the standard case. Our thesis, as now formulated (i.e., the thesis that seeing is nothing but the causal-reception of beliefs by means of using one's eyes), seems to have envisaged *only* this sort of case, and to have ignored the less common members of the series that we shall be coming to in a moment. Let us label these normal or standard cases, *First Cases*.

Before proceeding down our series of cases, let us pause here with the First Cases, and ask what sort of account can

[7] There are those who would question the legitimacy of using the word 'looks' this way in such normal situations, but I shall not stop to discuss their doubts, but simply refer the reader to H. P. Grice's article "The Causal Theory of Perception" (*Proceedings of the Aristotelian Society*, Supplementary Volume 35 [1961], 121-52), where the objection is discussed and, in my opinion, disposed of.

be given of the facts stated by sentences of type IIA *for these cases*—i.e., what sort of account in terms of the notion of causally-receiving certain beliefs. It might seem that the answer to this question is perfectly obvious—namely, that the account is

(*a*) *Q* causally-receives, by means of using his eyes,[8] the (perceptual) belief that there is an *x* at *u*.

But there is the following objection to this easy solution:

"(*a*) is too thin to capture the richness of IIA. For example, consider this statement of form IIA:

(1) It looks to Smith as though there is a tree outside the window.

The corresponding substitution instance of (*a*) would be

(2) Smith causally-receives, by means of using his eyes, the (perceptual) belief that there is a tree outside the window.

But (2) is not enough; on a belief-acquiring account of 'looks,' such as the one we are now discussing, (1) could not possibly be true unless Smith also causally-received lots of other beliefs in addition to the meagre one mentioned in (2)—beliefs, for example, about the (rough) distance and direction of the tree from Smith, about its

---

[8] This formulation may be satisfactory *for First Cases*, as these have just been characterized, but it certainly will not do for all kinds of cases in which (a) it looks to someone, *Q*, as though there is an *x* at place *u, and* (b) *Q* causally-receives the belief that there is an *x* at place *u*. It won't do, because (a) might be true when *Q* causally-receives the belief that there is an *x* at *u* in some way other than by using his eyes—e.g., by having his optic nerves, or certain areas of his visual cortex, electrically stimulated. It would not be difficult, however, to remove the restriction contained in (a) so as to have an account that applies more widely than just to First Cases. A rough formulation of one such modified schema might look something like this:

(*a'*) *Q* causally-receives, by means of using his eyes, the (perceptual) belief that there is an *x* at *u*; or *Q* causally-receives in some other way—probably by the stimulation of a part of his nervous system ordinarily involved in vision—a belief, essentially like the one mentioned in the previous clause, that there is an *x* at *u*.

branches and leaves, and others. Therefore, the proposed account is far too thin."

This objection recognizes the inherent richness of (1), but fails to see the corresponding richness of (2). I concede, indeed insist, that in order for (1) to be true, it is necessary that some set of the following propositions be true:

It looks to Smith as though the tree is roughly so big.
It looks to Smith as though it is roughly so far away.
It looks to him as though it is roughly in such-and-such a direction.
It looks to him as though it has leaves (or does not have leaves).
It looks to him as though its branches are disposed in such-and-such a way.
And so on.

How many, and which ones, of this indefinite set are true in any given case will depend upon the circumstances; normally, for example, fewer of them will be true if Smith merely glances quickly out the window than if he gazes steadily at the tree for a time. But some set of these subsidiary "looks"-propositions must be true, if (1) is true; one cannot deny all of them and maintain that it simply looks to Smith as though there is a tree outside the window. So (1), then, has a variable richness built into it, and this fact is recognized in the present objection.

But (2) has an exactly corresponding richness, a fact that is not acknowledged in the objection. The belief mentioned in (2) is a perceptual belief, not an ordinary one that a person might acquire by, for example, hearsay; and the only reasonable view to take of perceptual beliefs is that they include, as integral and essential parts, a variable set of subsidiary beliefs—just as its looking to a perceiver as though such-and-such is the case necessarily includes a variable set of subsidiary "lookings," as we have just seen. Thus the truth of (2) requires the truth of some set—

which set will again depend on the circumstances of the particular case—of the following propositions:

> Smith causally-receives, by means of using his eyes, the belief that the tree is roughly so big.
> Smith causally-receives . . . the belief that the tree is roughly so far away.
> Smith causally-receives . . . the belief that it is roughly in such-and-such a direction.
> And so on.

This set, it will be noticed, answers precisely to the set involved in the case of (1) and indicated in the last paragraph. Since perceptual beliefs must thus be viewed as having exactly the right amount of complexity, or richness, we can safely dismiss the objection and allow (a) to stand, so far, as an account of IIA for First Cases.

Nevertheless, our formulation of (a) is deficient in another way. This becomes evident when we remember that a person can use his eyes to gain beliefs about the world— even *perceptual* beliefs—in ways that are different from the way he uses them when he sees something. For example, he can place his eyes against a warm or cold surface, and learn thereby that it is warm or cold. Or, he can place his eyes on the edge of a table and, by tracing around the edge with his head, discover that its shape is circular. When he uses his eyes in these bizarre ways, the surface does not ipso facto *look* circular. Similarly, if Q uses his eyes in such a way that he *feels* with them that there is a pencil on the desk, the corresponding statement-instance of IIA will be false—that is, it will not *look* to Q as though there is a pencil on the desk. To rule out these unwanted cases of feeling things with one's eyes, and others, we must add some phrase to (a) to require that the using of the eyes involves the stimulation of their retinas by light rays. Perhaps the best way to do this would be to add the phrase 'in the standard visual way' to (a), thus yielding

(A) Q causally-receives, by means of using his eyes in
the standard visual way, the (perceptual) belief that
there is an x at u.

I want to say something about the role of the word 'perceptual' in this statement of (A). A person can use his
eyes in the standard visual way and causally-receive the
belief that there is an x at u (e.g., a tree outside the window), where it nevertheless does *not* look to him, in the
phenomenal sense, as though there is an x at u (a tree outside the window). This would be the case, for example, if
he were to read a statement, which he accepts, asserting
that there is a tree outside the window. If one were to
omit the word 'perceptual' in (A), then, (A) would be too
liberal to coincide, in the desired way, with IIA for First
Cases. So I need to impose a restriction on (A), and I do
it by insisting that the causally-received belief be a *perceptual* belief that there is an x at u. (And since Q causally-
receives it by means of using his *eyes*, the belief is a perceptual one of the specifically *visual* sort. In what immediately follows, I shall continue to use the generic label
'perceptual belief,' although I mean to be referring only to
the more specific kind just indicated).

But now I owe the reader a more explicit account than
I have so far given of exactly what I mean by a perceptual
belief that there is an x at u. As my recent remarks about
the "variable richness" of perceptual beliefs indicate, what
I mean by it is a belief that corresponds exactly, in its content and in the degree of its richness (or complexity), to
the state of Q whereby it looks to him as though there is
an x at u. To put the same thing more bluntly: by a perceptual belief that there is an x at u I mean one that a person has when, in First Cases, it looks (in the phenomenal
sense) to him as though there is an x at u. So although our
theory offers (A) as a contingent, substantive claim about
the nature of Q's state as specified in IIA, the claim is also
in part a necessary truth, since the meaning of the crucial

expression in (A) is fully explicable only by reference to the state of Q specified in IIA.

We need not be embarrassed by the partially contingent, partially necessary, character of the claims that make up our theory. I suspect that any philosophical theory of perception must share this feature. Certainly sense-datum theories do, as I shall now try to show. In place of (A), sense-datum theories give the following as an (at least partial) analysis of IIA: Q has a visual sense-datum of an x at u. But what are we to understand by a visual sense-datum of an x at u (e.g., of a tree outside the window)? For example, if someone were to read a statement that there is a tree outside the window, would he thereby have a visual sense-datum of a tree outside the window? A sense-datum theorist would of course reply in the negative: what he means by a visual sense-datum of a tree outside the window, he would say—indeed, would have to say—is just that sort of sense-datum a person has when it looks to him (in the phenomenal sense) as though there is a tree outside the window. So exactly the same sort and degree of necessity attach to the sense-datum theorist's claim as attach to ours. And yet his claim, like ours, is also in part contingent: for each account purports to tell us a substantive truth about what actually goes on in a person when it looks to him as though there is an x at u—and the two accounts are, after all, *incompatible* with one another.

If, now, we travel down our imaginary series of cases away from those in which the perceiver Q causally-receives the perceptual belief that there is an x at u (First Cases), we shall come to some that may be thought of as lying about half way between the two ends of the series: these are marked by the fact that although it looks to Q as though there is an x at u, nevertheless Q, for some reason or other, is not quite sure that there is, in fact, any such x at u. Suppose, for example, that an inexperienced automobile driver sees something up ahead on the road—something that looks like a pool of water, let us say. He may be

strongly tempted to think that there is a pool of water in
the road ahead, but at the same time be suspicious of it,
since everything else in the vicinity is dry and parched.
The driver, we may say, half-believes that there is a pool
of water on the road ahead, or, as I shall prefer to put it,
that he is inclined, or has an inclination, to believe that
there is such a pool. Let us call cases of this sort *Middle
Cases*. These offer no very formidable difficulties for us,
since inclinations to (perceptual) beliefs that such-and-
such will serve our purposes here just as well as (perceptual) beliefs did for First Cases. For Middle Cases, then,
the following account can be given of situations assertable
by sentences of type IIA:

> (B) Q causally-receives, by means of using his eyes in
> the standard visual way, an inclination to have the
> (perceptual) belief that there is an x at u.

Note, incidentally, that in (B) the inclination is to be construed in the same more or less "rich" way that we construed the belief in (A), for it is, after all, an inclination
to have a *perceptual* belief that there is an x at u.

We have now given accounts of what it is for it to look
to someone as though there is an x at u for First and Middle
Cases. Our imaginary series of cases contains additional
members, however; and to these we must now turn. We
have already encountered an example that belongs to this
new part of the series—that, namely, of the desert traveller who distrusts his eyes (or his judgment). Cases of this
type, which we may label the *Last Cases*, are marked by
the fact that although it looks to Q as though there is an
x at u, Q nevertheless does not causally-receive the perceptual belief that there is an x at u—on the contrary, he
acquires the firm belief that there certainly is not an x at u.
I think that in Last Cases, the perceiver may plausibly be
said to causally-receive an inclination to believe that there
is an x at u, but—and the following qualification is needed
to mark the difference between these cases and Middle
ones—it is an inclination that, for one reason or another,

he resists and indeed overcomes, one that he quashes or strongly suppresses, so that it is an attenuated inclination. I shall say that he causally-receives a *suppressed inclination* to have a perceptual belief that there is an x at u.[9] This kind of inclination is to be regarded as a theoretical perceptual state posited by our (new) theory of perception in order to account for certain difficult cases. It has analogues, however, in ordinary experience. Suppose, for example, that an appealing child accused of a misdeed tells you that he didn't do it, but that you have overwhelmingly good evidence that he did. It may well be that you *want* to believe the child, but can't. If so, your attitude towards what he says is weaker, even, than being inclined to believe it. You do have an immediate impulse to believe it, but you (reluctantly) suppress it: we may say that you have a suppressed inclination to believe what the child says, although in fact you believe the opposite.

Our account of its looking to Q as though there is an x at u, for Last Cases, then, is this:

(C) Q causally-receives, by means of using his eyes in the standard visual way, a suppressed inclination to have a (perceptual) belief that there is an x at u.

Although I have given separate accounts for the First, Middle, and Last Cases, the three kinds of states ascribed to Q in (A), (B), and (C) are obviously related: there is a unity to them provided by the concept of a perceptual belief that there is an x at u. The differences among them are attributable to differences in the perceiver, Q—mainly, to differences in his background beliefs. Exactly the same causal input can produce a perceptual belief (that there is an x at u) in one Q, an inclination to that belief in another, and a suppressed inclination to it in still another.

I confess that there are two huge, connected, problems that shall have to remain unsolved in this book, namely (a)

---

[9] I do not mean, of course, that the inclination is *totally* suppressed, i.e., that it is suppressed, so to speak, out of consciousness altogether. I mean only that it is partially, and perhaps even mostly, suppressed.

that of determining what the criteria are for establishing what beliefs in general, and what perceptual beliefs in particular, a given perceiver is capable of having, and (b) that of determining what the criteria are for establishing what perceptual beliefs (inclinations to believe, suppressed inclinations to believe) a given perceiver actually causally-receives on any given occasion. These are large issues, and I cannot go into them here, except to say that one of the requirements that seem to be necessary in order for a perceiver, Q, to be capable of causally-receiving the (perceptual) belief that there is an x at u, is that Q have the concept of an x. Thus I take it that a one year old child cannot causally-receive the (perceptual) belief that there is a digital computer before him, since he does not have that concept. If this is right, and if our analysis of locution IIA is correct, it follows that it cannot look to a one year old child as though there is a digital computer before him. And I think this consequence is in fact true. The way things look (even in the phenomenal sense) to a perceiver is partially dependent on what his repertoire of concepts is, a truth that our analysis of IIA fully acknowledges. Notice, too, that on our analysis, the way things look to a perceiver on a given occasion is also partially dependent on which of the concepts that are in his repertoire he actually uses on that occasion; thus if a person has the concept of a digital computer, and knows what one looks like, but does not take *this* object (which is, however, a digital computer) to be one, then our analysis implies that it does not look to him as though this is a digital computer. And I think this implication of the analysis is also true.[10]

Two minor points before pressing on: first, the terms 'First Case,' 'Middle Case,' and 'Last Case' are meant to

---

[10] Matters become more complicated, however, in the case of such 'looks'-locutions at 'It looks to Q as though the x is P'—e.g., 'It looks to Q as though the digital computer is turned on.' The truth of a statement of this form does not, I think, always require that Q have the concept of x (a digital computer), nor that, if he has it, he use it on this occasion, although its truth does seem always to require that Q have, and use, the concept of P (being turned on).

designate only vague ranges of a continuous series, not to mark off sharply distinguished types of cases. They melt into their neighbors, so that it might be difficult or impossible to determine whether, on a given occasion and relative to a certain aspect of the "visual field," the perceiver is in, say, a First Case or in a Middle Case.

A different point: it is evident that a perceptual situation need not be *entirely* a First Case or *entirely* a Middle Case, or *entirely* a Last Case. A perceiver may simultaneously find himself in a First Case situation relative to certain aspects or features of the things he sees, in a Middle Case situation relative to others, and in a Last Case situation relative to still others. Thus, if it looks to a chronic alcoholic, after a bout of heavy drinking, as though there are pink rats on the coverlet, he may well be in a First Case situation relative to the coverlet and a Last Case one with respect to the pink rats for he may know perfectly well that there are no such animals on the coverlet or anywhere else. It might even be possible for a person to be simultaneously in two different perceptual states relative to the *same* feature of his visual field—for example, to be inclined to believe that an object is elliptical (Middle Case) although believing at the same time that it really is round (First Case). In such a situation, the object would, in a way, look elliptical to him, and it would also, in a way, look round to him. This is a genuine possibility, for although nothing can *be* both elliptical and round (if that remark is suitably hedged), a thing can certainly *look* both elliptical and round.[11] (It must be confessed, however, that this sort of situation is puzzling; for while the perceiver might indeed express his uncertainty by saying something like "I know the thing can't be both elliptical and round, but darn it, it does look elliptical to me and it does look round to me right now," he could express it equally well

[11] To say that a thing looks both elliptical and round is not quite to say that it looks *as if it were* both elliptical and round—i.e., as if it had both predicates at once. Rather, it is to say that it looks elliptical and that it looks round.

by saying "Well, I simply can't decide whether the thing looks elliptical to me or whether it looks round to me.")

C. INFERENCE IN PERCEPTION

Before we go any further, there is one very important question to which we must address ourselves—namely, what, according to our theory, is to be the place of inference in perception? I have insisted that whenever in First Cases it looks (in the phenomenal sense) to someone, Q, as though there is an x at u (e.g., a tree outside the window), Q causally-receives, by means of using his eyes in the standard visual way, a set, normally extremely large, of beliefs about it. But suppose Q sees an object x at a place u and then infers something about it: does the belief he thereby acquires count as one that he acquires by means of using his eyes in the standard visual way? And should it therefore be included in the set of beliefs the acquiring of which constitutes his perceptual state? I must say something about these matters.

Actually, the acquiring of beliefs by *inference* is only one such way of acquiring them that is relevant here: for the same issues arise in connection with the acquiring of them by arbitrary leaps of thought, by association of ideas, by previous hypnotic suggestion, and so on. Still, inference is by far the most important of these ways of acquiring beliefs and so we may concentrate our attention on it. (I shall also confine the ensuing discussion largely to First Cases.)

There can be no doubt whatever that one often makes *conscious* inferences from what one sees. For example: a perceiver, Q, having been told that Miss Snead, whom he does not know, has a mole on her shoulder, sees a young lady with such a mole and infers—consciously—that she must be Miss Snead. He acquires this belief—that the lady is Miss Snead—by means of using his eyes in the standard visual way, and by then making a conscious inference. But surely we do not want to hold that the acquiring of this belief is in any way constitutive of Q's perceptual state:

his perceptual state (of its looking to him as though such-and-such) is complete, we feel compelled to say, before the idea of Miss Snead even occurs to him (or indeed *can* occur to him). Let us, then, rule out the acquiring (or, more generally, the causal-reception) of beliefs by any conscious process akin to inference; let us, in other words, construe the words 'by means of using his eyes in the standard visual way' in formula (A) (as well as in (B) and (C)) in such a way as to exclude such processes.

This restriction, though obviously a needed one, accomplishes almost nothing. For one thing, it does not rule out very many beliefs, and for another, those that it does eliminate, it eliminates, so to speak, only for an instant—because after a belief has been acquired by a conscious process, further observation of the relevant object (event, scene, or whatever) almost always results in the belief's being causally-received *without* any such conscious process, i.e., unconsciously. Let us turn at once, then, to the far more important and difficult question of what to do about the acquiring of beliefs in perception by unconscious processes.

I think there is no denying that in many cases of perception, and perhaps even in all, processes go on that may not altogether inappropriately be called unconscious ones —the unconscious making of assumptions, unconscious inferences, and the like. For example, when, under standard conditions, someone sees a sofa or a chair, he naturally assumes, or takes it for granted, *without thinking*—i.e., not consciously and therefore, presumably, unconsciously —that the thing has a back side to it of a kind normally met with in sofas and chairs. Again, when an experienced furnaceman looks at a red, glowing poker freshly removed from the roaring fire, he infers—not, in all probability, consciously, and so unconsciously—that it is exceedingly hot. These seem to be undeniable facts, ones that must somehow be accommodated in any adequate theory of perception.

To meet this requirement, it is not in the least necessary to grant the existence of a new faculty—the unconscious mind—that makes our unconscious assumptions and inferences for us, nor even to grant the intelligibility of that notion. I shall certainly have no recourse to the unconscious mind, at any rate: I shall appeal rather to something whose existence cannot be doubted by anyone, not even by a philosopher—namely, to the brain. We do not, it is true, yet know very much about the internal workings of the brain; but at least it is possible to think of it on the model of a computer, as more and more psychologists are beginning to do. We may think of the signals reaching the brain from the various sense organs as being so many inputs to the brain-computer. The person's past conditioning and the built-in characteristics of his central nervous system would determine the "program" and capabilities of his brain-computer. And the various perceptual beliefs (inclinations to believe, suppressed inclinations to believe) that the person acquires on a given occasion would correspond to different states that the brain-computer gets into on that occasion. Although it is not at all essential to my argument, it will be convenient to assume—and so I shall assume— that an adequate model of the brain as a fantastically complicated computer can be developed.

If this assumption be granted, then it is easy to see how something very like unconscious inferences can occur. Stimulated by sensory inputs, the brain-computer is put into a number of different states—i.e., the perceiver acquires a number of perceptual beliefs (inclinations to believe, suppressed inclinations to believe). If the logical and other (e.g., temporal) relationships among these states are of the right sort, as they surely sometimes are, we are entitled to say that the perceiver infers some of them from some of the others. And if the (incredibly rapid) transitions from one brain-computer state to another are not experienced as conscious occurrences by the perceiver, as they often are not, we are free to say that the inferences are unconscious. In this way, unconscious inference may be allowed into our theory of perception without introducing, along with it, any undesirable metaphysical mechanisms.[12]

Granted, then, that unconscious inferences occur when perception does, we now face the problem of determining what specific role, if any, beliefs so acquired play in perception itself. In particular, we want to answer the question (call it question (A)):

> Does the acquiring of a belief in perception by a process of unconscious inference (at least partially) constitute the perceptual state of the perceiver (that is, the state whereby it looks, in the phenomenal sense, to him as though such-and-such)?

I think there may be, or may have been, some philosophers who would hold that the acquiring of beliefs by any process of inference, whether conscious or unconscious, has nothing to do with perception properly so called. Their idea is that perceptual states (of the visual kind) really consist in nothing but the awareness of colors, shapes, locations, and other "purely visual" qualities—an idea that, when translated into our theory, becomes the idea that perceptual states (of the visual kind) really consist in the acquiring of perceptual beliefs[13] concerning *only* colors, shapes, locations, and the other "purely visual" qualities. All the other, higher-level beliefs[14] acquired in perception are derived from these basic ones by inference (or some such process), and the acquiring of them cannot constitute a *perceptual* state at all. But is there any good reason to accept this view?

It will be best to split the question into two sub-questions: (a) Why should anyone think that *all* of the more

---

[12] For his sort of view about unconscious inference I am indebted to Gilbert Harman. See his "Knowledge, Inference, and Explanation," *American Philosophical Quarterly*, 5 (1968), 164-73.

[13] To simplify the discussion, I shall consider just perceptual beliefs, and ignore inclinations to believe and suppressed inclinations to believe.

[14] I mean beliefs that are not merely about visual qualities: for example, the belief that there is a tree outside the window, that there is a man standing before one, that there is a book on the table.

complex, or higher-level beliefs must in every case be in-ferred from the allegedly more basic beliefs concerning just colors, shapes, and the other purely visual properties? (b) Even if one grants that the higher-level beliefs are all in-ferred from the basic ones, why should anyone think that the acquiring of them cannot be allowed to constitute a perceptual state? I shall take up these questions in order.

(a). The most plausible line of reasoning—and the only one I shall consider here—that might lead to this view is the following. Look at this sequence of propositions:

> (i) There is a surface of such-and-such a shape, col-ored in such-and-such a way, and located in such-and-such a direction and distance from me.
>
> (ii) There is a physical object of a certain shape and having certain colors in that place (i.e., the place mentioned in (i)).
>
> (iii) There is a living being of a certain kind in that place.
>
> (iv) There is a male human standing in that place.
>
> (v) My brother is standing in that place.

Surely anyone who causally-receives, by means of using his eyes in the standard visual way, belief (v)—so the argu-ment would go—must first acquire some combination of the other beliefs (i)-(iv);[15] because if he didn't think that the object he was looking at had most or all of those charac-teristics mentioned in (i)-(iv)—e.g., that it was a male hu-man being—he could not possibly believe that it was in fact his brother. In other words, he acquires belief (v), if he does, *because* he acquires (i)-(iv). But if the acquir-ings of (i)-(iv) are among the causes of his acquiring (v), he must acquire them *before* he acquires (v). Since the logical relationship between (i)-(iv), on the one hand, and (v) on the other, is of a suitable kind, and since anyone who acquired them all would first have to acquire (i)-(iv)

---

[15] Or of some similar series of beliefs: I do not mean to suggest, of course, that (v) can be reached *only* via the particular series (i)-(iv) that I have used as a typical example.

before he could acquire (v), we may conclude that he must *infer* (v) from (i)-(iv). The same argument would show that (iv) must be inferred from (i)-(iii), (iii) from (i)-(ii), and (ii), finally, from (i). So all other perceptual beliefs acquired visually must be inferred from such basic beliefs as (i) which are themselves acquired directly—i.e., without inference.

There is a lot wrong with the foregoing argument. For one thing, it confuses a logical relationship among propositions with a temporal, and indeed causal, relationship among the acquirings of beliefs corresponding to those propositions. Thus although the proposition (v)—that my brother is standing in a certain place—logically presupposes proposition (iv)—that a male human being is standing in that place—this does not make it in the least necessary that anyone who acquires beliefs answering to (iv) and (v) must acquire the one answering to (iv) *before* he acquires the one answering to (v). Given the fantastic complexity of the human brain, there is no a priori reason why a person, when his eyes are stimulated by light rays reflected from his brother, should not causally-receive all the beliefs (i)-(v) *simultaneously*. And if this should happen, there would seem to be no basis for the claim that any of them are inferred by that person from any of the others. To be sure, there might, on occasion, be inferential relationships among (i)-(v) in the case of some perceivers; my only point is that the above argument does not provide any valid a priori reasons for thinking this must always be so. To be sure, when a complete, satisfactory computer model (or some other model) of the brain is worked out, it may turn out to be of such a kind that one will have to concede that what I have been calling higher-level beliefs (e.g., beliefs (v), (iv), and so on) are always inferred (or at any rate "inferred") from basic beliefs such as (i). All I am insisting on now is that there does not seem to be any good a priori reason to think that the completed brain model *must* be of this sort.

The argument I am criticizing seems to suggest that there

is always a simple, hierarchical, uni-directional structure to
the acquiring of the perceptual beliefs a person acquires on
any given occasion. In the example employed, it claims that
the perceiver acquires (i), (ii), (iii), (iv), and (v) in that
(temporal) order, and seems to imply that no belief
higher up in this hierarchy—i.e., toward the (v)-end—can
influence in any way the content of a belief that is lower
down in the hierarchy—i.e., nearer the (i)-end. But this
suggestion, whether or not it is implied by the argument, is
difficult to reconcile with the actual facts. There is, for example, quite a bit of experimental evidence pointing to the
conclusion that the kind of thing a perceiver takes an object to be may affect the size, shape, color, slant, or motion
the thing looks to have, and the distance away it looks to
be.[16] That is to say, the acquiring of a higher-level belief
such as (iv) may in part determine the content of a basic
belief such as (i). It is obvious that the content of a basic

[16] See, for example, W. H. Ittelson and F. P. Kilpatrick, "Experiments in Perception," *Scientific American*, 1951, 50-55; J. S. Bruner
and A. L. Minturn, "Perceptual identification and perceptual organization," *Journal of General Psychology*, 53 (1955), 21-28; J. S.
Bruner, L. Postman, and J. Rodrigues, "Expectation and the perception
of color," *American Journal of Psychology*, 64 (1951), 216-27, reprinted in Beardslee and Wertheimer (eds.), *Readings in Perception*,
pp. 267-78; R. C. Bolles and D. E. Bailey, "Importance of object
recognition in size constancy," *Journal of Experimental Psychology*,
51 (1956), 222-25; A. C. McKennell, "Visual size and familiar size:
individual differences," *British Journal of Psychology*, 51 (1960),
27-35; A. H. Hastorf, "The influence of suggestion on the relationship
between stimulus size and perceived distance," *Journal of Psychology*,
29 (1950), 195-217; J. S. Bruner and L. Postman, "On the perception of incongruity: a paradigm," *Journal of Personality*, 18 (1949),
206-23, reprinted (in part) in Beardslee and Wertheimer (eds.), *op.
cit.*, pp. 648-63; A. J. Dinnerstein, "Image size and instructions in the
perception of depth," *Journal of Experimental Psychology*, 75 (1967),
525-28.
    There is an excellent comprehensive review of this literature in
William Epstein, *Varieties of Perceptual Learning* (New York:
McGraw-Hill Book Company, 1967), Chaps. 2-4. More recent work
in this area includes H. W. Leibowitz and L. O. Harvey, Jr., "Effect of
instructions, environment, and type of test object on matched size,"
Journal of Experimental Psychology, 81 (1969), 36-43, and H. Ono,
"Apparent distance as a function of familiar size," *ibid.*, 79 (1969),
109-15.

perceptual belief such as (i) will largely determine what the higher-level beliefs acquired along with it shall be. It would seem, then, that there is normally a very complicated *inter*action, a mutual interplay, among the various perceptual belief-states of the perceiver, rather than the simple one-way, step-by-step influence suggested by the argument we have been criticizing. And where this complicated interplay exists among a set of perceptual beliefs (as I suspect that it does in most, if not all, cases of perception) it would seem to be not altogether appropriate to speak of the perceiver *inferring* any of the set from some of the others. At any rate, it would seem to be wrong to speak of the relationship among the beliefs as being one of just inference alone; at the very least, we ought to speak of inference *plus* some sort of feed-back operation.

The particular set of logical relationships that hold among the propositions (i)-(v) of our example represents, of course, only one quite special set of such relationships that might unite a group of perceptual beliefs causally-received by a perceiver on a given occasion. But whatever the character of these relationships may be, the most plausible general position to take on the issue of whether the perceiver acquires some of his beliefs by *inference* from the others seems to me to be this: although there undoubtedly are cases where a perceiver acquires one or more of his perceptual beliefs by inferring them—either consciously or unconsciously—from some of his other beliefs, these cases are perhaps rather special; it is probably far more commonly the case that there is an "organic unity" among the perceptual beliefs acquired on any given occasion, with each exerting some sort of "influence" on the others. In these latter cases, if one can speak of inference at all, one can speak of it only in conjunction with an accompanying process of feed-back.

I think there may be other quite common cases of perception that are different in certain respects from the kind we have just been considering, and where good reasons can be produced for denying that acquired beliefs are connected

by anything like inference at all. Consider the following. When you are straightening a picture hanging on a
wall, do you acquire by *inference* the belief that the sides
of the picture are vertical—e.g., by noting such things as
that the top looks parallel to the ceiling line and inferring
that therefore the sides must be vertical; or is it possible for
you simply to look at the picture and acquire straight off,
without inference from anything, the belief that it is
straight? It might seem perfectly evident, if one appeals
to "what goes on" in one's consciousness when he straightens
a picture, that the latter is certainly possible. But one's
judgment of the position, relative to the vertical, of objects
and lines in the environment depends on one's perception,
or feeling, or whatever it is—it is surely not, in any case, a
sensation or group of sensations—of the position of one's
own body relative to the vertical. Do we have to say, therefore, that a person must always acquire by inference the
perceptual belief that a picture is straight, since he can acquire such a belief only on the basis of how he thinks his
own body is positioned relative to the vertical?

In opposition to this, one might maintain that it is implausible to hold that a perceiver's awareness of the position of his body relative to the vertical is (part of) his
grounds for inferring that a picture is straight, and that
it seems much more reasonable to hold that this awareness
is merely one of the *conditions* that allows him to tell—without inference—whether or not a picture is straight. We
know, in fact, that one of the main ways a person tells how
his own body is positioned relative to the vertical is by noting how it seems to be aligned with what *looks* to be vertical in his environment—e.g., with the way the lines formed
by the meeting of two walls look. This factor counts so much
with some people, that when they are placed in a tilted
room, they feel themselves to be upright despite the fact
that they may actually be tilted as much as 35°![17] So it can

---

[17] See the fascinating experiments described by Herman Witkin in
"Development of the Body Concept and Psychological Differentia-
tion," in Wapner and Werner (eds.), *The Body Percept* (New York:
Random House, 1965), pp. 26-47.

hardly be the case that a person infers, on the basis of how he feels his body to be disposed relative to the vertical, that a picture is straight; if he infers anything here, it appears as though he must rather infer, from what looks to him to be vertical in his surroundings (e.g., the way pictures are hanging), how his own body is positioned relative to the vertical.

But ought we to adopt *either* of these two opposing points of view? Must we say either that a person normally infers what is vertical in his surroundings from the way his body feels disposed relative to the vertical, *or* that a person normally infers how his body is disposed relative to the vertical from what looks to be vertical in his environment? I would answer this question in the following way. I would concede that there are certain special cases where one may properly speak of a person inferring that a picture is straight —e.g., he may measure the distances of the two top corners from the ceiling and, finding them to be the same, infer that the picture must be straight (although it may still *look* disturbingly crooked to him). Indeed, there no doubt are (unusual) cases where a person may be said to infer that he is upright *from what looks to him to be vertical in his surroundings*; this might be an appropriate thing to say, for example, of those people who are strongly influenced by "visual cues" and who, when placed in Witkin's tilting room, suppose that they are upright when in fact they are merely aligned with a room that may be tilted as much as 35° from the true vertical. I would admit, too, that there may be very rare and unusual situations in which a person infers that a picture is straight from the way his body feels disposed relative to the vertical. For example, suppose that a person who is one of those who can "just tell" when he is upright, no matter what his surroundings are like, is placed in an adjustable tilting chair in a tilting room and asked to adjust a picture on the wall until its sides are aligned with the true vertical. If he adjusts his chair until he feels upright, and then aligns the picture with his body, he might be said to infer that the picture is straight (in the sense, at least, of hanging straight up and down) from the way his body feels disposed relative to the vertical.

But while admitting the existence of such inferences in certain special or rare situations, I would want to deny that one can appropriately speak of them at all in the ordinary, run-of-the-mill cases. As a person moves about in the normal course of events, his brain receives a steady stream of signals from his vestibular mechanism (the sense organ for bodily equilibrium) and from his eyes. There is most certainly a mutual interplay between what he learns via the two senses; but it seems wildly inappropriate to speak of this interplay in terms of inference. He can tell, by means of (using?) his vestibular mechanism and by means of using his eyes, such things as whether he is upright or not, and whether pictures are straight or not. But it would surely be wrong to say, in the normal case, either that he infers the first bit of information from the second or that he infers the second from the first. There just does not seem to be any such simple, straightforward relationship between them. But again, this conclusion can only be a reasonable guess; a definitive characterization both of what the various bits of information are that one receives in such cases and of the relationships among them, must await a satisfactory model of the workings of the brain.

So much for question (a) (p. 99f.) and its ramifications. Let us turn now to question (b). I suppose the main reason for thinking that the acquiring of perceptual beliefs by inference ought not to be allowed to constitute any part of a perceptual state is that inferring is something one does with one's mind, and a perceptual state ought really to be the result of something one does with just one's *eyes*. But of course this is an incredibly bad reason for thinking that; for surely the mind, or anyway the brain, plays an essential part in the acquiring of any perceptual belief, even those basic ones about the colors and shapes of seen things.

Consider a set of beliefs, such as the set (i)-(v)

(p. 100), which are all acquired on a single occasion by the perceiver's using his eyes in the standard visual way. And let us focus our attention on what may be rather special cases of a perceiver's so acquiring them—those cases, namely, in which some of the set are acquired by (unconscious) inference, or at any rate by a computer-model process analogous to inference, from some of the others. Are we to allow the acquiring of each one of the inferred beliefs to constitute (part of) the person's perceptual (visual) state? The response to this question that seems to me to be the most reasonable is this: there really is no single correct answer to the question in the abstract. The concept of a perceptual state (or, for vision, and expressed more colloquially, the concept of "how things look to someone") just is not sharply enough demarcated to permit anything but an arbitrary decision as to where in the series of perceptually acquired beliefs, such as the series (i)-(v), the line should be drawn that would separate, once and for all, and for all cases, perceptual states from non-perceptual states. Given certain specific problems, certain specific interests, certain contexts of inquiry, there might well be good reasons for drawing the line in one place rather than another. In a courtroom, for example, where someone's life may depend on the accuracy and caution with which a witness reports what he saw, there would doubtless be good cause to restrict rather drastically the scope of his perceptual state and to distinguish it as sharply as possible from his (acts of) inference, interpretation, or whatever. Depending on the special circumstances of the case, this justifiably restrictive attitude could result, to put it in our own theoretical terms, in confining the witness's perceptual state to the acquiring of just beliefs (i), (ii), and (iii), or to the acquiring of just (i) and (ii), or perhaps even to the acquiring of just (i); the remainder of the set of beliefs (i)-(v) would then be dismissed as being produced by the witness's having (merely) inferred them from "the appearances" or the way things looked to him, or by his

having interpreted what he saw, or by his having made
an unthinking assumption, or something of the sort. But
why should the courtroom situation be made the paradigm for all cases? For most practical purposes of everyday life, there seems to be no compelling reason to rule
out any perceptually acquired belief. None of the alleged
reasons for pursuing this ruthless course that we have considered, at any rate, ought to persuade us to do so, as we
have seen; and I cannot think of any more cogent ones.

So if I were positively forced to give a general answer
to the question "Should we allow the causal-reception (e.g.,
the acquiring) of beliefs by means of using one's eyes in
the standard visual way *and* an (act of) unconscious inference (association of ideas, and so on), to partially constitute a person's perceptual state?" (which is just question (A), p. 99), I would answer as follows. First, I would
point out that all it can mean, as far as I can see, to say
that "the acquiring of a certain belief does, or does not,
partially constitute a person's perceptual state" is this: that
the acquiring of it does, or does not, make a difference to
how things look (in the phenomenal sense) to him, or to
the "look" of something in his "visual field," or something
of the sort. This is vague enough; but the vagueness of
'makes a difference to how things look . . . etc.' seems to me
to correspond exactly to the vagueness of 'perceptual
(visual) state.' Second, there seems to be no good a priori
reason to deny that the acquiring of any belief at all, in
the ways indicated in question (A), can partially constitute, or contribute to, a person's perceptual state. Third:
there would seem, intuitively, to be good reason to hold
that, on the contrary, the acquiring of beliefs in those ways
can make a difference to the way things look to a person.
Thus consider a belief such as (v) (viz., that one's brother
is standing in such-and-such a place) in the example we
considered earlier. Does it not seem entirely plausible to
hold that the way a man looks to a perceiver, Q, might well
be affected by Q's knowledge that the man is his brother?
But fourthly, and finally, I would stress the fact that the

question of whether the acquiring of a certain belief does or does not partially constitute a person's perceptual state on a given occasion is entirely an empirical question; there is no way of answering it a priori. It seems perfectly conceivable to me that the acquiring, in the ways we have been talking about, of the very same belief might contribute to one person's perceptual state and not contribute at all to another person's. For instance, suppose two brothers, Q and R, are both looking at a certain girl who resembles, and reminds them both of, their mother. The acquiring of the (perhaps unconscious) belief that the girl resembles their mother might very well affect the actual phenomenal look of the girl for one of the brothers, Q: I see no reason in principle why this should not happen, nor even why there couldn't be a laboratory experiment dealing with the influence of such beliefs on the way one person looks to another. On the other hand, the acquiring of this same belief might not work that way at all with the other brother, R: the girl might look in every respect the same whether he acquires the belief or not. If so, then the acquiring of the belief would partially constitute Q's perceptual state on this occasion, and would not make any contribution to R's.

To summarize. Consider any belief, B, that is acquired by someone, Q, on a given occasion by means of using his eyes in the standard visual way *and* by a process (or act) of unconscious inference. There is no a priori reason to suppose that the acquiring of B cannot partially constitute Q's relevant perceptual state on that occasion: whether it does or not is entirely an empirical question. And if we consider beliefs such as (ii)-(v) of our well-used example in the (perhaps more common) cases where the relationships among them cannot be characterized in terms of inference alone, but are rather of the "organic" type I described earlier, then I think we must say that the acquiring of them certainly does partially constitute the perceiver's perceptual state.[18]

---

[18] We should not forget, however, that in certain situations (e.g., in

So much for question (A) (p. 99), to which we have now given a qualified affirmative answer. Our discussion of the issues involved in this question has brought to light the need to make a distinction between two different kinds of beliefs that one may acquire by using one's eyes in the standard visual way: I mean the distinction between (ordinary) perceptual beliefs on the one hand, and what I shall call *thin perceptual beliefs* or, for short, *thin beliefs*, on the other. I have already said what I mean by an (ordinary) perceptual belief: it is a relatively rich, complex belief, containing a certain (variable) amount of specific detail. A thin perceptual belief does not have this kind of richness; it contains much less detail and normally has little specificity. Although this distinction is obviously not a remarkably clear or sharp one, the following example will show, I hope, that there is a genuine, if only rough, distinction to be made here. Suppose that a perceiver, Q, is looking directly at an exposed scar on a girl's back under "standard conditions of observation" (whatever they are!), and that he thereby acquires the belief that there is a scar on the girl's back. This is an ordinary, or full-blooded, perceptual belief, rich and specific: in acquiring it, Q necessarily acquires some subset of the following huge set of beliefs—that the scar is of such-and-such a (more or less specific) size, has such-and-such a (more or less specific) color, is of such-and-such a (more or less specific) shape, is located at place ———, is or is not covered by a shadow, has such-and-such a (more or less specific) texture, is surrounded by such-and-such, and so on and on. But suppose, now, that a perceiver, R, is talking to the same girl at a cocktail party and, though he is not acquainted with the intimate details of her anatomy, he for some reason unconsciously infers that she has a scar on her back. The belief he thus acquires is a thin perceptual belief: in acquiring it, R may not, and doubtless does not, acquire *any* of the above-indicated set of beliefs concerning the spe-

---

a courtroom), there may be special reasons for confining someone's perceptual state within more stringent limits.

cific size, shape, and so on, of the scar. And if he should happen to acquire one or two of them, they will doubtless lack the specificity or determinateness of the corresponding beliefs in the case of Q. The acquiring (or, more generally, the causal-reception) of an ordinary perceptual belief constitutes, on our theory of perception, a perceptual state—i.e., a state of its looking (in the phenomenal sense) to the perceiver as though such-and-such. But the acquiring of a thin perceptual belief does not: thus in the example just discussed, it does not look (in the phenomenal sense) to R as though there is a scar on the girl's back. The acquiring (or, more generally, the causal-reception) of a thin perceptual belief can at most affect the phenomenal look of something (no doubt in this case, the girl); it can contribute to the person's perceptual state, but not wholly constitute it.[19]

The distinction, just drawn, between an ordinary (or full-blooded) perceptual belief and a thin one allows us to cope with objections to our theory that might otherwise prove embarrassing—objections that charge us with being too liberal in allowing even beliefs acquired by inference to (wholly or partially) constitute perceptual states. Here is one such objection: "Consider the case of an experienced motorist who suffers from red-green color blindness—all red things look a kind of muddy grey to him. When he catches sight of a red stop light it is very unlikely that he goes through any process of conscious inference, arriving at the conclusion that the light is bright red. No, he immediately acquires the belief that the thing is red; he does it by unconscious inference. According to the account of 'looks' that you have defended in these pages, then, you must say that the stop light looks bright red to him. But it doesn't; it looks muddy grey. So it appears that your ac-

---

[19] For convenience, we might as well allow a thin belief that is causally-received by means of using one's eyes in the standard visual way and then making an inference to count as a *perceptual* belief, whether or not it in fact contributes to a perceptual state of the perceiver.

count is too permissive; the motorist's acquiring of the belief that the light is red should not be allowed to count as the light's looking red to him."

If the example cited in this objection causes any embarrassment to our allegedly too liberal account, it is not because our account has the consequence that the stop light does *not* look muddy grey to the experienced but color blind motorist. The motorist acquires either an inclination to believe, or a suppressed inclination to believe, that the stop light is muddy grey. He presumably gets into one or the other of these states without indulging in any inference: he has, in fact, an inclination to have an ordinary, or full-blooded, perceptual belief. So the light, on our view, looks (in the phenomenal sense) muddy grey to him. The embarrassment, rather, if any, lies in the alleged fact that our view implies not only that the light looks muddy grey to the motorist, but also that the light looks red to him. But in view of our recent distinction this second implication does not exist. The motorist's belief that the light is red is acquired by inference (from the fact, perhaps that the light looks muddy grey to him, or from the fact that it is a stop light, or whatever), and is clearly only a *thin* perceptual belief. It is indeterminate, in that the motorist has no idea of what determinate shade of red the light might be. Indeed, on a dispositional account of belief (which I accept), his acquiring the belief amounts to little more than his becoming disposed to *say* that the light is red. By contrast, acquiring an *ordinary* perceptual belief that something is red, as we shall see when we discuss colors in Chapter IV, consists in becoming disposed to do a great many other things; we shall also see that if the disposition to say that the thing is red plays any part at all in the perceptual state of something's looking red to someone, it plays only a minimal, peripheral role. I conclude that the case of the color blind motorist does not cause any embarrassment to our theory by showing it to be too liberal or permissive.

D. SEEING

I shall assume that we now have a satisfactory account, couched in our theoretical terms, of what it is for it to look to someone as though there is an x at u, for all the different sorts of cases—First, Middle, and Last. This account constitutes a kind of analysis[20] of 'looks'-locutions of type IIA, where 'looks' is construed, as always in these pages, in what I called the phenomenal sense.

This book is concerned with the nature of sense perception: and it is one thing to have an account—or at any rate the promise of an account—of what it is for something to *look* such-and-such to someone, and quite another to have an account of what it is for someone to *see* something, to indulge in that form of sense perception. We must now turn to the task of trying to provide such an account.

I shall make no effort to survey all the different possible kinds of 'see'-locutions and to reduce them to a small number of basic forms, so that I could then proceed to give an analysis of each of these latter. That strikes me as a hopeless venture, and pointless as well. Instead, I shall try, as I did in the case of 'looks,' to give a fairly detailed account of only one important kind of 'see'-locution. It will be relatively clear, I hope, how the principles involved in this account can readily be applied to other 'see'-locutions.

The kind of locution I shall pick for special attention may be schematized as follows: 'Person Q sees an x that is

[20] By an *analysis* of a declarative sentence form (or schema) F, I mean here a certain kind of interesting or informative list of the necessary and sufficient conditions for the truth of any categorical statement made by using just a sentence of form F. (Whether such a list is "interesting or informative" will depend on the purposes that the theory in which it is embedded is meant to serve.) I do not think such a list necessarily amounts to a statement of the meaning of the form (or schema) F: in particular, I certainly do not think that schemas (A), (B), and (C), taken together, give the meaning of the 'looks'-locution in schema IIA. If this conception of an analysis is thought unclear or unsatisfactory, I do not by any means insist on it—i.e., I do not insist that (A), (B), and (C) provide an *analysis* of IIA.

at place u (or in direction u).' I shall refer to this as *Locution Schema L*, or sometimes as *Locution L*, or even more simply as *L*. An instance of the use of Locution L is the statement "Jones sees a tree in front of him," or the statement "Smith sees a bottle of port at the end of the table." It might seem, if it be granted, as I hope it is, that we already have a satisfactory account of 'looks'-locutions of type IIA (viz., 'It looks to someone, Q, as though there is an x at u'), that the analysis of L must be very close at hand. It might seem in fact, as though that analysis must consist simply of the following two parts: (a) It looks to Q as though there is an x at place u (or in direction u), and (b) There is an x at place u (or in direction u). But this account will not do. For one thing, it will not work for any situation in which things look to the perceiver other than they are. Suppose, for example, that a warship is cleverly camouflaged to look exactly like a whale. A sailor on another vessel may very well see this extraordinary object over there on his starboard hand, but it will most probably not be true that it looks to him as though there is a warship in that direction. On the contrary, it will doubtless look to him as though there is a whale there. And so the suggested easy analysis does not work for this example. Again, someone may see, in a system of mirrors, a dog that is actually on the person's left side, but the mirrors make it look as though the dog is on his right side. Here, too, the easy analysis will not do; for although the perceiver sees a dog that *is* on his left, it is not the case that it looks to him as though there is a dog *on his left*.

Here is a slightly more complicated analysis that I think will constitute a move in the right direction. It consists of the following two propositional schemas:

(c) There is an x at place u (or in direction u),[21] and
(d) It looks to Q as though there is a y at place w (or in direction w).

[21] There is one respect in which both L and schema (c) are badly formulated; for if what I said in the last chapter in reply to the

Before trying to defend this (partial) analysis of L, I want to say a word or two by way of clarifying it. I have used the two different letters 'x' and 'y' in formulating schemas (c) and (d) because in many cases the thing that is seen (the x) looks to the observer to be other than what it is (it looks as though it is a y). But although I used two different letters, I do not by any means wish to rule out the possibility that in certain single substitution instances of (c) and (d), the words that occupy the places of 'x' and 'y' may be exactly the same word. Indeed, if this possibility were ruled out, so would all the standard, straightforward cases of someone's seeing something; for in the overwhelming majority of cases of seeing, the thing seen (e.g., a tree) looks to the perceiver to be exactly what it is (viz., a tree). For the same reason, place w (or direction w) may be, and usually is, the same place (or direction) as u.

It is no doubt also true that if the kind of thing referred to by 'x' is too radically different from the kind of thing referred to by 'y,' and/or the place (or direction) w is too radically different from the place (or direction) u, then we will not allow that Q sees an x at u (or in direction u) at all. And this will be true even after we have added, as we must, the extra element (e) to our analysis of Locution Schema L. This means that in our statement of condition (d), some limitations on the possible disparity allowable between the kind of object y and the kind of object x, and between the place (or direction) w and the place (or direction) u, ought, ideally, to be specified. The

---

time-lag argument is correct, then although the x that Q sees may indeed now happen to be at place u (or in direction u), nevertheless since he inevitably sees it *as it was some time ago*, it would be more felicitous to change L in the following way: 'At time t person Q sees an x that was at place u (or in direction u) at time t-Δ,' where Δ is, roughly speaking, the time it takes the light rays to reach Q from x. (c) should be similarly altered. For obvious reasons of simplicity and clarity of exposition, however, I ignore these temporal complications.

amount and type of disparity allowable, however, will vary
with several factors. They will change, for example, as
the conditions of observation change: roughly speaking,
the better the conditions, the less disparity is allowed. And
it seems to me that there is no way of specifying such
limitations, even for a perfectly determinate, concrete sub-
stitution-instance of L and (d)—and a fortiori there can be
no hope of specifying them for L and (d) in general.

But I think there is a much better way of thinking of the
necessary restrictions. If, instead of confining ourselves
to the terminology of (d) as now formulated, we appeal
to our account of what it is for it to look to someone, Q, as
though there is a y at w, we can say that the required limitations amount simply to this: that some significant aspects,
or components, of the perceptual belief that there is a y at
w must be *true*—where by the phrase 'the perceptual belief
that there is a y at w' I mean the belief that Q actually does
causally-receive (in First Cases), that Q causally-receives
an inclination to have (in Middle Cases), or that he causally-
receives a suppressed inclination to have (in Last Cases).
But here again, there is no saying in advance, for every
possible situation, exactly (or even roughly) *how much* of
that perceptual belief must be true. I do not think that
this is a defect in our (partial) analysis—for the roughness, or vagueness, of condition (d) probably corresponds
exactly to a roughness, or vagueness, in our concept of
seeing itself.

When we demand that some significant aspects, or components, of the perceptual belief that there is a y at w
must be *true*, we obviously do not mean merely that these
aspects, or components, happen to be true—we mean more
specifically that they are true *of the x at u*. I suggest that
we revise (d) in order to incorporate this demand, yielding

> (d') It looks to Q as though there is a y at place w (or
> in direction w) where some aspect(s) or compo-
> nent(s) of his relevant perceptual belief is(are) true,
> and true, furthermore, of the x at u (or in direction u).

Notice, now, that there are at least two possible senses we may attach to the expression 'is true of' in (d').[22] There is a weak sense in which p is true of an object x if, and only if, p is a true description of x (and no doubt of many other things as well). And there is a strong sense in which p is true of x if, and only if, p is true of x in the weak sense *and* p refers to, or is about, just x alone, and no other thing. In construing (d'), we must insist on weak true-of-ness at least: but should we demand strong true-of-ness as well? I hope not, because it is a difficult notion at best. For what are we to understand by a belief's referring to, or being about, just one particular object x and no other? This would seem to require that the believer perform an act of intending, thus attaching his belief to just x, and no other object. We should of course be loath to introduce any such acts into our theory. Perhaps strong true-of-ness can be handled behavioristically, but grave difficulties would certainly arise when we tried to deal in this way with inclinations to believe and (especially) suppressed inclinations to believe. So the best strategy must surely be to assume for the moment mere weak true-of-ness in (d'), and see if it works. I hope, and think, it will.

The notion of true-of-ness, even in the weak sense, is certainly not a perfectly precise one. Consider the following examples. I see the track of a meson in a cloud chamber: is the perceptual belief expressed by the words "There is a meson track in that cloud chamber" true of some *meson*? Again, if I see a patch of sunlight on the grass, is my perceptual belief "There is a patch of sunlight on the grass" true of the *sun*? A negative answer to these questions is in the best interests of our analysis of L, for positive answers might make our analysis have the undesirable implication that in the foregoing examples I was seeing a meson (whereas we want to say that I was merely seeing a meson track) and seeing the sun (whereas we want to say that I was merely seeing a patch of sunlight). To avoid this danger, we must construe 'true of' narrowly enough so that

[22] Here I am indebted to John Wallace.

belief-statements which are, on any reasonable interpretation, true of something, x, are not ipso facto also true of the causes or effects of x. But I do not think this rule really makes the notion of true-of-ness very much more precise than it was. Nor do I entertain the hope that I should ever be able to formulate other rules to make it precise enough to guarantee that for any conceivable example of a perceptual belief, it would always be perfectly certain whether or not that belief was, or was not, true of any given object x. So instead of trying to do that, I shall simply rest content with an intuitive understanding of 'true of'; for our very abstract purposes, this kind of understanding of the notion should serve well enough.

Before continuing the main line of argument, I want to enter a caveat about the relationship between L and (d'). I think that with the overwhelming majority of statement-instances of L, the forms of words embodied in schema (d') are suitable, perhaps even the most suitable, ones for stating the relevant truth conditions for the statement-instance. But I do not want to deny either that there are other forms of words—i.e., other 'looks'-locutions—that may sometimes be as suitable as they, or even that for certain special cases of statement-instances of L, the 'looks'-locutions embodied in (d') may be positively unsuitable. In offering (c) and (d') as a partial analysis of L, I am simply offering *one* form of words that can be used, and that I think can almost always be used, to state what statement-instances of L assert or entail. I showed earlier how the expressions in schema (d') may be analyzed in the terms of our theory of sense perception—i.e., in terms of the perceiver's acquiring certain beliefs, or inclinations to believe, in certain ways. In putting forth (c) and (d'), then, what I think of myself as doing is showing a, or the, major route by which we can proceed from one kind of perceptual statement expressed in ordinary language (viz., statements embodying Locution L) to the corresponding statements couched in the terms of our theory of sense perception. I have no doubt that there are other avenues, but I cannot hope to trace out all, or even many, of them. In indicating where a, or the, main thoroughfare lies leading away from a large number of statements embodying L, I must simply trust that the reader will agree with me that other avenues exist leading away from the *rest* of the statement-instances of L that end in the same desirable place that my main thoroughfare does—namely, with statements that are couched in the terms of our theory and that state exactly what the necessary and sufficient truth conditions for the corresponding statement-instances of L are.

Let us proceed, now, to the task of determining whether (c) and (d') together provide a satisfactory analysis of L. It is easy to show that they are not enough. To see what is lacking, we may consider a situation in which a pair of statement-instances of (c) and (d') are true, but in which the corresponding statement-instance of L is nevertheless false. Grice provides us with a convenient example of such a situation.[23] Suppose that someone, Jones, is in a room that has a clock on a shelf. Jones is facing in the direction of the clock, but unknown to him, there is a large mirror before him hiding the clock from his view and reflecting a different, but exactly similar, clock on a different, but similar, shelf behind him. So although Jones thinks he is seeing a clock on a shelf straight ahead of him, in reality he is seeing a (similar) clock on a shelf behind him reflected in the mirror. Take as our instance of L, the statement: Jones (Q) sees a clock (x) that is on a shelf straight ahead of him (u). This statement, as we have seen, is false. But the corresponding instances of (c) and (d') are true, for there is a clock (x) on a shelf straight ahead of Jones (u), and it looks to Jones (Q) as though there is a clock on a shelf straight ahead of him, where—we may readily suppose —all aspects or components of his relevant perceptual belief are true, and true, furthermore, of the clock (x) on the shelf straight ahead of him (u). Since these instances

[23] "The Causal Theory of Perception," *op. cit.*, p. 142.

of (c) and (d') are true, but the corresponding instance of
L is false, (c) and (d') together obviously cannot constitute a satisfactory analysis of L.

One could be tempted at this point to bring in the notion
of strong true-of-ness to resolve the difficulty for us. If the
'true of' of (d') were to be understood in the *strong* sense,
it might seem as though the instance of (d') in Grice's
example would then turn out, happily, to be false, on the
grounds that Jones' perceptual belief is not strongly true
of the original clock (x) on the shelf straight ahead of him
(u), but is strongly true, rather, of the duplicate clock behind him. But this would provide only very shaky support indeed for our present analysis, because it is doubtful that any plausible account can be given of strong true-
of-ness that would render Jones' perceptual belief strongly
true of the duplicate clock behind him. For example, suppose one tries to explicate strong true-of-ness in terms of
an act of intending or meaning: according to an account
of that sort, it would seem that if Jones' perceptual belief
is strongly true of any clock at all, it would have to be not,
as we wanted, the duplicate clock behind him, but rather
the original clock ahead of him—for he surely *thinks* he is
seeing a clock that is straight ahead. Nor is it clear that a
behavioral account would fare any better.

Strong true-of-ness, then, is not helpful in meeting Grice's
counterexample. Looking back at the example, we notice that
what prevents us from being able to say that Jones sees the
original clock is that there is no causal connection of the
right kind between that clock and Jones' perceptual state
(as described in the appropriate instance of (d')). And what
allows us to say that he does, on the other hand, see the duplicate clock is precisely that there is the right sort of causal connection between it and Jones' perceptual state. In order to have an adequate analysis of L, then, what must be
added to (c) and (d') is a schema whose statement-instances assert the right sort of causal connection between
the thing seen and the perceiver's perceptual state. The invoking of strong true-of-ness may now be viewed as the

result of looking for the right thing in the wrong place. The "right thing" is a suitable connection between the perceiver's perceptual state and the object perceived. But this tie cannot, it seems, be found entirely within that perceptual state itself (the "wrong place"): rather it is, as I believe, just the causal connection to which we are now appealing.

But how is the required causal connection to be characterized? Part of the connection, let it be noted, already lies buried in (d′), if our analysis of (d′) is correct. As we analyze (d′), it is a necessary condition for the truth of (d′)-statements that the perceiver, Q, gets into a certain kind of state *as the result of using his eyes, or by (means of) using his eyes*, in the standard visual way. If (d′) is part of the analysis of L, then the perceiver's eyes must figure in the causal tie between what is seen and the seeing of it. Even this harmless-looking claim is controversial: the claim could be thought to be too strong on the grounds that although it is granted that as far as we know all cases of seeing do *in fact* involve the use of organs that are undoubtedly eyes, it is still conceivable that creatures might be able to see even though they had no eyes, or, if they did have eyes, to see without using them. Suppose, for example, that men from Mars land on the earth, and we discover that they can detect the colors, shapes, and locations of things at a distance, and that they do this by using long antennae that project from the sides of their heads. Wouldn't they be seeing things, and by means of their antennae? Or consider ordinary earthmen with eyes. One can easily conceive of a machine that has, as its input, light rays reflected from objects, and as output, a signal that directly stimulates a person's visual cortex in exactly the same way that it would be stimulated if he were looking at the same objects in the normal way. (We may imagine the subject to be blindfolded). Wouldn't he *see* those objects, despite the fact that he does not use his eyes?

It is impossible to deal adequately with examples of this kind in short order. We need to know a lot more about the

situations we are being asked to imagine before we can begin to answer the crucial questions about them: and even
if we did know everything that is relevant, it is not certain
that conclusive answers could then be given. In the example
of the Martians: how is it supposed to be determined
whether those creatures can detect the *colors* of things or
not? Presumably, by noticing what sorts of discriminations
they make among things of different colors. But what sorts
of discriminations, exactly? Even if they knew how to apply
our color-terms to things correctly, it is not clear that we
would be forced to admit that this proved that they could
detect *colors*. For what if the things they called colors did
not play a role in their lives which was at all like the role
that colors play in ours? For example, what if they never
used color at all in picking out, or identifying, an individual
thing, or a kind of thing? What if they were totally unper-
turbed by what we would call a violent clash of colors, or
were unmoved, or perhaps made sick, by what we would
consider to be a ravishingly beautiful combination of colors? Or what if we discovered that their antennae were sensitive not to light rays, but to energy of some quite different range of frequencies? Might we not have to suppose
that they were detecting some qualities which were merely
correlated with colors (coextensive with colors)? Or what
if, on dissecting one of these creatures, we found that the
nerves from its antennae led not to anything like a brain,
but rather directly to its vocal chords and limbs; and what
if the best theory we could devise to explain its behavior
was that it is the signals that travel along these nerves that
activate the various parts of the creature's body, rather
than signals from its brain, if indeed it has one? All of
these questions, and more, would have to be answered before we would want to commit ourselves to the thesis that
the Martians are able, or are not able, to detect the very
same qualities that we refer to as colors—and the same
goes, of course, for the other "visual properties." One can
think of answers that would lead any reasonable man to
judge that the Martians can indeed detect all the same "vis-

ual properties" that we do, and therefore that they really do *see* with those antennae, and one can think of other answers that would lead to the contrary judgment, and of still others that would lead to hopeless indecision.[24] But if the details were filled out in such a way that we ought to judge that they *do* in fact see, would this show that here we certainly had a case of seeing without eyes? Not at all. For we might very well wish to say that their antennae *are* their eyes, that their eyes are merely constructed in a different way from ours.

The question, then, of whether functioning eyes are or are not essential to anything that can properly be called seeing (or ears to hearing, and so on) is an exceedingly difficult and complicated one. So are the questions of whether or not the organs of seeing must be sensitive to *light rays*, in particular, of whether or not the organs of seeing must be structurally similar to ours and connected with something that serves roughly the same purposes as our brain, and so on. As things now are, it is, I assume, a fact that every creature that is capable of seeing does have eyes that are structurally similar to ours and that are sensitive to light rays. Whether we should, or ought to, say of some imaginary creatures who apparently showed evidence of being able to see but whose (alleged) eyes failed to have one or more of these *now* universal characteristics, that they can see or that they cannot see, is a topic for prolonged debate. So is the question of whether we should say of a blindfolded person whose visual cortex is being stimulated by the machine imagined earlier, that he sees, or does not see, the relevant objects. Questions of this sort cannot be settled, and the attempt should not be made to settle them, simply by introspecting and asking oneself "What would I say if . . . ?" As Jerry Fodor remarks:

It is notorious that the disconfirmation of any of our more

---

[24] For an extremely acute discussion of the criteria we might use in distinguishing one sense from another, see H. P. Grice, "Some Remarks about the Senses," in R. J. Butler (ed.), *Analytical Philosophy* (Oxford: Basil Blackwell, 1962), pp. 133-53.

firmly entrenched beliefs may be an occasion for considerable conceptual revision and that neither the direction of such revision nor its impact upon our ways of talking is likely to be predictable ahead of time.[25]

I feel that I have nothing interesting to contribute to the prolonged debate that would be necessary if these questions are ever to be settled in a respectable way. I also have the suspicion that in the absence of problems and purposes that are no more concrete than our highly abstract ones, even a very prolonged debate would probably yield few, if any, results, since it would have to be conducted in a partial vacuum. But the important point for us now is that none of this really matters. The fact is that we can safely ignore all these disquieting considerations: we do not lie under the slightest obligation to become embroiled in discussions of the kind just envisaged. The reason is this: as I use the term 'analysis,' an analysis of a sentence is a (certain kind of) list of the necessary and sufficient conditions for the truth of statements that are made by using the sentence. As the preceding discussion has made clear, by 'necessary,' I do not mean *absolutely* necessary—i.e., necessary in any conceivable situation, or in any possible world. I mean necessary for the truth of the statements *in our world as it now is*. Given the present laws of nature, I take it that everyone would admit that it *is* a necessary condition for the truth of statements asserting that someone sees something, that he have eyes, and that these organs play an essential role in the causal connection between what is seen and the seeing of it. If the basic relevant facts known to us now should change—well, that possibility needs to be faced only if, and when, it becomes actualized. But until then, we are justified in allowing our analysis of L to include (d′), which in turn contains in *its* analysis the phrases 'as the result of using his eyes' and 'by means of using his eyes.'

But in using these phrases, we still assert only *part*, or only one aspect, of the causal tie between what is seen and

[25] "On Knowing What We Would Say," *The Philosophical Review*, 73 (1964), 211.

the seeing of it, and the problem remains of characterizing, somehow, the rest of it. Grice thinks the best way to indicate the nature of the causal tie is to do it by reference to examples. He writes:[26]

> I suggest that the best procedure for the Causal Theorist is to indicate the mode of causal connexion by examples; to say that, for an object to be perceived by x, it is sufficient that it should be causally involved in the generation of some sense-impression of x in the kind of way in which, for example, when I look at my hand in a good light, my hand is causally responsible for its looking to me as if there were a hand before me, or in which . . . (and so on), *whatever that kind of way may be*; and to be enlightened on that question one must have recourse to the specialist.

It has been argued[27] that this account, although not explicitly circular, is implicitly so. For we need to know what the principle is that governs the selection of the examples; and evidently it can only be that they must all be genuine cases of seeing. Strawson himself puts it this way:

> So the generalized statement of the doctrine comes to this: *for an object to be perceived by x,* it is sufficient that it should be causally involved in the generation of some sense-impression of x's in any one of the ways in which, *when x perceives an object,* that object is causally responsible for (or causally involved in the generation of) x's sense-impression. This is a plain circularity.

As against this, I want to urge that Grice's account is *not* circular in any invidious sense. It seems impossible, in a venture such as ours, to avoid making some sort of covert appeal to the concept of seeing (or, more generally, to the concept of perceiving). Suppose we tried to formulate a *general* characterization of the required causal tie—in terms, say, of light rays being reflected by, or emitted from,

---

[26] "The Causal Theory of Perception," *op. cit.*, p. 143.
[27] By P. F. Strawson in an unpublished paper entitled "Perception."

the object. One criterion we would have to employ in deciding whether or not to accept any given characterization that we might hit upon is this: does it capture all those cases that, as we think, anyone would call cases of genuine seeing, and does it also exclude all those that clearly are not cases of genuine seeing? So the use of this criterion constitutes an appeal to the concept of seeing no less than Grice's procedure does. Grice has to pick his examples one by one, whereas someone who attempts a general characterization picks his examples all at once, as it were—but neither is any more, or less, guilty of an *illicit* appeal to the concept of seeing; neither procedure is illegitimately circular.

There are, of course, important differences between Grice's ostensive characterization of the causal tie and a general descriptive one. For example, Grice's does not in any way increase our knowledge about, or understanding of, the causal connection, while an adequate descriptive characterization, by picking out common features, would throw light on the nature of that connection. But for three main reasons, I shall go along with Grice's proposal and spurn any effort to formulate a general description of the causal tie. First, I have grave doubts that any such description is possible. My suspicion is that there is a family of cases here, and that we may well have to rest satisfied with merely pointing out (or pointing *to*, anyway) a handful of clear, representative examples, in the manner suggested by Grice. These doubts, it must be confessed, were instilled by my long, but fruitless, efforts to discover the essence of the required connection. Second, even if there were such an essence, my major aims in this book would in no way be served by finding out what it is. I am far more concerned with what goes on in the perceiver as the result of, or as an effect of, the relevant causal influences than I am in the precise nature of those influences. And third: even if we were successful in formulating a satisfactory general characterization of the causal tie for seeing, we would still have on our hands the job of doing the same thing for the other senses—and in view of the obvious and important differences in the causal media for the various senses, it seems unlikely that we could learn anything from this characterization that would materially aid us in accomplishing this new task. But if our descriptive characterization really would apply only to vision, with little or no relevance to the other senses, it is difficult to see how it could be of very much philosophical interest.

In accordance with this decision, let us formulate a third condition to be added to (c) and (d') in our analysis of schema L. The expression '(d')-state of Q' in the following formula means: that state of Q whereby condition (d') is true of him.

(e) The x at place u (or in direction u) is causally involved in the generation of the (d')-state of Q in the kind of way in which, for example, when I look at my hand in a good light, my hand is causally responsible for its looking to me as if there were a hand before me, or in which . . . (and so on), whatever that kind of way may be.

(Note that everything after the expression '(d')-state of Q' is a direct quotation from the passage in Grice cited above.)

This way of characterizing the causal connection between the object x and the (d')-state of Q represents continued adherence to the policy we adopted a while back of being satisfied with current universal truths about perception in giving the necessary conditions for the truth of statements of form L. For example, given our fund of common knowledge about vision, (e) implies that light rays are involved in the generation of the (d')-state of Q. Therefore, by including (e) in our analysis of L, we are in effect making the intervention of light rays essential to the seeing of an object. And suppose someone should object as follows: "Look here, (e) is much too limiting; for if there were a demon—or a Berkeleyan God—who, without recourse to anything as vulgar as light rays, made it look to people as though there were an x at u, and did so when, and only when, there really was an x at u (which is more than can be said for light rays), how could it then be denied that people would really see those objects? And yet according to what is implicit in (e), if there are no light rays, there is no seeing." Our answer to this objection is that we are going to treat light rays here as we treated eyes in the case of the antenna-ed Martians. We have no idea what we should say, what would happen to our concept of seeing, if it should turn out that there really were such an epistemologically benevolent demon loose in the world. To be sure, we might say that he causes people to *see* objects; but then we might say instead that he causes them to have demonvisions of them. For the purposes of our investigations, however, there is no need to pursue these matters, for we have decided to eschew all such conjectures; light rays, for us, will be necessary if anything that can properly be called seeing is to occur.

Before going on, I want to point out that by including condition (e), as now worded, in our analysis of L, we have effectively swept a number of knotty problems under the rug, safely out of sight. For example: how much, and what part(s), of an object x must reflect (or emit) light rays into our eyes in order for it to be correct to say that we see it? How does this vary from one type of object to another? From one set of conditions to another? In some cases, it seems as though no part of the object reflects (or emits) light rays into our eyes, and yet we can be said to see it: thus if I come across a moored boat that is completely and tightly covered with a tarpaulin, so that its shape is clearly outlined, I can, in certain circumstances, properly speak of seeing that boat.[28] How can we account for this fact?

To mention just one of the many more specific problems that (e) hides: what principle(s) determines whether a

[28] This example is taken from R. Firth, "The Men Themselves: or the Role of Causation in our Concept of Seeing," in H.-N. Castañeda (ed.), *Intentionality, Minds, and Perception* (Detroit: Wayne State University Press, 1967), pp. 357-82. See p. 375.

certain kind of intermediary in the causal chain between a person and an object prevents one from being able to describe him as *seeing* the object? Binoculars, ordinary spectacles, mirrors, and periscopes, for example, are clearly all right: one *sees* things through (or in) them. But other intervening "devices" are clearly not all right: thus if someone looks at an object and writes down a description of it which Q then reads, Q does not thereby see the object. Still other intermediaries are perhaps doubtful: for instance, do we *see*, in the literal sense, people and events on live television? The expression 'the kind of way' in (e) represents a policy of saying nothing in answer to this problem.[29] I very much doubt that any general condition(s) could be formulated to replace (e) that would settle these matters ahead of time for all possible cases. Our concept of seeing is just too complex for that. Condition (e), with its 'and so on,' stands as a symbol, or as a promise, for a whole host of different sets of causal conditions that vary with the perceptual situation—it falls pitifully short of actually delivering the goods. So in effect it throws up an innocent-looking smoke screen around a lot of ugly problems. I shall let it stay there, however, since I have no inclination to try to cope with these problems. My main concern in these pages is clearly with condition (d'); I am satisfied to let (e) stand as it is. I have mentioned the difficulties and complexities that (e) hides only to keep us from falling into a false sense of security—that is, to keep us from thinking that the concept of seeing is a simpler and more easily analyzable one than it is.

Here, then—to summarize—is the analysis I offer of the Locution Schema L, viz., 'Person Q sees an *x* that is at place *u* (or in direction *u*)' (where 'see,' as always, is to be understood in the *liberal* sense):

[29] Problems of this kind are discussed in G. J. Warnock, "Seeing," *Proceedings of the Aristotelian Society*, 55 (1954-1955), 201-18; in R. M. Chisholm, *Perceiving* (Ithaca, N.Y.: Cornell University Press, 1957), pp. 142-56; and in R. Firth, *op. cit.*

(c) There is an x at place u (or in direction u).

(d′) It looks to Q as though there is a y at place w (or in direction w), where some aspect(s) or component(s) of his relevant perceptual belief is(are) true, and true, furthermore, of the x at u (or in direction u).

(e) The x at place u (or in direction u) is causally involved in the generation of the (d′)-state of Q in the kind of way in which, for example, when I look at my hand in a good light, my hand is causally responsible for its looking to me as if there were a hand before me, or in which . . . (and so on), whatever that kind of way may be.

Locution L is, of course, only one kind of 'see'-locution, albeit a most important kind; but if we assume for the moment that we are now in possession of an adequate analysis of it (or at any rate the bare bones of an adequate analysis of it), as I think we are, then analyses of any other 'see'-locution can easily be formulated in terms of 'looks,' along with such notions as are expressed in (c) and (e). Since we know how to interpret states of affairs such as are described in (d′)-like schemas in the terminology of our theory of sense perception—i.e., in terms, roughly, of Q's causally-receiving, by use of his sense organs in standard ways, certain perceptual beliefs, inclinations to believe, or suppressed inclinations to believe—this would mean that our theory is able to yield a satisfactory interpretation of any 'see'-locution.

III

Evidence for the Theory

I HAVE now presented the outline of a (philosophical) theory of perception. What I propose to do in the present chapter is to put some flesh on the bare bones of this theory, primarily by examining some of its implications. I shall also describe some experimental evidence, culled from the psychological literature, showing that many of these implications are fully borne out by the facts of sense perception. In this way, I hope to make clearer exactly what the theory amounts to, and at the same time to persuade the reader that he ought to accept it.

It seems to me that any philosophical theory of perception, including ours, has certain connections with empirical science, mainly, of course, with psychology and secondarily with physiology. At one time, this would have been considered a heretical view. When the various natural sciences finally managed to dissociate themselves from philosophy, leaving the latter as a separate discipline with its own special areas of concern, philosophers began to assume a lofty, not-interested attitude toward empirical facts in general, and toward the find-

ings of the sciences in particular. Thus, in the field of sense
perception, they tended deliberately to ignore the experimental results in physiology and psychology, considering it
sufficient, for their purposes, to know the broadest—i.e.,
the crudest—general principles of those sciences; or, even
if they did bother to consult the scientific literature, they
still normally dismissed what they found there as irrelevant to their problems.

There is now beginning to be a reaction against this philosophical isolationism, and I, for one, welcome it; for if I
am right that a philosophical theory of sense perception is,
at least in part, an explanatory theory, or something akin
to it, it behooves the theorist to know what the range of
facts is that he is called upon to explain. So I think it is im-
proper for a philosopher of perception to dismiss the results of psychological and physiological investigations,
treating them as if they had nothing whatever to do with
him. This is not to say that he ought to abandon his arm-
chair altogether and take to the laboratory, for he is certainly not any kind of scientist. But he ought to philoso-
phize with one eye on the actual facts of perception, as
revealed by the experiments of psychology and physiology; for although those facts may not be able straightforwardly to confirm or disconfirm his theories, as they
might do a scientific hypothesis, nevertheless they are
relevant to his theories, in that they may either "fit in," or
fail to "fit in," with them. When I say that certain empirical facts may "fit in" with a philosophical theory of perception, I mean something weaker than that they are
in any way implied by it. I mean only that once one accepts the theory, those facts are seen to be things that one
might very naturally expect to be the case; for the theory
gives a general theoretical framework within which the
phenomena are readily intelligible. So one is able to see, in
light of the theory, if only in a very general or sketchy
way (that is, without necessarily knowing the details of
the actual mechanisms involved) how those perceptual
phenomena might well occur. And when I say that certain

empirical facts may fail to "fit in" with a philosophical theory of perception, I do not mean that it would be inconsistent to accept both the facts and the theory; I mean rather that in order for the theory to be able, as it must, to encompass the facts, it must be subjected to ad hoc and perhaps implausible modifications or supplementations. In what follows, I want to make these still rather abstract and no doubt fairly unclear contentions somewhat clearer by citing a few examples of perceptual facts established more or less recently by psychological experiments. I shall try to show that these facts do in all cases "fit in" nicely with our theory of perception, and at least sometimes fail to "fit in" with certain other theories, for example, with sense-datum theories.

A. PERCEPTION AND VALUATION

I believe that sense perception cannot be properly understood in abstraction from all other aspects of the perceiving organism. If his seeing is viewed, for example, as having nothing to do with anything but his eyes, optic nerves, and the visual centers of his brain, or just these things and his "mind," it will be viewed inadequately and partially. Perception is obviously an important function of the organism and serves its needs; therefore it seems entirely natural to suppose that it cannot be fully understood apart from its connections with various other aspects of the whole organism.

Anyone who accepts our theory of perception must admit that in one way, at least—namely, via the *contents* of certain perceptual beliefs causally-received by a person as the result of using his sense organs[1]—there surely *are* connections between seeing (hearing, and so on) and what would ordinarily be thought of as quite different aspects or functions of the perceiver. Thus, on our theory, a person may causally-receive, by using his eyes in the standard visual way, the perceptual belief that, and therefore it may

[1] I shall usually make no reference to inclinations, or suppressed inclinations, to have perceptual beliefs in what follows.

look to him as though, something is warm, or dangerous, or delicious, or sickening, or sexually desirable—or perhaps all of these at once. But now I am interested in a rather different way in which perception is connected with other aspects of the perceiver: this second way has to do not with the contents of perceptually acquired beliefs, but with their causes, and in particular with certain causal conditions that lie within the perceiving organism.

I begin with his conative and affective nature, that is, with his wants, desires, likes and dislikes, feelings, emotions, and so on. It is common knowledge, of a rough and ready sort, that the way things look to a person is often strongly affected by his emotions, desires, feelings of elation, and the like. We have all noticed, for example, that everything—even wholly familiar scenes and objects—can become transformed in our eyes by the receipt of some wonderfully good news. "The world of the happy man," as Wittgenstein remarked (*Tractatus* 6.43), "is a different one from that of the unhappy man." Again, the same peaceful street looks different to the man calmly returning home from work and to a hunted man who is frightened to death, thinking that his enemy may be lurking behind any tree or bush. And everyone knows that a platter of raw oysters has one look to a hungry gourmand who delights in them, and quite another to a sick man who, even at the best of times, loathes them.

It might easily be thought that examples of this sort do not embody bits of real knowledge that we have learned, but only illustrate quasi-literary ways of talking that we sometimes indulge in. "Things don't really look different to us when we are happy, frightened, sick, and so on," one is tempted to suppose, "but we only speak as if they did, and hence perhaps deceive ourselves, because the total experience, which includes the feelings, desires, emotions, or whatnot, *is*, indeed, radically different under those circumstances." But there is now a fair amount of solid experimental evidence to show that our alleged "quasi-literary ways of talking" actually represent hard fact, and that our emotions, desires, feelings, as well as our much less color-ful evaluations of things, affect the way things look—even their "visual properties"—in quite determinate, measurable ways.

Before citing any of this evidence, I want to mention—what is perhaps obvious anyway—that one has to exercise caution in interpreting the results of psychological experi-ments, especially of those that purport to prove something about how things look (sound, taste, etc.) to subjects. If, for example, the results of an experiment are based mainly or entirely on what the subjects said or wrote about the apparent color, let us say, of a person's skin, then there can be several different hypotheses to explain why they said or wrote what they did, only one of which is the hypoth-esis that the thing really did look that way to them. I can-not, of course, give detailed descriptions of the procedures that were followed in all of the experiments I shall be citing; but I shall describe some of them, and in the other cases, the reader can take my word for it—although, if he likes, he can always consult the original sources—that I have hon-estly tried to mention only those experiments that seemed really to show, as unambiguously as is possible in these matters, something about how the relevant objects (prop-erties, or whatever) actually looked to the subjects.

Pioneering work in this area was done by J. S. Bruner and C. C. Goodman. In a famous experiment,[2] ten-year-old children were instructed to adjust the area of a disc of light so that it looked to them to be exactly equal to the size of a variety of coins and cardboard discs. It was found that they tended to overestimate both the sizes of the coins and of the cardboard discs, but that the error was greater with the coins than with the discs. But the most interesting fact is that the poor children in the group consistently made larger errors of overestimation, in the case of the coins, than did the rich children. The conclusion seems warranted

[2] J. S. Bruner and C. C. Goodman, "Value and need as organizing factors in perception," *Journal of Abnormal and Social Psychology*, 42 (1947), 33-44.

that the coins looked larger to all the children than the cardboard discs, and that any given coin looked larger to the poor children than it did to the rich ones. It is true that when other psychologists repeated this experiment, using similar methods, the results were not always in accord with those of Bruner and Goodman;[3] but at least there appears to be general agreement that children tend to overestimate the sizes of the larger (i.e., more valuable) coins, and that their error here is greater than it is in the case of the larger cardboard discs. These data seem to support the following hypothesis: things that people desire, or at least value fairly highly, tend to look larger to them than similar objects that they desire less (or not at all), or that they value less highly (or not at all).

Other experiments seem to confirm this hypothesis. In one of them,[4] some nursery school children were conditioned as follows: after turning a crank a number of times, they received a white poker chip which, when put into a slot, automatically paid them a piece of candy. One group performed this operation once a day for ten days, another group five times a day for ten days. Using the same size-estimation device that Bruner and Goodman used, the experimenters found that with both groups of children, the apparent size of the poker chip increased significantly after the ten days of conditioning. This was in marked contrast to a control group of children who, for the same ten day period, received candy directly after turning the crank,

[3] See L. F. Carter and K. Schooler, "Value, need and other factors in perception," *Psychological Review*, 56 (1949), 200-07; J. S. Bruner and J. S. Rodrigues, "Some determinants of apparent size," *Journal of Abnormal and Social Psychology*, 48 (1953), 17-24; H. Tajfel and S. D. Cawasjee, "Value and accentuation of judged differences," *ibid.*, 59 (1959), 436-39; H. Tajfel, "Value and perceptual judgment of magnitude," *Psychological Review*, 64 (1957), 192-204; B. G. Rosenthal, "Attitude toward money, need, and methods of presentation as determinants of perception of coins from 6 to 10 years of age," *Journal of General Psychology*, 78 (1968), 85-103.

[4] W. W. Lambert, R. L. Solomon, and P. D. Watson, "Reinforcement and extinction as factors in size estimation," *Journal of Experimental Psychology*, 39 (1949), 637-41; reprinted in Beardslee and Wertheimer (eds.), *Readings in Perception*, pp. 458-64.

without the mediation of the poker chip: for them, there was no significant increase in the apparent size of the chip. What is more, the overestimation, on the part of the experimental group, no longer occurred on the eleventh day, when they performed the same work but did not receive their candy reward. In another experiment,[5] young children were required to judge the heights of desirable 3-inch toys; their heights were consistently overestimated, as compared with the heights of control blocks. The children were first allowed to keep the toys and were promised that they would continue to receive them. Then, when the experimenters broke their promise and did not permit the children to play with them, it was found that the apparent size of the toys increased still further. There was no such increase in apparent size for a control group of children who were not treated in that unjust fashion.[6] Our hypothesis is also borne out by the experiment in which it was shown that foods liked by the subjects, all children, looked larger to them than foods they did not like.[7]

Things that people like, or desire, or in some way value, not only tend to look larger to them, it would seem; they also tend to look brighter. In one experiment[8]—this time conducted, for a change, with adults as subjects—it was demonstrated that pictures of food and drink looked

[5] L. Postman and J. S. Bruner, "Satisfaction and deprivation as determinants of perceptual organization": paper read at the meetings of the Eastern Psychological Association, spring, 1949.

[6] It is presumed that the forbidden toy became more attractive and desirable. This presumption has been shown to be generally true: see L. Festinger, "Cognitive dissonance," *Scientific American*, 207 (October 1962), 93-102. As Festinger demonstrates, there are conditions under which a forbidden toy does not become more attractive to a child; but in the conditions that presumably obtained in the Bruner-Postman experiment—i.e., no mild or severe threat of punishment in case the child tried to play with the forbidden toy—the toy does become more desirable.

[7] H. L. Beams, "Affectivity as a factor in the apparent size of pictured food," *Journal of Experimental Psychology*, 47 (1954), 197-200.

[8] J. C. Gilchrist and L. S. Nesberg, "Need and perceptual change in need-related objects," *Journal of Experimental Psychology*, 44 (1952), 369-76.

brighter to hungry and thirsty people than did pictures of things unrelated to food or drink. The apparent brightness increased with time, until it had been eight hours since the subjects had drunk anything. Then, after being allowed to drink as much as they wanted, the apparent brightness disappeared, and the pictures of food and drink looked no brighter than they had at the beginning of the experiment.[9]

One might well feel compelled to accept these crude hypotheses of ours—the hypotheses, namely, that other things being equal, objects that have, for one reason or another, some value for an observer tend to look larger and brighter to him than similar objects that have less, or no, value for him—were it not for the fact that there is another experiment which, if it does not directly subvert them, at least seems to contain the wherewithal for their destruction. The experimenters[10] denominated lines that fell within certain ranges of lengths, more or less arbitrarily, as "short," "intermediate," and "long." Similarly, they called weights that fell within certain ranges of magnitude "small," "intermediate," and "heavy." The experiment was divided into three periods. In the first (or pre-training) period, the subjects were required to estimate the lengths of lines and the magnitudes of weights, and to determine the movements of a spot of light (right, left, or no movement). In the second (or training) period, which lasted for seven weeks, with two sessions held each week, the subjects were conditioned in the following way. For each

[9] A partial explanation of this phenomenon is afforded by the work of E. H. Hess of the University of Chicago. By using a pupillograph, a device that can measure small differences in the size of a person's pupils, he discovered that when someone looks at an object that he considers to be attractive or pleasant, his pupils tend to expand. This reaction would naturally let more light from the object into the perceiver's eyes, thus causing the object to appear brighter. See Hess's article "Attitude and pupil size," *Scientific American*, Vol. 212, No. 4 (April 1965), 46-54. (See also J. D. Barlow, "Pupillary size as an index of preference in political candidates," *Perceptual and Motor Skills*, 28 (1969), 587-90.)

[10] H. Proshansky and G. Murphy, "The effects of reward and punishment on perception," *Journal of Psychology*, 13 (1942), 295-305.

"long" line, "heavy" weight, and movement of the light to the right, the subject was rewarded (by receiving fifteen cents); for each "short" line, "small" weight, and movement of the light to the left, the subject was punished (by losing fifteen cents); and for the "intermediate" stimuli, the subject was sometimes rewarded and sometimes punished, in accordance with a prearranged random schedule. The third and final (or post-training) period was simply a repeat of the pre-training period; the subject was again required to estimate the lengths of lines and the magnitudes of weights, and to determine the movements of a point of light. It was found that there were significant shifts in the subjects' estimations, and in the direction of the rewarded stimuli; this means, I take it, that lines now looked longer to them, that weights felt heavier, and that the point of light seemed to move more often to the right.[11] There were no significant shifts of this sort for a group of control subjects, who went through exactly the same routine as the experimental group, except that they were neither rewarded nor punished in the training period.

It is true that in the post-training period the lines looked longer to the conditioned subjects, but this result nevertheless does not appear to offer any very solid support to our hypothesis that valued things tend to look larger; for it seems reasonable to think that if the "short" lines had been rewarded in the training period, lines would then have looked shorter to the subjects in the post-training period. (I sincerely hope that someone will carry out such an experiment, if it has not already been done.) In that case, a valued thing would look smaller, rather than larger, to the subjects. But what, then, are we to make of the results of the experiments, described earlier, which seem to suggest that a valued thing ought to look *larger* to the valuing observer?

[11] It is true that this experiment used the verbal responses of the subjects, and it is possible that it was the verbal responses, and not the ways things looked and felt, that were altered by the conditioning; but, as the authors explain (p. 303), the behavior of the subjects in the post-training period would seem to quell such doubts.

I think that all the data can be accommodated if we dig a bit deeper, and examine our earlier hypothesis with a critical eye. *Why*, we may ask, should something on which a person places, for whatever reason, some positive value tend to look larger and brighter to him? It is no good trying to pass the proposition off as a self-evident truth, with some such words as "*Of course* things that a person values loom larger and brighter in his experience"; for what really does seem self-evident is that the thesis requires some explanation. As noted earlier, we already have a partial explanation in the results of Hess; valued things look brighter —and perhaps also larger—because the perceiver's pupils tend to dilate when he observes them. But we can reasonably ask for a deeper-going explanation, for we have as yet no idea why a perceiver's pupils should dilate when he observes a valued object.

One plausible explanation that goes deeper can be gleaned —paradoxically—from the very experiment, just described, that seemed to upset it. What is strongly suggested by that experiment, to put it bluntly, is that rewarded perceptual responses tend to establish or preserve themselves (that is, tend to be repeated), and that punished perceptual responses tend to be extinguished (tend not to be repeated). A basic tenet of learning theory is thus applied to sense perception. In the post-training period, the physical stimulus on the eyes of a subject caused by a line of a given length L_1 was the same as that in the pre-training period; and yet it now looked longer than L_1 to him. The difference, presumably, since it was not due to a difference in the stimulus, must have been due to the subject's responses to the stimulus—where under the heading of his 'responses,' I include anything that went on in him (e.g., in his brain) that (a) was caused by his receiving the stimulus, and (b) was responsible for the fact that the lines looked to him the way they did. These responses were of such a kind, as we know, that the lines looked longer to him than they had in the pre-training period. It is entirely reasonable to assume, I think, that these responses were of the same general type as the responses that had been rewarded in the training period—that is, they were "long"-responses, rather than "short"- or "intermediate"-responses. So I shall make the following rough conjecture: if, in a certain kind of situation, an organism responds to a certain kind of perceptual stimulus in such a way that what he perceives looks (or sounds, or feels, and so on) R to him and this kind of response is consistently enough and often enough rewarded [punished], then the organism will become so conditioned that in subsequent situations of that sort, he will be more [less] likely to respond to similar perceptual stimuli in that same way than if the responses had not been rewarded [punished]. The effect of his so responding will be that what he perceives will [will not] look (sound, feel, or whatever) R to him, or will look (sound, feel, etc.) more [less] R than it otherwise would, depending on the nature of the stimulus and the character of the property R. (I shall call this our *first* principle of perceptual conditioning.)

This principle, as I have formulated it, is little more, really, than an almost empty schema of a principle; in effect, it says merely that the properties things appear to have in sense perception are subject to some kind of conditioning. Stated in this abstract way—or, if you prefer, in this crude or rough way—the principle is of virtually no practical (i.e., scientific) interest. For that, it must be fleshed out with details, so that it may be more directly applicable to concrete cases. And the details will be different for different kinds of cases. For example, what is rewarding or punishing for one class of perceivers may not be so for another class. A kind of conditioning that is effective for one sort of perceptual property may be totally ineffective for a different property. And so on. A vast amount of work has been done, and is being done, in the laboratories of experimental psychologists, to discover just what the appropriate details are—that is, to discover exactly what the less abstract, more directly testable, hypotheses are that our crude general schema gets fleshed out into; to discover, in other words, what its concrete applications are.

Although, then, our first principle of perceptual conditioning is not of much practical use or interest to the working psychologist, I hope that my abstract, or crude, formulation of it will serve our purposes well enough. In light of the huge quantities of experimental evidence,[12] there can be no doubt whatever that some such principle is at work in all perceptual learning.

Our earlier hypothesis—namely, that things people desire, or at least value fairly highly, tend to look larger and brighter to them than similar objects that they desire less (or not at all), or that they value less highly (or not at all)—can now be viewed as nothing more than a special instance of our basic first principle of perceptual conditioning. In order for it to be so viewed, one need only make the plausible assumption that when, on receiving a perceptual stimulus from a kind of thing it values more or less highly, an organism responds to it in such a way that the thing looks relatively large and/or relatively bright to it, that kind of response will generally be rewarded. It will be generally rewarded because a thing that looks relatively large and/or bright is more likely to be noticed, recognized for what it is, and so obtained, than is an object that does not look that way. The "large"-and "bright"-responses are generally rewarded, then, by the organism's obtaining, more easily and more often, that which it values. If the truth of this plausible assumption be granted, we can now apply our principle of perceptual conditioning; and it tells us that the organism will tend to respond to stimuli from things it values in such a way that those things will look larger and/or brighter to it than they would have if its earlier responses of that kind had not been rewarded. Our earlier hypothesis, then, is just a consequence of our first principle of perceptual conditioning.

Our earlier hypothesis, it must now be admitted, has

[12] For reports of some of this evidence, see C. M. Solley and G. Murphy, *Development of the Perceptual World* (New York: Basic Books, Inc., 1960), and I. Rock, *The Nature of Perceptual Adaptation* (New York: Basic Books, Inc., 1966).

been disputed by certain experimental psychologists, and there is, in fact, quite a bit of evidence to support an alternative hypothesis that is incompatible with it. Tajfel[13] argues that whatever may be true in other cases, in cases where physical magnitudes and value vary concomitantly in a series of stimuli (e.g., the more candy, toys, phonograph records, books, or whatever, the better) the true hypothesis is not that the relevant physical magnitude of a series member is simply overestimated according to its value, but that the person accentuates the perceived *differences* of the relevant physical magnitude. For adults, anyway, the differences among the sizes of silver coins is more important than their absolute sizes. Perceptually "playing down" the size differences would court confusion in our petty monetary dealings, while accentuating the differences leads rather to harmony and efficiency. (There is seldom any comparable reward for perceiving the coins as being precisely the objective size that they are.) Therefore, what we actually do, according to Tajfel, is to accentuate the size differences. Then, the overestimating of the sizes of quarters and half-dollars would be the result of this accentuating process, rather than the direct result of our placing value on them. On this hypothesis, one might naturally be led to expect that we would tend to underestimate the size of dimes; and there is evidence that this is, in fact, the case.[14] There is also evidence showing that if what is rewarded is the objective accuracy with which we perceive the sizes, weights, or whatever, that things have—whether we value the things themselves or not—then we do tend to make accurate estimations of the relevant property.[15]

[13] H. Tajfel, "Value and the perceptual judgment of magnitude," *Psychological Review*, 64 (1957), 192-204. See also H. Tajfel and S. D. Cawasjee, "Value and the accentuation of judged differences: a confirmation," *Journal of Abnormal and Social Psychology*, 59 (1959), 436-39.

[14] See the Carter and Schooler article cited in n. 3, p. 136.

[15] See K. R. Smith, G. B. Parker, and G. A. Robinson, "An exploratory investigation of autistic perception," *Journal of Abnormal and Social Psychology*, 46 (1951), 324-26.

Whether Tajfel's hypothesis or our original one (namely, that valued things tend to look larger) is more nearly correct is a question for further empirical investigation. Actually, however, what the upshot of that enquiry ultimately turns out to be is not a matter of great moment for us, because Tajfel's conjecture, no less than our original hypothesis, is nothing but a specification of our first principle of perceptual conditioning—and our interest at the moment is primarily focused on the truth of that abstract first principle. We are only secondarily concerned with the question of which of the indefinitely many possible detailed hypotheses that fall under our first principle happen to be true.

Perceptual conditioning might be expected to affect not only the apparent qualities of things, but also our ability to recognize them. That is to say, one would expect the following principle to be true (let us call it our *second* principle of perceptual conditioning): if, in a certain kind of situation, an organism responds to a perceptual stimulus in such a way that he recognizes what he perceives as x, or an x, and this kind of response is consistently enough and often enough rewarded [punished], then the organism will become so conditioned that in subsequent situations of that sort, he will be more [less] likely to respond to similar perceptual stimuli in that same way than if the response had not been rewarded [punished]. And there is, in fact, some experimental evidence that tends to confirm this thesis. In one famous experiment,[16] subjects were presented with various different pictures of faces. Among them were the two pictures (a) and (b) of Figure I; these two pictures, as one can tell from (c), are "interlockable" faces. Whenever one of them—Fig. I (a), say—was presented to a subject, he was rewarded with money; and whenever the other (Fig. I (b)) was presented, he was punished by having money taken away from him. (Precautions were

[16] R. Schafer and G. Murphy, "The role of autism in a visual figure-ground relationship," *Journal of Experimental Psychology*, 32 (1943), 335-43.

taken to ensure that the subjects were not aware that it was these figures as such that were being rewarded and punished.) When, after this period of conditioning, subjects were presented with Fig. I (c), they saw it (recognized it) as the rewarded face, rather than as the punished face, in the great majority of cases. The experiment

Figure I

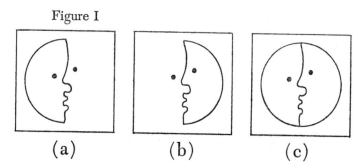

(a)   (b)   (c)

has been repeated a number of times,[17] and each time, this general result has been confirmed. But it was also discovered that there are large individual differences: children tended to see the rewarded face more often than adults did, and subjects who did not care, particularly, whether they were rewarded or punished (i.e., whether they received the money or were deprived of it) did not tend to pick out the "rewarded" face more often than the "punished" one. Individual differences of this sort should not surprise us at all if we accept our second principle of per-

[17] See I. Rock and F. S. Fleck, "A re-examination of the effect of monetary reward and punishment on figure-ground perception," *Journal of Experimental Psychology*, 40 (1950), 766-76; D. N. Jackson, "A further examination of the role of autism in a visual figure-ground relationship," *Journal of Psychology*, 38 (1954), 339-57; C. M. Solley and R. Sommer, "Perceptual autism in children," *Journal of General Psychology*, 56 (1957), 3-11; R. Sommer, "The effects of rewards and punishments during perceptual organization," *Journal of Personality*, 25 (1957), 550-58.

For a discussion of the literature in this area, along with some harsh words about the way most of the experiments were conducted, see William Epstein, *Varieties of Perceptual Learning*, pp. 144-51, 160-63.

ceptual conditioning; for the principle would seem to have the plausible corollary that, other things being equal, one who receives a "richer" reward for the recognition-response—and we may assume that children value the small monetary reward more highly than adults, in general —would be likely to exhibit it more often than adults, and much more often still than those who do not value the "reward" at all.

We noted earlier that a certain hypothesis—namely, that things people desire, or otherwise value relatively highly, tend to look larger and brighter to them—could be derived, with the help of some plausible assumptions, from our first principle of perceptual conditioning. In an exactly parallel fashion, one can derive, from our second principle of perceptual conditioning, the following subsidiary hypothesis: people tend to be able to recognize more quickly and under more adverse conditions, things that they desire or otherwise value fairly highly, than things they desire less (or not at all) or things they otherwise value less (or not at all). And again, there is experimental evidence to support this hypothesis. In one experiment,[18] pictures of food, projected badly out of focus on a screen, were gradually brought into sharp focus. It was found that hungry subjects recognized the food depicted earlier than non-hungry subjects did.

It might be thought that with the help of further plausible assumptions, one could derive some such subsidiary hypotheses as the following: (a) that things people loathe, do not like, find unpleasant, or otherwise disvalue, tend to look smaller and duller to them than similar objects that they disvalue less or not at all; and (b) that people tend to be less able to recognize quickly, and under adverse conditions, things they disvalue than they are to recognize things they disvalue less or not at all. But to accept any such sweepingly general hypotheses as (a) and (b)

18 D. McClelland and J. Atkinson, "The projective expression of needs. I. The effect of different intensities of the hunger drive on perception," *Journal of Psychology*, 25 (1948), 205-22.

would betray a lack of sensitivity to the complexities that beset the relationship between perception and punishment (in the learning theorist's sense of the term). And the complexities are formidable indeed. Our special interests would not be well served by going into the details of the numerous experiments that have been conducted in this area—experiments that have tried to determine what the relevant variables are and how they affect our perception. I shall content myself simply with giving an illustration of just one kind of experiment, and indicating briefly how the results accord well with our principles of perceptual conditioning.[19]

The kind of experiment I select as my example is the kind that tests what effect the pairing of electric shocks of various different intensities with the presentation of certain things (e.g., nonsense syllables, pictures of faces) has on the subjects' subsequent ability to recognize them. One result of these experiments that seems to be fairly well established is this: when the perceived item is followed by a punishing stimulus (i.e., an electric shock) and the subject can take some action to avoid the punishment, he will tend to recognize it more quickly and accurately than others—but where the subject cannot avoid the punishing stimulus, he will tend to recognize it less quickly and accurately than others.[20] This result will come as no surprise to anyone who accepts our principles of perceptual conditioning. In circumstances where the punishing stimulus can be avoided by appropriate action, it will obviously pay the perceiver (i.e., he will be rewarded) to recognize quickly and accurately the thing that is normally paired with the noxious stimulus; our principles tell us that this response of quick recognition, since it is rewarded, will tend to be repeated, to become part of the perceiver's repertory of responses—i.e., that he will become good at recognizing

[19] For a lucid discussion of the work that has been done on the connections between punishment and perception, see Chapter 6 of Solley and Murphy's *Development of the Perceptual World.*

[20] See Solley and Murphy, *op. cit.*, p. 109.

the normally punished item. And this, as we saw, is just
what happens. On the other hand, in circumstances where
there is no possibility of avoiding the noxious stimulus,
the response of *not* recognizing the item that is paired with
the electric shock will be rewarded—albeit rather poorly
(although it is the best that can be made of a bad job)—
by the person's remaining unaware of something unpleasant. Our principles of perceptual conditioning would lead
us to expect the perceiver in these circumstances to become
less good at recognizing the shocked item; and this expectation, too, as we know, is borne out.

The relationship between punishment and perception is
a fascinating and complex subject. Even the single result that we have just very sketchily discussed holds, I
would imagine, only for the most part; all sorts of qualifications would have to be made for special cases—e.g., for
extremely high intensities of electric shock. And, as we
might expect, there are large individual differences. As I
stated earlier, we need not go into all these complexities;
my hope is that what little we have said on this subject
gives some indication that here, too, our principles of perceptual conditioning hold good.

In an attempt to show how perception is affected by
the conative or affective state of the perceiver, I have been
presenting experimental evidence that relates almost exclusively to his likes (and dislikes), desires, wants, and so
on. Carried away by the intrinsic interest of the experiments,
I fear I have already spent more time on this presentation
than its importance for our investigation would strictly
warrant. But I cannot resist the temptation to prolong
the discussion just a bit more, by very briefly describing one
final experiment that deals with a somewhat different aspect of the perceiver's affective nature. This experiment,
or rather, *set* of experiments,[21] studies the perception of
one person by another, where the relationship between the
two makes the perceiver anxious to some degree. In one of

[21] W. J. Wittreich, "Visual Perception and Personality," *Scientific American*, 200 (April 1959), 56-60.

the experiments, newly-married people viewed their spouses and strangers as they (the spouses and strangers) walked about in a large Ames room or as they looked back at the viewers from the windows of a small Ames room.[22] It was found that although the strangers underwent the usual distortions of apparent size while the Ames room looked normal, the spouses tended to undergo smaller changes and the Ames room tended to look distorted. The spouses, in other words, looked much closer to their actual sizes than the strangers did. In another experiment, the subjects wore distorting glasses that normally make it look to the wearer as though other people seen through them are bent forward, or have distorted limbs, or as if the whole lower halfs of their bodies are broadened. It was discovered that when mutilated persons (e.g., amputees) are looked at through these glasses, they look much less distorted than people with normal bodies. Furthermore, when a group of Navy recruits wore the glasses, their petty-officer superiors looked much less distorted to them than did their fellow recruits. From the results of these, and similar, experiments, it seems reasonable to conclude, with the experimenters, that at least as far as shape and size are concerned, we tend to see people who cause feelings of anxiety in us more accurately than we see other people, at least under difficult conditions of visual observation—i.e., they tend to look to be closer to their actual shape and size than other people do. Here again we discover that where there is need for perception to have certain characteristics—and presumably it will, on the whole, serve our best interests if we perceive important features of anxiety-causing persons more accurately than those of others—we are somehow able to bring

[22] An Ames room is a specially constructed space that is designed to look rectangular when viewed from a certain point, but is not in fact rectangular. The wall opposite the viewer looks to be placed at right angles to his line of sight, but actually the left side of it is much farther away from him than is the right side. The result is that an object placed in the far left corner of the room looks much smaller than it looks when placed in the far right corner.

it about that our perceptions do in fact have those characteristics.

So much for the experimental evidence. I think it shows quite conclusively that sense perception is not an isolated process totally unrelated to other aspects of the perceiver's nature. In particular—since virtually all the experiments in this area have dealt with vision—I think it shows that the way certain objects (or persons) look to someone is affected to some extent and in specifiable ways by such things as his likes, needs, wants, bodily appetites, and feelings of anxiety. And when I speak of "the way they look," I do not speak vaguely or metaphorically: I refer to the sizes they look to be, the shapes they look to have, and the like. I shall assume that this empirical thesis has now been proven to the reader's satisfaction.

Earlier I said that any philosophical theory of perception has connections of a peculiar sort with empirical facts; and my main purpose in giving the foregoing accounts of psychological experiments was to show that their results do "fit in" very nicely with our theory of perception and do not "fit in" with certain others. By 'certain other theories' it is no doubt clear that I mean sense-datum theories, primarily. The time has now come to justify both of these claims.

I begin with our own theory. According to this theory, the way things look to a perceiver (to consider just vision) is a matter of the perceptual beliefs, inclinations to believe, and suppressed inclinations to believe he causally-receives, under certain conditions, by means of using his eyes in the standard visual way. As I have already indicated, these perceptual states are to be construed as being dispositional ones; thus, to have a perceptual belief, for example, is just to be disposed to act—or, more generally, to behave—in a certain variety of ways. This dispositional account of perceptual beliefs, and the other kinds of perceptual states, is no mere accidental supplement, or accompaniment, of our general theory of perception: it is an essential part of it. It is an essential part because without it, our theory has very little, if any, plausibility. Thus no one would experience a temptation to accept our theory if we were to maintain, for example, that to have a perceptual belief is to make a conscious judgment, or to entertain a proposition and assent to it, or to do anything else of that general sort. So although at one level, our theory of perception might perhaps be called a belief-theory, it would be more accurate to call it a *behavioral* theory, for that is what, at bottom, it is.

And when our theory is viewed in this light, all of the phenomena discovered in the experiments we have been discussing are seen to "fit in" very nicely with it; our theory renders all of them intelligible. That it does so may be shown as follows. Our two principles of perceptual conditioning, if we can accept them, certainly provide at least the form, or heart, of an explanation of these perceptual phenomena; for given that perception is conditionable along the lines sketched in the two principles, we have no further difficulty in understanding, if only in a general way, how, and why, the phenomena happen. It is something of a problem, however, to see how those principles of conditioning can actually work—to see, in other words, how perception *can* possibly be conditioned in the ways indicated. But this problem dissolves into nothingness the moment our theory of perception is accepted. The reason for this is that our theory, as we saw, is basically a behavioral one, and it is readily understandable how the modes of behavior, and hence the dispositions to such modes, that on our theory constitute perceptual states, are subject to conditioning. All behavior is subject to conditioning, and so it is only to be expected that the special kinds of behavior, and the dispositions to it, that according to our theory go to make up the way things look (sound, feel, and so on) to people, should also be subject to conditioning. The point may be put this way: our theory allows us to see our two principles of perceptual conditioning as being nothing more than perfectly standard, widely accepted principles of *general* behavioral conditioning applied to the special case of sense perception. The two principles then become wholly intelligible, and so, therefore, do the various perceptual phenomena that they, in turn, explain. So given our behavioral theory of perception plus ordinary principles of behavioral conditioning, the experimental perceptual phenomena that we have been describing—which are otherwise very puzzling—are just the sorts of thing one would expect to exist. That is what I mean when I say that they "fit in" nicely with our theory.

These same perceptual phenomena do not, however, "fit in" at all well with sense-datum theories of perception: for it is obvious that there is nothing whatever inherent in such theories that would lead one to expect that perception had anything to do with what may be called the affective, or valuing, nature of the perceiving organism. Sense-datum theories may be able to provide some account to explain the kind of experimental results we have been discussing, but not, I should imagine, without appealing to extremely dubious, ad hoc conjectures. Any such account will inevitably look as though it were simply "tacked on" to the sense-datum theory, since that theory, unlike ours, just does not provide a conceptual framework that creates the slightest antecedent expectation that perception might have connections with the affective, or valuing, state of the perceiver. Sense-datum theories have no implications that run in that direction. So the experimental results do not "fit in" with sense-datum theories nearly as well as they do with ours.

B. Perception and Motion

I want now to consider the relationship between visual perception—in particular, the visual perception of certain spatial properties—and physical movements of various kinds on the part of the observer. The spatial properties I have in mind include the following: the straightness or curvature of a line, the radial location of an object relative to the direction one is facing (e.g., straight ahead, off to the left or right), the size and shape of an object, the verticality or tilt of an object or line, and so on. Our theory implies that there is an intimate connection between the visual perception of such properties and bodily movements, or at any rate the dispositions to bodily movement, by the observer. I shall now try to indicate, in very broad strokes, what the nature of this connection is.

As an example, let us consider the straightness or curvature of a line. Imagine a straight black line of three or four yards length drawn on a plain white surface. Imagine further that a perceiver, Q, sees this line and that it looks straight to him. Given that he is in a First Case situation relative to the shape of the line, our theory says that the line's looking straight to him is essentially a matter of his causally-receiving, in a special way, the (perceptual) belief that it is straight. But for him to causally-receive a belief of that sort and in that way, according to the dispositional account of belief that is an integral part of our general theory of perception, is for him to get (or be put) into such a state that he is disposed to act or behave in a certain variety of ways with respect to the line. And plausible candidates for the most basic ways of behaving in the present case are surely the making of bodily movements of one sort or another. It is not possible to list the indefinitely many different movements that would be relevant in even this relatively simple case, but I shall try to describe a few representative examples: (Q is the perceiver in all cases)

(a) (When the black line is flush with the floor, Q is standing at one end of it, and the line stretches out in front of him) Q is in such a dispositional state (or is so disposed) that if he wanted to walk along the line, he would move in such-and-such a particular way.

(b) (Under the same conditions as in (a)) Q is so disposed that if he wanted to lie along the line, he would move in such-and-such a way.

(c) (When the black line is on a wall in front of Q, about three feet straight ahead of him) Q is so disposed that if he wanted to trace along the line with his

right forefinger, he would move his trunk and right
arm in such-and-such a particular way.

(d) (When the black line is placed obliquely on a wall,
with Q sitting directly before it, the lower end of the
line being opposite Q's head) Q is so disposed that
if he wanted to look along the length of the line
without standing up or moving his head, he would
move his eyes in such-and-such a particular way.

(e) (Under the same conditions as in (d)) Q is so disposed that if he wanted to inspect the entire length
of the line, keeping it constantly the same distance
before his eyes, he would stand up, obliquely, in
such-and-such a way.

One could obviously go on indefinitely listing the various
different ways Q is disposed to move his body as a whole
and/or its parts (including his eyes) under a variety of
conditions—ways he is disposed to move in virtue of the
fact that the line looks straight to him. But (a)-(e) will
have to do for now as typical examples. According to our
theory of perception, the line's looking straight to a perceiver Q ultimately *is* (i.e., is ultimately identical with)
his being in just such a fantastically complex dispositional
state to move in the sorts of ways I have indicated in (a)-
(e), where his being in that state is the result of his using
his eyes, with respect to the line, in the standard visual
way. So our theory forges a very close tie indeed between
the visual perception of the straightness or curvature of
a line and the perceiver's bodily movements. And of course
it makes the same sort of intimate connection to bodily
movements for the perception of the other spatial properties as well.

In so far as our theory of perception does forge these
connections, it receives something like a degree of confirmation, so I want to argue, from recent work by experimental
psychologists on our ability to adapt to prism spectacles
and other devices that distort our perception of spatial
properties—that distort the apparent curvature of lines, for

example, or the radial direction of objects in our visual
field, or the apparent visual size of objects, and so on. It
has been found that subjects wearing devices of this sort
can, under certain conditions—and, in fact, under a rather
surprisingly wide range of conditions—adapt to them partially or entirely, so that the original distortion of the relevant spatial property is either diminished significantly or
altogether eliminated.[23]

The earliest experiments of this sort were among the
most dramatic. For example, Theodor Erismann, at the University of Innsbruck, designed a pair of spectacles that
made everything look upside down, but did not affect the
viewer's right-left orientation. A group of (adult) subjects
were required to wear these spectacles continuously for
an extended period, and while doing so to engage in a wide
variety of normal—and hence, in those circumstances, haz-
ardous—activities. At first, the subjects found it difficult
to co-ordinate their movements, experienced great discom-
fort, and were sometimes even made sick. Several of the
subjects thought the strain was too much for them, and
resigned after a day or two. But gradually the others were
able to do—smoothly and well, too—all sorts of quite complicated and difficult things: to ride bicycles, walk along
crowded streets, and so on. The world, however, still looked
upside down to them. But as their overt behavior got better and better, the subjects began to experience moments
in which the inverted world was suddenly seen as right
side up, only to lapse again, just as suddenly, back into up-
sidedownness. As the experiment progressed, however,
these moments became more and more frequent, until finally all of the subjects but one[24] saw the world right side

[23] Chapter 9 of William Epstein's book *Varieties of Perceptual
Learning* contains a comprehensive and judicious survey of the recent
psychological literature. Readers seriously interested in this topic
should consult Epstein; his point of view is quite different from mine.

[24] This subject's way of dealing with the experimental situation was
very special. His case is discussed and explained in J. G. Taylor, *The
Behavioral Basis of Perception* (New Haven and London: Yale University Press, 1962), pp. 180-81.

up continuously. When the inverting spectacles were then removed, the world looked upside down once again, but its proper erect position was very soon re-established.

In most of the more recent experiments, investigators have used optical devices that distort spatial properties less drastically; and they have been more concerned than their predecessors to collect quantitative data on the exact amount of adaptation achieved by their subjects. They have tried to find the answers to such questions as these: whether active (i.e., self-produced) movement on the part of the subject is a necessary condition for adaptation; what correlation there is between, on the one hand, the kind and amount of bodily movement and, on the other hand, the degree and speed of adaptation; whether it is a necessary condition for adaptation that the subject receive informational feedback as to the success or failure of his bodily movements; and so on. But the bare fact that partial or complete visual adaptation to all sorts of optical devices that distort spatial characteristics can and does occur is not a matter of dispute.

Anyone who accepts our behavioral theory of perception will not be the least bit surprised to discover that people can visually adapt to such distorting devices; on the contrary, he would positively expect it. Let us try to see why. (In the account that follows, there will necessarily be a lot of oversimplification but otherwise, I trust, no essential distortion of facts.) Imagine a normal perceiver, Q, placed in an artificial environment: all the lines he can see are either straight, convex to the left, or convex to the right (as in Fig. II). I shall use the following symbols:

P(s) : the patterns of retinal stimulation caused in Q when he looks at the straight lines.

P(cl) : the patterns of retinal stimulation caused in Q when he looks at the curved lines that are convex to the left.

P(cr) : the patterns of retinal stimulation caused in Q when he looks at the curved lines that are convex to the right.

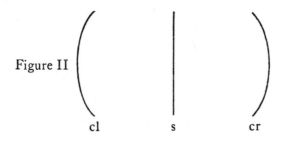

Figure II

cl   s   cr

R(s)   : the set of responses that Q is disposed to make when a line looks straight to him—e.g., those described in (a)-(e) (above). (I shall call these Q's *straight-responses*).

R(cl)   : the set of responses Q is disposed to make when a line looks curved to him and convex to the left. (I shall call these Q's *convex-to-the-left-responses*).

R(cr)   : the set of responses Q is disposed to make when a line looks curved to him and convex to the right. (I shall call these Q's *convex-to-the-right-responses*).

We may imagine that the conditions of observation (lighting, and so on) are standard. Since Q is a normal perceiver, the straight lines look straight to him, the curved lines curved. On our theory, a line's looking straight [convex to the left, convex to the right] to a normal perceiver in standard conditions just *is* (identical with) the line's causing him, in a certain way, to be disposed to make some of the R(s) [R(cl), R(cr)] responses. Hence

(A) When Q's retinas are stimulated in one of the P(s) ways, Q is thereby disposed to make R(s) responses.

(B) When Q's retinas are stimulated in one of the P(cl) ways, Q is thereby disposed to make R(cl) responses.

(C) When Q's retinas are stimulated in one of the P(cr) ways, Q is thereby disposed to make R(cr) responses.

But suppose, now, that Q dons a pair of distorting spectacles that (a) make the straight lines look curved, convex to the right, (b) make the curved lines that are convex to the right look as though they have a greater degree of curvature in that direction, and (c) make the curved lines that

are convex to the left look straight (as in Fig. III). To
simplify the discussion, we are to imagine that in Q's special
environment, the curved lines that are convex to the left are
all of exactly the same degree of curvature, and that this
degree of curvature is such that the lenses make the lines
look straight. So when Q dons such a pair of spectacles,

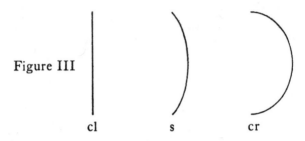

Figure III

cl   s   cr

(D) the straight lines cause a P(cr) (whereas before
they had caused a P(s)), and

(E) the curved lines that are convex to the left cause a
P(s) (whereas before they had caused a P(cl)).[25]

Since (A) and (B), however, are still true of Q when he
first puts the spectacles on, we may say that his straight-
responses and his convex-to-the-right-responses are now all
wrong. In virtue of (A) and (E), when Q is confronted
with a curved line that is convex to the left, he is now disposed to make inappropriate *straight*-responses (R(s));
and in virtue of (C) and (D), when he is confronted with
a straight line, he is now disposed to make inappropriate
convex-to-the-right-responses (R(cr)). As a result, any of
these R(s) or R(cr) responses that he actualizes will result in confusion, or at any rate in ensuing perceptual and
other states that are unexpected, unwanted, and hence
"punished." For example, suppose Q is standing at one end

[25] It is also true that any given curved line L that is convex to
the right now causes a P(crr)—that is, a pattern of retinal stimulation
that would normally be caused by a curving line that is convex to the
right and of a degree of curvature greater than L. But I shall ignore
these cases in what follows.

of a curved line, convex to the left, 3 or 4 yards long, drawn on the floor: the line, as we know, looks straight to him. When he tries to walk along the line, he is naturally disposed to move his body in a relevant R(s) way—i.e., to move his body in the way he normally would to walk along a straight line. His effort fails dismally, however: instead of moving easily and smoothly along the line, he finds that his course keeps diverging from the line. His R(s) response, in other words, is punished. However, if Q tries this same experiment over again a number of times, we should expect that he would eventually learn to move his body in appropriate ways—that is, to make suitable R(cl) responses. Such responses would be rewarded because they would enable Q to walk easily and smoothly along the line. We know from countless experiments that Q can and will learn to do this, despite the fact that the objectively curved line still continues to look straight to him.

It might be thought that our theory runs into trouble at this point. On our account, a line's looking straight to an observer is a matter of his being disposed to respond to visual stimuli from the line in such a manner as to behave in ways appropriate to a straight line—i.e., to make straight-responses to it. But after Q has been conditioned in the way just described, he is disposed to make convex-to-the-left-responses, not straight-responses, to the line. How, then, can we consistently hold that the line nevertheless still looks straight to him? The answer to this objection is not far to seek. Our theory holds that a line's looking straight to an observer is a matter of his being disposed to make a vast number of straight-responses to it, not just a few isolated ones. Since all but a few of Q's responses to the line are presumably still not conditioned to the new circumstance of the distorting prisms[26]—that is, since he is still disposed to make straight-responses to it in virtually every

---

[26] I assume here that there is little, if any, generalization of the few convex-to-the-left-responses—i.e., that Q's adaptation in this one particular kind of perceptual situation does not "spread" to other kinds of cases involving curved lines that are convex to the left.

case—it is positively to be expected, on our theory, that the line will still look straight to him, despite the few convex-to-the-left-responses that he has conditioned himself to make. So our theory runs into no trouble on this score—although, of course, it gathers no garlands of credit either.

From here on, however, our theory does, as it seems to me, begin to win some laurels. On our theory, we would naturally expect that as Q continues to wear the distorting spectacles and as he learns the appropriate responses to make to this and other curved lines under an ever wider variety of circumstances—that is, as he conditions himself to make more and more different kinds of $R(cl)$ and $R(cr)$ responses to objectively curved lines—curved lines would begin to look less distorted to him, would look to him, more and more, to have just the degree and kind of curvature that they really have, and eventually would look to him just as they objectively are. Similarly, we would expect that straight lines would eventually look straight to him no matter how he viewed them, and no matter what bodily movements he made involving them. The reason we would expect this, of course, is that on our theory, a line's looking straight (convex to the left, convex to the right) to a person just *is* his being disposed, as the result of a certain kind of causal process, to make a host of suitable straight-(convex-to-the-left-, convex-to-the-right-) responses to it. And there is a vast amount of experimental evidence that beautifully corroborates our expectation.[27]

Suppose that Q does finally achieve complete perceptual adaptation to the distorting spectacles; since (D) and (E) are still true, this means that

(F) when Q's retinas are stimulated in one of the $P(cr)$ ways, Q is thereby disposed to make $R(s)$ responses.[28]

[27] See, for example, Chapter 6 of I. Rock's *The Nature of Perceptual Adaptation.*

[28] There is a complication here that is worth mentioning. All of the $R(s)$ responses that Q has conditioned himself to make after a prolonged period of wearing the distorting spectacles are indeed the same as his original (i.e., pre-spectacles) $R(s)$ responses, but many of them

(G) when Q's retinas are stimulated in one of the P(s) ways, Q is thereby disposed to make R(cl) responses.

Very well: suppose that Q now takes off the spectacles; because of (F) and (G), we would expect that curved lines that are convex to the right would look *straight* to him, and that straight lines would look as though they were curved and convex to the left. This means that the visual distortion is exactly the opposite of what it was when Q first donned the spectacles (cf. (a) and (b), p. 157). And again our expectation is borne out by the experimental facts; indeed, experimenters commonly measure the extent of a subject's perceptual adaptation to distorting prisms by measuring the amount of this reverse distortion that he exhibits on first taking the glasses off.

I think our theory has a marked advantage over other philosophical theories of perception in its ability to deal with the foregoing facts about the perceptual adaptation to distorting prisms. Our theory does not win its victory here merely by virtue of the double fact that (a) observers

---

—notably those involving the way he moves his eyes—are the same *only under a certain description*. To take a particularly pure example, consider the R(s) response (d) described on p. 154. Suppose we were to describe the way Q is disposed to move his eyes as follows:

(W_1) Q moves his eyes in such a way as to keep the line constantly in the center of his visual field.

Under this description, Q's R(s) response of the (d)-sort after he has become perceptually adapted to the distorting spectacles is the same as his R(s) response of the (d)-sort before he put them on. But we are free to describe his eye movements in a different, and perhaps more basic, way—viz.:

(W_2) Q moves his eyes so that they move in such-and-such a way in space (or relative to their sockets).

Under this description, Q's R(s) response of the (d)-sort after adaptation is quite different from the corresponding R(s) response before he donned the glasses: indeed, because of the optical characteristics of the lenses, Q would *have* to move his eyes physically in a different way when he is wearing the spectacles if he is to succeed in keeping the line constantly in the center of his visual field. In other words, his post-adaptation R(s) response of the (d)-sort *must* be different under description (W_2) if it is to be the same under description (W_1).

wearing distorting spectacles eventually learn to adapt all of their behavior, and all of their dispositions to behave, to curved and straight lines and (b) curved (straight) lines eventually come to look curved (straight) to them. Any theory of perception whatever, of course, can accommodate fact (a). And almost any theory could easily hold that fact (a) is the result, or an effect, of fact (b); that the two facts are distinct, but causally related. But then they need some independent explanation of fact (b); we need to be told why, when people wear distorting spectacles long enough, visual adaptation to them eventually occurs. I do not say that no explanation of this puzzling fact will be forthcoming from adherents to other theories of perception, but only that the explanation will have to constitute some sort of complicating addition to their theories. And it is precisely here that our theory has a notable advantage over the others. For on our theory, facts (a) and (b) are the same fact. We, like anyone else, can easily explain fact (a) by appeal to familiar principles of behavioral conditioning or learning. But on our theory, and on our theory alone, this explanation is at the same time an explanation of fact (b), since our theory, and only our theory, identifies facts (a) and (b). To be sure, our theory must here appeal to principles of conditioning, but this is no ad hoc appeal; such principles must be considered to be virtual parts of our theory (since it is a behavioral theory at bottom) and are anyway pretty well established over a far wider range of human phenomena than just sense perception. So I think we can safely claim that the facts of visual adaptation to distorting prisms provide something like strong confirmation of our theory of perception. These otherwise amazing facts become, when seen from the point of view of our theory, entirely natural and intelligible.

If a subject wears distorting spectacles over a relatively long period of time, but if while doing so he drastically restricts the kinds of activities he engages in, our theory of perception would lead us to expect that his perceptual adaptation would not be complete or perfect; for then whole ranges of movements or actions would not become re-conditioned to the spectacles, so that those aspects of his "visual field" answering to those ranges of behavior would undergo no change with the passage of time. Again, this implication of our theory has been borne out. Taylor reports an experiment[29] in which he wore, for several hours each day for thirteen days, a pair of prism spectacles that have the following two effects, among others: they make flat surfaces look curved; and when the wearer rotates his head about its vertical axis, they make it look as though the widths of things constantly change. He spent most of his time while wearing the glasses sitting at a table, reaching out with his hands, and manipulating various objects on the table. He did not take any action with respect to objects beyond the reach of his hands, such as throwing balls or darts at them. At the end of the experiment, the shapes of the table and the things on it looked perfectly normal—that is, flat surfaces looked flat, not curved, and their apparent widths no longer varied with the rotation of his head. The distortion and instability in the shapes of all the more distant objects (i.e., all those beyond arm's reach), however, remained just as great as at the beginning of the experiment.

The explanation of what happened in Taylor's experiment, within the framework of our theory of perception, is roughly as follows. (I shall confine the discussion to just one of the kinds of distortion caused by the prisms—namely, that whereby flat surfaces were made to look curved.) We may assume that when Taylor first put on the glasses, he causally-received inclinations, or suppressed inclinations, to believe that all the flat surfaces he saw were curved—for since he was thoroughly familiar with the effects of such spectacles, he did not causally-receive the (perceptual) belief, and perhaps not even the inclination to believe, that those surfaces actually were curved. As I would wish to construe these perceptual states, this

[29] J. G. Taylor, *The Behavioral Basis of Perception*, pp. 207-22.

means that all of the actions he was spontaneously disposed to perform were appropriate to curved surfaces, and not to flat ones, although he was not disposed to act in the confident way characteristic of having perceptual *beliefs*, of course. And in fact Taylor reports that his actions at the table in the beginning *were* indeed appropriate to a curved, and not to a flat, surface; and since the table top *was* flat, these actions were of course "punished" by not meeting with complete success, in one way or another. For example, "in writing, [he] tended to press the pen too hard against the paper at the beginning of each line and to decrease the pressure toward the end of the line."[30] With constant and prolonged practice, however, all his actions, and therefore presumably all the actions he was disposed to perform, became perfectly and harmoniously adjusted to a flat surface. Therefore, since Taylor never had any doubts that his table top was flat, we may say (if my account of belief is correct) that at the end of the thirteen day experiment, he kept causally-receiving the perceptual belief, by means of using his eyes in the standard visual way, that the table top was flat. But on our theory of perception, to say this is to say that the table top looked flat to him—and we know that it did. On the other hand, since Taylor did nothing whatever to objects beyond his arm's reach during the experiment, except passively look at them, all the modes of behavior he was disposed to adopt towards them at the end of the experiment were the same as those at the beginning of it. That is to say, at the end of the experiment, as at the beginning, whenever he looked at flat surfaces beyond arm's reach, he still causally-received inclinations, or suppressed inclinations, to have the perceptual belief that they were curved. In other words, they still looked curved to him.

Experimental psychologists in the field of perceptual adaptation to distorting optical devices are concerned, among other things, with the role of active (i.e., self-produced) motion on the part of the subject in such adapta-

[30] Taylor, *op. cit.*, p. 219.

tion. Is active motion a necessary condition for adaptation or not? What our theory would lead us to expect, I think, is that active motion would at least be a very great aid to adaptation, but that in all probability it would not always be an absolutely necessary condition of adaptation—for it seems likely that in an organism as complicated as man, some kinds of responses might well become conditioned to changed circumstances without the organism actually making the response, and having it rewarded, in the changed circumstances. I should also be inclined to expect, on the basis of our theory of perception, that if the subject wearing distorting spectacles is to adapt to them, he must receive some information as to how things really are in his environment. Thus, for example, when the subject makes active movements, it seems that, unless artificial rewards and punishments are introduced by the experimenter, the subject must get informational feedback as to the degree of success (or failure) of those movements, since otherwise his responses would not receive the usual reward (or punishment), and hence would not be conditioned.[31] And in those cases, if there are any, where a subject can adapt without any sort of movement, it seems reasonable to suppose that he must have, or receive, some independent information about the relevant objective property—for otherwise it is difficult to understand how he should be able to adapt at all.[32]

What the facts really are on the foregoing issues, and other related ones, is by no means finally settled; psychologists are still hotly debating them, and experiments are being conducted in an effort to discover where the truth

[31] But see R. Held, "Plasticity in sensory-motor systems," *Scientific American*, Vol. 213, No. 5 (November 1965), 84-94.

[32] I do not believe that the well-known Gibson effect is a counterexample to this claim, since it is not a phenomenon of *adaptation* or *learning* at all, but rather one of mere change: it occurs, for example, when a subject views curved lines without wearing distorting spectacles—the lines, after even quite a short time, look straighter to him than they really are. For a discussion of the Gibson effect, see Irvin Rock, *The Nature of Perceptual Adaptation*, pp. 185-93.

lies. I shall make no effort to discuss or summarize the results of these investigations; the time and effort that would
have to be expended for such an undertaking would be
excessive for our purposes, and anyway the job has already
been done with great skill by an expert in the field—Irvin
Rock, in his admirable book *The Nature of Perceptual Adaptation*, already referred to. I shall have to content myself
with the bare assertion that as far as I can determine from
reading accounts of what has gone on in the laboratories so
far, it seems very likely indeed that the expectations
sketched above, or at least something quite like them, will
turn out to be confirmed. Here, for example, is part of
Rock's summary of his chapter on "Adaptation to Optical
Distortion of Form":

> The work of several . . . investigators . . . clearly indicates
> that, above and beyond the adaptive change predict-
> able in terms of the Gibson effect, there is prism adapta-
> tion to curvature, based on information as to the prop-
> erties of objects in the environment. In all such research
> thus far performed, movement of the observer or his
> head or his eyes alone was a necessary condition for adap-
> tation, as is to be expected on the basis of defining prop-
> erties of subject-relative curvature. Feedback from move-
> ment provides the crucial information that points are not
> located where they at first appear to be. There is evi-
> dence which suggests that *active* movement by the ob-
> server is a necessary condition. If further research con-
> firms this finding, the explanation may lie with the ambi-
> guity of information about the direction of movement of
> the observer when such movement is passively imposed.
> However, [in this chapter] procedures were suggested by
> which passive movement would be expected to yield
> adaptation to prismatic changes of curvature, and it was
> pointed out that familiarity with the scene might produce
> an effect even in a stationary observer.[33]

[33] Irvin Rock, *op. cit.*, p. 215. For some recent work in this area
see S. M. Fishkin, "Passive vs. active exposure and other variables

I have said it before, and no doubt it is perfectly obvious to the reader anyway, but I want to emphasize once again that our theory of perception, including a dispositional or behavioristic account of beliefs, inclinations to believe, and suppressed inclinations to believe, is by no means a scientific theory, although it has connections with scientific theories. It may be said to provide a very general theoretical framework within which genuine scientific hypotheses can be formulated. The part of our theory that is relevant to the present topic asserts no more than that the way things look to a perceiver is a matter of the ways he is disposed to act towards them as the result of using his eyes in the standard visual way—to put it much too crudely. This very general contention is compatible with a great many different specific and testable hypotheses that fill in the details, as it were, that our theory says nothing whatever about. They would explain, ideally, every perceptual phenomenon that has so far been discovered, and predict others that have not. For example, they would specify which "phenomenal properties" are determined by dispositions to which particular modes of behavior, and explain why this is so. At present we are a long way from having any such complete and adequate scientific theory of perception; the nearest and best approach to it that I know of is the theory expounded in Taylor's very important book, *The Behavioral Basis of Perception*, to which I have referred several times.[34]

My claim about the results of experiments with distorting spectacles, then, is not that they serve to confirm directly our theory of sense perception, but rather that they

---

related to the occurrence of hand adaptation to lateral displacement," *Perceptual and Motor Skills*, 29 (1969), 291-97, and R. B. Welch and R. W. Rhoades, "The manipulation of informational feedback and its effects upon prism adaptation," *Canadian Journal of Psychology*, 23 (1969), 415-28.

[34] For recent elaborations of Taylor's theory, see his articles "The behavioural basis of perceived size and distance," *Canadian Journal of Psychology*, 19 (1965), 1-14, and "Perception generated by training echolocation," *ibid.*, 20 (1966), 64-81.

confirm certain scientific hypotheses—e.g., those espoused by Taylor—that may be regarded as specifications of our theory, as fleshed-out versions of the bare skeleton that our theory essentially is. It is in this sense that I want to say that these experimental results "fit in" beautifully with our theory of perception, and lend it additional plausibility.

I should perhaps add here, what may be obvious, that the line between a philosophical theory of perception, such as ours, and a very general psychological theory of perception is not at all a sharp or clear one. Among the ways of telling whether a theory is a psychological one, I suppose, is to note whether it is propounded by undoubted psychologists and whether it is published in a reputable psychological journal. On this test, there is at least one very general psychological theory of the visual perception of shape (or contour) that is indistinguishable from ours. It is put forward by the psychologists L. Festinger, H. Ono, C. A. Burnham, and D. Bamber in their monograph "Efference and the conscious experience of perception."[35] In the concluding section of their monograph, the authors write:

> . . . [We] have stated an experimentally testable theory of visual perception of contour. This theory, which seems to fit known facts, holds that visual perception of contour is determined by the particular sets of preprogrammed efferent instructions that are activated by the visual input into a state of readiness for immediate use. (p. 34)

This is precisely the account we have given, couched in different terms. Reporting on the experiments described in the main body of the monograph, the authors continue their summing-up as follows:

> Four experiments were done to test whether or not the conscious experience of visual perception is determined by

[35] *Journal of Experimental Psychology Monograph*, Vol. 74, No. 4 (August 1967), 1-36.

the efferent readiness activated by the visual input. In three of these experiments [subjects] wore prism spectacles producing apparent curvature of straight lines and made arm movements corresponding to the objective contour of the lines while viewing them through the prisms. In each experiment one set of experimental conditions was designed to facilitate learning to issue new efference to the arm in response to the retinal contour and one set of conditions was designed to hinder such learning of a new afferent-efferent association. In all three experiments there was significantly more change in the visual perception of "straight" in the conditions that encouraged learning a new afferent-efferent association. . . . In a fourth experiment change in the visual perception of curvature was measured for three [subjects] who viewed a line monocularly through a wedge prism mounted on a contact lens. For each [subject] the head was fixed by a biteboard and the only movement relevant to the contour was movement of the eyes. . . . All three [subjects] showed appreciable change in the visual perception of curvature as a consequence of simply scanning the line while wearing the contact lens. This occurred whether [the subject] viewed an apparently straight line or an apparently curved line. . . .

While the data are not conclusive with regard to an "efference readiness" theory of visual perception, they do support the theory. (pp. 34-35)

To the extent that these experiments support the psychologists' "efference readiness" theory, they also support our theory of the visual perception of shape (or contour)—for the two theories, as far as I can tell, are one.[36]

[36] Further corroboration for the theory of Festinger *et al.* is provided in R. S. Slotnick, "Adaptation to curvature distortion," *Journal of Experimental Psychology*, 81 (1969), 441-48. In another experiment designed to test the "efferent readiness" theory of perception (C. A. Burnham, "Consistency between motor activity and perceived direction of rotation," *Perception and Psychophysics*, 5 [1969], 29-32), it was found that when subjects simultaneously turned a crank and viewed a stimulus capable of apparent reversal of direction, "the

I do not think that defenders of sense-datum theories would experience much trouble finding explanations of the foregoing perceptual phenomena that are compatible with their theories. They could suggest, for example, something like this: the conditioning undergone by a person wearing distorting spectacles gradually brings it about that his brain produces sense-data (or the awareness of sense-data) that reflect, more and more accurately, the relevant spatial characteristics of the objects in his visual field. But such explanations obviously constitute additions to the sense-datum theories—they have to be imposed on them from the outside, as it were. In contrast to ours, sense-datum theories, once again, create no antecedent expectation that perception has any connections with the bodily movements a perceiver is disposed to make. In this sense, the experimental results we have been discussing do not at all "fit in" with these theories, and therefore cause them yet further embarrassment.

C. PERCEPTION AND LANGUAGE

One of the significant kinds of things that human beings are disposed to do, as a result of using their sense organs, is to use language in a variety of ways. Thus, if a person sees a tree, for example, he is for that very reason so dis-

---

perceived initial direction of rotation was more stable when it was consistent with the motor activity of the viewer than when it was inconsistent" (*ibid.*, p. 29) and "when [subjects] were instructed to perceive a particular direction of rotation for a period of time they tended to engage in motor activity consistent with that direction. The results were interpreted as supporting an efference theory of perception." (*ibid.*, p. 29)

Further support for the efferent readiness theory is claimed in L. Festinger, C. W. White, and M. R. Allyn, "Eye movements and decrement in the Müller-Lyer illusion" (*Perception and Psychophysics,* 3 [1968], 376-82) and in C. A. Burnham, "Decrement of the Müller-Lyer illusion with saccadic and tracking eye movements" (*ibid.*, 424-26); these claims are disputed in S. C. McLaughlin, M. J. DeSisto, and M. J. Kelly, Jr., "Comments on 'Eye movements and decrement in the Müller-Lyer illusion'" (*Perception and Psychophysics,* 5 [1969], 288) and in R. C. Bolles, "The role of eye movements in the Müller-Lyer illusion," (*ibid.*, 6 [1969], 175-76.)

posed that if he were to describe or characterize what he saw, he might say that he saw a tree, or say something that at least entails that he did. Such dispositional states as these may well be among the important elements that constitute a human perceiver's perceptual beliefs, inclinations to believe, and suppressed inclinations to believe. If this be granted, then it follows from our theory of perception that the ways things look (sound, feel, etc.) to human users of language may in part be determined by the ways they are disposed to use language. So it might well be the case, first, that things look (sound, feel, etc.) generally different to people whose language is different in certain relevant respects. (I do not claim to know what the relevant respects are.) And second, on any given occasion, the way a thing or quality looks (sounds, feels, etc.) to a language-using human perceiver might well depend in part on which particular words, or at least on which kinds of words, he is disposed to use to characterize it. To the extent that these two remarkable implications (or possible implications) of our theory can be substantiated, to that extent would the theory receive yet further support.

I propose to say nothing about the first (possible) implication. As is well known, Whorf and Sapir, among others, have done a great deal of work in this area; but the issues involved are so complex and difficult that I would not want to risk embarrassment by trying to discuss them even if, contrary to fact, such a discussion would not take us too far off our main course. On, then, to the second implication.

Before turning to the relevant experimental evidence, I should like to make one or two general points. First, it is unlikely that a human perceiver's dispositions to use certain words, rather than others, in a perceptual situation to characterize what he sees will play anything like as important a part in determining the way it looks to him as do his dispositions to move his body in various ways, for example. A human can certainly see things before he acquires the ability to use language; moreover, some humans and most, if not all, other animals cannot use language at all, and yet this does not seem to prevent them from being expert at seeing. By contrast, it is not at all evident that if any organism were perpetually deprived of his ability to *move*, he could then see all things as well as his mobile colleagues, or that he would be able to detect certain aspects of things visually at all. These considerations are far from conclusive, of course; it might just happen that things do look radically different to users of language and non-users of language, but I would be inclined to doubt it until there is some powerful evidence to the contrary. The real truth of the matter is, though, I suppose, that it is idle to discuss the question at all until we have a clearer idea of what sort of evidence there might conceivably *be* that would weigh on one side or the other.

Second, I must concede that the very idea of there being just the sort of connection between perception and language that I have been suggesting strikes one immediately as implausible; for the alleged connection seems, if I may put it so, to run in the wrong direction. No one, I take it, would want to deny that when a person sees something, he is so disposed that if he were to characterize what he sees, or thinks he sees, he would probably use certain words rather than others. But the natural presumption is that this linguistic disposition owes its distinctive features entirely to the character of the perceiver's "visual field"—for example, that he might be disposed to apply the word 'red,' rather than 'blue,' to something he sees only because it first, and independently, looks red to him, and not blue. But what I have darkly and oddly hinted, in the name of our theory, is that the influence may work, at least to some extent, in the opposite direction—for example, that a thing's looking red to a person may in part be determined by his being disposed, if he were to apply an adjective to it, to use the word 'red,' rather than 'blue,' 'green,' or whatever. And that, I confess, sounds somehow absurd.

In reply to this concession of mine, I want to defend the following two points. (1) Despite the contrary appearances, the sort of connection between language and perception that I have hinted at is a perfectly possible one that ought not to be ruled summarily out of court. (2) I did not mean to claim that the existence of such a connection certainly *is* an implication of our theory of perception, but only that it might well be. I begin with the second point. It is true that on our theory, the way things (phenomenally) look to a perceiver is a matter of the beliefs, inclinations to believe, and suppressed inclinations to believe that he causally-receives in a certain specified way. It is also true that I maintain that all beliefs and inclinations to believe are constituted by dispositions to act in a variety of ways, and that these ways normally include linguistic behavior when the believer is human. But there is nothing in all this to rule out the possibility that causally-received *perceptual* beliefs and inclinations to believe are special states, and that they are constituted *only* by dispositions to behave in non-linguistic ways. If that were so, the perceiver's disposition to say certain things about what he sees would be a mere consequence of the way it looks to him, and this would be in accord with what I called the "natural presumption." Since I have not yet said very much by way of marking out the class of behavioral dispositions that constitute the way things look to perceivers, on our theory of perception, our theory is so far compatible with this "natural presumption." On the other hand, it is also compatible with the contrary view that the way things directly look to a perceiver is in part determined by his dispositions to use certain words to characterize what he sees, or thinks he sees. And this brings us to point (1).

I certainly would never wish to deny that many of a perceiver's dispositions to say certain things follow after, and are mere consequences of, his pre-existing perceptual awareness. But there is no reason to suppose that the way things look to a language-using perceiver cannot be in part determined by the dispositions he acquires, on the occasion in question, to use certain words, rather than others, to characterize what he sees, or thinks he sees. One naturally—although wrongly—assumes that this must be impossible, because one is strongly tempted to imagine that an observer's perceptual awareness must already exist complete and full-blown before he can develop any dispositions to describe what he is thus aware of. For how could a person have a disposition to describe that of which he is perceptually aware, unless he was already aware of it? But this natural—and wrong—way of thinking is fostered by an oversimplified picture of the workings of a human organism, and in particular, of his central nervous system, including his brain. As far as I can tell, there is not the slightest reason to doubt that the human brain is sufficiently complex so that the following might very well happen: signals from a perceiver's optic nerves stimulate the appropriate regions of his visual cortex, and, because of his previous conditioning, dispositions to act in a variety of ways immediately arise, among which are dispositions to use certain words. I cannot see why such linguistic dispositions must necessarily wait upon the others, or upon anything else except some sort of brain stimulation caused by the perceived things. And if they need not, then they may be elements of his perceptual beliefs (inclinations to believe, or suppressed inclinations to believe), and they may therefore partly determine the way the objects of his "perceptual awareness" look to him. I do not say that this certainly does happen, but only that no incoherence, or even implausibility, is involved in thinking that it might. That it might is a real—and to my mind, a fascinating—possibility, and one that our theory of perception immediately suggests. I urge that we keep an open mind on the question, and that we "look and see" whether this real and important possibility is actualized or not.

Having said this, I must confess at once that, as the reader will soon discover, it is difficult to evaluate the relevant experimental evidence;[37] it by no means points unambigu-

---

[37] This lugubrious assessment I share with William Epstein: see Chapter 6 of his *Varieties of Perceptual Learning* for a survey of the pertinent literature.

ously to the conclusion that there exists the sort of connection between perception and language that is (at least)
suggested by our theory. Part of the trouble, although not all
of it, is that few of these experiments were specifically designed to test the hypothesis that there is just this kind of
connection—evidently because that hypothesis is such a
novel one, as well as an initially implausible-sounding one.
Nevertheless, I shall persist in my intention of briefly mentioning some of the evidence, for aside from its own intrinsic interest, it contains, I think, some indications that
there really is such a connection.

One final point, however, before presenting the experimental evidence. There might be thought to be, and indeed
there may be, a real distinction between the following two
hypotheses about the nature of the connection between a
perceiver's disposition to apply a certain word to what he
sees and the way that thing looks to him in the relevant
respect: (a) the linguistic disposition is no part of the perceptual state, but causally influences it, and (b) the linguistic disposition is a constitutive part of the perceptual
state, and (partially) determines it not by way of being a
causal antecedent of it, but by being part of it. I shall not
raise the question of whether (a) and (b) are really different, as they at least seem to be at first glance; instead, I shall
simply point out that since no way has yet been devised for
distinguishing (a) from (b)—for obvious reasons—I shall
treat them as equivalent in what follows.

And now, at last, for the actual evidence, such as it is.
In one experiment,[38] patches of grey paper were cut out in
the following shapes: tomato, tangerine, lemon, neutral
oval, lobster claw, carrot, banana, neutral elongated el-
lipse. The patches were placed on a sheet of blue-green
paper; the contrast of colors made them all look a kind of
brownish-orange. Subjects were assigned the task of ad-

[38] J. S. Bruner, L. Postman, and J. Rodrigues, "Expectation and the
perception of color," *American Journal of Psychology*, 64 (1951),
216-27; reprinted in Beardslee and Wertheimer (eds.), *Readings in
Perception*, pp. 267-78.

justing a variable color-wheel made up of yellow and red segments until its color matched that of each of the patches of paper. As each patch was presented, the subject was told what it was supposed to represent—e.g., "This is a lemon. Make the color-wheel the same color as it." It was found that the patches depicting normally red objects (tomato, lobster claw) were judged to be considerably redder than the neutral patches, that the patches depicting normally yellow objects (lemon, banana) were judged to be considerably yellower, and that the patches depicting normally orange objects (tangerine, carrot) were judged to be about the same color as the neutral patches.

The apparent colors of the various patches differed from that of the neutral patches because, surely, the subjects believed that each of them represented the sort of thing (lemon, tomato, or whatever) that it did represent. But where the believer is a language-using human, an important part of his believing that something is, or depicts a lemon (say) is his being disposed to apply the word 'lemon' (and hence, normally, also 'yellow') to it. It is to be expected that the subjects in this experiment, at any rate, had such linguistic dispositions, for they were told, just before each presentation of a patch, what it was supposed to represent. It seems plausible to assume, then, that the linguistic dispositions were at least partially responsible for the variations in apparent color. I confess that in our present state of ignorance, this can be nothing more than a (perhaps wishful) conjecture; for it just might be the case that the other, non-linguistic, dispositions making up the subject's belief (that the patch represents a lemon) are the only ones that influence the way its color looks to him, and that his being disposed to apply the word 'lemon' to the patch is a mere idle accompaniment of the process. I hope some obliging and ingenious psychologist will one day conduct an experiment analogous to the Bruner-Postman-Rodrigues one, but designed specifically for non-users of language. But until that day, I think one may be justified in feeling fairly confident that our earlier conjecture is at least a plausible hypothesis. It might not be possible to have quite as much confidence in the efficacy of the linguistic dispositions if the experiments had dealt not with mere patches of paper cut out in the shapes of lemons, tomatoes, and so on, but rather with realistic three-dimensional objects—for example, with real dyed lemons, tomatoes, and the rest. For in that case, a subject would presumably acquire the perceptual belief that the object is an actual lemon (tomato, or whatever), and such a belief no doubt consists of a great many dispositions to behave in a variety of ways, of which the disposition to apply the word 'lemon' ('tomato,' etc.) is but one, and perhaps an insignificant one at that. But when the visual objects are patches of paper, so that the relevant perceptual beliefs are that they (merely) represent, or depict, lemons (tomatoes, etc.), it is reasonable to suppose that the linguistic dispositions figure more prominently in their make-up, and therefore it is more likely that those dispositions bear some responsibility for the quality of the object's apparent color.

Before leaving the Bruner-Postman-Rodrigues experiment, I want to mention the fact that with one group of subjects, well saturated color patches were used and the color-mixer was placed directly alongside the test patch of color, so that simultaneous comparisons were possible. (With the other groups, there was an eighty degree arc between the color patch and the color-mixer, making simultaneous comparisons impossible). Under these ideal conditions, there was no change in the apparent color of the patches; the subjects judged their colors to be just what they objectively were. This shows that the effect of linguistic dispositions, if indeed there is any, is not a major factor in determining the way things look to us, at least as far as their color is concerned. But then no one could reasonably think that it is a major factor.[39]

[39] I confess that it would probably be unwise to place too much reliance on the experiment of Bruner *et al.*: the methods they used have been sharply criticized and their results disputed, although their findings have also been corroborated by other investigators. The se-

It should be pointed out that I am, in a sense, creating more trouble for our theory than is strictly necessary; that is, I am trying to defend a much stronger consequence of it than I really need to. For I could plausibly take the following weaker line: "Consider the Bruner-Postman-Rodrigues experiment. The subjects in that experiment (leaving aside those in the group mentioned in the last paragraph) acquire the perceptual belief that a certain colored patch is the picture of, say, a lemon. Such a belief would normally include the belief that the thing is yellow, since lemons are usually yellow. We may suppose, then, that the acquiring of the belief that the thing represents a lemon arouses in these subjects, conditioned as they are by their past experience with yellow lemons, the disposition to act in ways that correspond to the perceptual belief that the thing is yellow. (This disposition does not 'win out' altogether, of course, because the actual color of the patch is at the same time influencing the subject in the direction of having a disposition to act in slightly different ways, in ways corresponding to the perceptual belief that the patch is brownish-orange in color). I have not yet specified what these ways of acting are that correspond to the perceptual belief that something is yellow, but presumably they form a group of which the purely linguistic acts— such as calling it 'yellow'—are only one, perhaps minor, element. And it is the existence of the dispositions to act in the whole group of ways that accounts for the patch looking yellower to the subject than it really does look, not just the existence of the disposition to act in the purely linguistic ways."

This weaker line would be easier to defend, and would yet be strong enough to give some support to our theory of perception, for there is nothing in that theory which demands that dispositions to act in purely linguistic ways should determine a person's perceptual states. I have chosen to pick out from the relevant bundle of behavioral

---

quence of relevant experiments is clearly described in William Epstein, *Varieties of Perceptual Learning*, Chapter 4.

dispositions just one element—the dispositions to act in linguistic ways—for special attention. I have done this simply because I think it happens to be an extremely fascinating possibility that the way things look to us may be in part determined by the things we are disposed to say about them—a possibility that seems to be at least suggested by our theory of perception.

An experiment conducted by T. H. Howells[40] provides further evidence of the connection between language and color-perception. The subjects were conditioned in the following way. One of two musical tones was sounded and, just after the sound began, a red or a green patch of colored light was switched on. In 95% of the cases, the red patch was preceded by sounding the lower tone, and the green patch was preceded by the higher tone. In the other 5% of the cases—the test trials—this association was reversed. Each subject had about 5,000 trials during this conditioning period. In each trial, the subject reported the color he saw as soon as the stimuli ceased, and was immediately told whether he had judged rightly or wrongly. Very few errors were made by any of the subjects during these first 5,000 trials. There then followed a series of 20,000 additional trials (including, therefore, 1,000 test trials in which the tones were switched) of exactly the same kind for each subject, except that the saturation of the two colors was greatly reduced on every other trial. During the progress of this second series, there was practically a straight line curve of a steadily increasing proportion of errors for those test trials in which the weaker color-stimulus was shown: that is, in more and more of the test trials, the pale green looked red to the subjects and the pale red looked green. (A supplementary experiment was conducted to rule out the possibility that it was merely the subjects' verbal responses of saying 'red' and 'green' that had been conditioned thus accounting for the increasing number of wrong reports; it was shown that their actual

---

[40] T. H. Howells, "The experimental development of color-tone synesthesia," *Journal of Experimental Psychology*, 34 (1944), 87-103.

perception of the colors was what had been conditioned.)

The subjects in this experiment were deliberately conditioned to give the verbal response 'red' when they
heard the low note, and to give the verbal response 'green'
when they heard the higher note. We may assume that after,
and as a result of, this conditioning, when they heard the
low note, they were disposed to apply the word 'red' to what
they saw, and to apply the word 'green' to what they saw
when the higher note was heard. And these verbal dispositions, I would contend (or at least I would suspect), are at
least partially responsible for the fact that the pale green
light very often looked red to them when it was accompanied by the low tone, and for the fact that the pale red light
very often looked green to them when it was accompanied
by the higher tone.

I must confess, however, that it is possible that the conditioning to which the subjects were submitted forged a
direct link between the hearing of the low (high) tone
and the awareness of the color red (green), so that their
dispositions to report 'red' ('green') had nothing to do
with their subsequent misperceptions of those two colors. And there is, in fact, a significant amount of experimental evidence showing that changes in stimuli of one
sense modality do, under certain conditions, directly affect one's awareness in another sense modality,[41] a phenomenon known as synesthesia. But even if we admit—as
I am perfectly willing to do—that the musical tone might
have had some direct effect on the conditioned subjects'
awareness of the two colors in the Howells experiment, it
nevertheless seems not improbable that their appropriate
verbal dispositions had some additional effect.[42]

[41] See, for example, W. Börnstein, "On the functional relations of
the sense organs to one another and to the organism as a whole,"
Journal of General Psychology, 15 (1936), 117-31; and E. D. Turner
and W. Bevan, "The perception of auditory patterns as a function of
incidental visual stimulation," *Psychonomic Science*, 1 (1964), 135-36.

[42] Howells himself thought that his results were due to synesthesia,
although he concedes that "it cannot be denied that the conditioned

So much for the influence of language on the perception of color. I turn now, briefly, to its influence on the perception of shape. The available evidence here, alas, is even more indecisive. In a famous experiment,[43] subjects were shown a series of ambiguous pictures: drawings that could be interpreted equally well as the numeral 2 or the numeral 8, as a pair of eyeglasses or a pair of dumbbells, and so on. As each drawing was presented, the subject was told what it was supposed to be; half the subjects were given names corresponding to one of the two most plausible possibilities (e.g., '2,' 'eyeglasses'), while the other half were given names corresponding to the other possibility ('8,' 'dumbbells'). Then the subjects were required to reproduce what they had just seen as accurately as possible. It was found that there was a marked tendency on the part of the subjects to produce drawings that differed radically from the presented ones, and that the direction of change was towards the thing normally named by the word each subject happened to be given. For example, subjects told that a certain ambiguous figure was a 2 (or an 8) tended to produce figures that were much more like 2's (or 8's) than the original figure was. From this evidence, one cannot infer with certainty that the ambiguous figures actually looked different to the two groups of subjects; but since they were all presumably trying to reproduce accurately what they saw, it is not unlikely that the figures did look different. And if they did, then there seem to be some

---

verbal response was actually a part of the total organismic response, and undoubtedly contributed its share in determining decisions about color. . . . Perhaps the best interpretation is that the verbal response was as much a means by which the perception was mediated as was the word a resultant of the perception" (p. 98).

Another well-known experiment in which, as it seems to me, the influence of certain verbal dispositions on the perception of color is strongly suggested is reported in J. S. Bruner and L. Postman, "On the perception of incongruity: a paradigm," *Journal of Personality,* 18 (1949), 206-23; reprinted in Beardslee and Wertheimer (eds.), *Readings in Perception,* pp. 648-63.

[43] L. Carmichael, H. P. Hogan, and A. A. Walter, "An experimental study of the effect of language on the reproduction of visually perceived form," *Journal of Experimental Psychology,* 15 (1932), 73-86.

grounds for thinking that the subjects' dispositions to apply different words to the drawings were largely, or perhaps even entirely, responsible for the differences.[44]

There is some evidence that if a perceiver is conditioned to apply the same label to different objects, the effect will be to make the objects look more nearly alike to him than they otherwise would. Katz,[45] for example, trained some 7- and 9-year-old children to apply the same name to two different polygon shapes. When the polygons were then presented tachistoscopically, the children reported that they looked the same more often, and they then also experienced more difficulty in learning to make discriminatory responses to the polygons, than did a second group of children who were trained to apply different names to the polygons and a third group who were not conditioned to apply any labels at all to the figures.[46]

Next, I want to mention the effect of a perceiver's readiness to make verbal responses on the so-called *visual stability* of what he sees. When, under certain specifiable conditions, a perceiver looks at an object continuously, there comes a time when it begins to fragment visually in "perceptual units" (i.e., organized parts of it appear to become dissociated from one another) and even to disappear altogether. The visual stability of an object for a perceiver is its resistance, for him, to visual fragmentation and disappearance. Recent experiments have shown that the readiness of a perceiver to attach a verbal label to an ob-

[44] For the reports of other relevant experiments, see D. T. Herman, R. H. Lawless, and R. W. Marshall, "Variables in the effect of language on the reproduction of visually perceived forms," *Perceptual and Motor Skills*, 7, Monograph Supplement 2 (1957), 171-86; and J. S. Bruner and A. L. Minturn, "Perceptual identification and perceptual organization," *Journal of General Psychology*, 53 (1955), 21-28.

[45] P. Katz, "Effects of labels on children's perception and discrimination learning," *Journal of Experimental Psychology*, 66 (1963), 423-28.

[46] For related work, see P. A. Katz and E. Zigler, "Effects of labels on perceptual transfer: stimulus and developmental factors," *Journal of Experimental Psychology*, 80 (1969), 73-77.

ject affects its visual stability. McKinney[47] demonstrated that when subjects were conditioned to apply specific names to certain geometrical designs (in fact, the designs were letters of the alphabet, printed as large capitals), they were more stable than the very same designs when subjects were conditioned *not* to apply specific names to them. McKinney writes:

> The results of this study demonstrate . . . that the perceptual advantage of a "familiar" object arises, at least in part, from verbal identifiability. Targets which were given alphabetic names were more stable perceptually than the same targets viewed as simple designs. . . . Visual perception is, in this instance, enhanced by verbal labelling. (p. 241)

In another experiment,[48] each subject was shown three circles simultaneously; the circles had discriminably different diameters. The subjects were conditioned to apply a common label (viz., a letter name) to two of the circles, and another label to the third. It was found that the two circles that had been assigned the common label were more likely to fragment at the same time than two circles with different names.

> Our experiments show that discriminably different stimuli react as if they became more "identical" following common-[verbal]-response training. (p. 28)[49]

If, as our theory of perception implies, or may imply, there is some sort of intimate connection between an observer's perceptually caused dispositions to apply certain words, or labels, to what he sees and the ways things look to

[47] J. P. McKinney, "Verbal meaning and perceptual stability," *Canadian Journal of Psychology*, 20 (1966), 237-42.
[48] D. C. Donderi and E. Kane, "Perceptual learning produced by common responses to different stimuli," *Canadian Journal of Psychology*, 19 (1965), 15-30.
[49] See also P. Arnold, P. R. Meudell, and K. G. Pease, "Influence of meaning on fragmentation of visual afterimages," *Perceptual and Motor Skills*, 27 (1968), 965-66.

him,[50] then we should expect that there might be certain
ways in which a person's command of language could be so
radically defective that certain kinds of things would look
markedly different to him from the way they look to people whose command of language is normal. I mention this
further (possible) implication of our theory, not as a prel-
ude to the listing of vast amounts of corroborating experimental evidence, but rather as a plea to psychologists to
devise and execute new experiments that would test the
implication, in the hope that vast amounts of corroborating evidence would then be forthcoming. As things stand
now, however, it is virtually impossible to evaluate the extent to which the available evidence supports this implication of our theory. There are a great many detailed descriptions of the behavior of persons whose ability to use
language is faulty in a variety of ways, but—for obvious
reasons—it is even more difficult in these cases to corre-
late items of behavior with characteristics of the person's visual (auditory, or tactual, etc.) field than it usually is. Furthermore, most of the evidence pertains to people with serious brain damage, and so even if one knew
in precisely what ways things looked (sounded, felt, and
so on) distorted to them, it would still be almost impossible to determine exactly, or even roughly, what part of
the distortion, if any, was due to shortcomings in the person's ability to use language.

Here are one or two examples of the sort of evidence
that is now available. Goldstein[51] reports the case of a
woman suffering from amnesic aphasia. Although not
color-blind, she could not sort objects according to their
colors. Presented with the standard Holmgren colored
wool skeins, she was unable to make heaps of various dif-

---

[50] For evidence indicating that a readiness to apply a range of
verbal labels to a visual stimulus object might have some effect on
the apparent distance of the object, see H. Ono, "Apparent distance
as a function of familiar size," *Journal of Experimental Psychology*, 79
(1969), 109-115.

[51] K. Goldstein, *Language and Language Disturbances* (New York:
Greene and Stratton, 1948).

ferent reds or blues. She could pick out a skein of exactly the same hue as a given one, but not other skeins of different hues of the same color. Did the colors look different to her from the way they do to normal language-users; or was she merely incapable of applying the color-words with any competence? It seems impossible to say.

After many days of tests with the colored yarns, the patient suddenly began sorting them correctly, just as a normal person might, apparently on the basis of their hues; and she even applied the color words correctly to the different piles she made. But it soon became clear that she was not basing her choices on any seen similarities of color; for when she was asked whether the words 'red,' 'green,' and so on, fit all the different hues in the separate piles, she replied "They do not fit any one." She had simply remembered that the doctors had called this, that, and the other hue 'blue'; this, that, and the other hue 'red'; and so on—but she did not think that the hues so named really belonged together. She had put them together only because she thought the doctors wanted her to, and had applied the words 'red,' 'green,' and so on, to the different piles simply to please the doctors. These facts might lead one to think that the colors must have looked different to the patient from the way they look to us; but could it not be argued that the various hues looked to her just as they look to us, but she was unable to get it through her head that the word 'blue' ('red,' and so on) really does properly apply to this, that, and the other hue? I am strongly inclined to think that colors did look different to the patient from the way they look to us—indeed, I think this may even be a necessary truth, given the evidence—but I have no idea how much, if any, of this difference is attributable to her language-using deficiencies. The most one can say, apparently, is that these deficiencies might very well have had some effect, direct or indirect, on her perception of color—but to say that, of course, is to say very little.

There is also some flimsy evidence that certain sorts

of deficiencies in one's ability to use language may cause (or constitute) faults in one's perception of shape. Visual agnosia is a disorder, usually caused by brain damage, in which the patient is unable to recognize visually presented objects, although he can recognize them at once if he hears them, feels them, or whatever. It is typical of this malady that the patient finds it difficult or impossible to make anything like an accurate copy of even the simplest visually presented figures.[52] This would seem to indicate that the shapes of things look distorted to the visual agnostic. But, again, how are we to tell whether the distortions of apparent shape result wholly or in part from the language deficiency, or whether the latter instead results wholly or in part from the former, or whether the two are not directly connected with each other at all? I can only repeat my expression of hope that further work will be undertaken in this area. The thesis that a person's dispositions to use language in certain ways to characterize what he sees (hears, feels, etc.) may affect, or partially constitute, the way things look (sound, feel, etc.) to him—a thesis that is strongly suggested by our theory of perception— seems to me to be an interesting and important one, if true, and one that deserves the serious attention of experimental psychologists.

D. THE DIRECTIONALITY OF SOUND;
   KINAESTHETIC PERCEPTION

I want to conclude this chapter by considering two far less exotic perceptual phenomena than the ones we have been discussing. The first is the perfectly familiar ability we have, in most cases, of being able to tell, just by hearing alone, the direction from which a sound is coming. I shall begin by arguing that one group of leading contenders for the title of "Most satisfactory theory of perception," namely sense-datum theories, cannot give a coherent account of this commonplace ability, and I shall then argue

---

[52] See, for example, W. R. Brain, "Visual object-agnosia with special reference to the Gestalt Theory," *Brain*, Vol. 64, Part 1 (1941), 43-62.

that our theory of perception is easily able to deal with it.

It is, indeed, a well-known fact that in addition to hearing the pitch, timbre, and loudness of sounds, we are also usually able to hear the direction from which they come. In the cases I have in mind, we do not simply infer that the sound is coming from a certain direction (from the facts, for example, that the sound is a bird call and that there is a bird singing over there in that direction); rather, we hear the sound as coming from that direction. Psychologists know what the features of the sound stimulus are that enable us to have this kind of direct perceptual knowledge.[53]

There seem to be only two possibilities open to sense-datum theorists in dealing with this familiar aural phenomenon:

(A) They can hold that the apparent or phenomenal directionality of the sound is an inherent characteristic of the hearer's aural sense-datum, or aural "field"; and they could add that it is the physical features of the sound stimulus, alluded to at the end of the previous paragraph, that determine which direction the sound appears to be coming from.

(B) On the other hand, they can hold that an aural sense-datum is characterized only by pitch, timbre, and loudness, and not by directionality. The relevant features of the sound stimulus, on this view, produce some accompaniment, x, of the aural sense-datum, and it is this x that constitutes our awareness of the direction from which the sound is coming.

This second position (i.e., (B)) that the sense-datum theorist might choose to defend is not very promising. It runs the risk of not doing justice to the phenomenological facts; for surely the directionality of the sound *seems* to be just as much an inherent feature of the aural datum as

[53] To simplify our inquiry, I ignore the role of head movements, which are sometimes necessary if we are to know, by hearing alone, the direction from which a sound is coming.

are its pitch, timbre, and loudness. To this the sense-
datum theorist is bound to reply: "It is a mere illusion that
the directionality of the sound seems to be one of its intrinsic features along with its pitch, timbre, and loudness.
It seems that way to us only because our awareness of the
direction from which the sound seems to be coming, x,
accompanies the aural datum so regularly and so automatically—that is, without our having to make any conscious
inferences or performing any conscious acts of interpretation. This intimate association seduces us into attributing
to the aural datum itself something that is merely an accompaniment of it." This is not a very auspicious line for
the sense-datum theorist to take, because what he has admitted, now, is that sense-data can appear to have characteristics that they do not really have. But sense-data are
introduced in the first place in the role of objects of immediate awareness, and that, therefore, is of their essence.
The point of positing such objects is to have something in
perceptual experience about which we cannot be wrong
(or cannot, anyway, be very wrong), something that explains the difference between perceptual appearance and
reality, something that answers to our need for a foundation of human knowledge. All of this is undermined when
the distinction between appearance and reality is allowed
to break out within the realm of sense-data themselves—
especially when it is allowed to break out in such a violent form as in (B), where what is countenanced is that
sense-data should appear to have a whole separate kind of
characteristic (viz., directionality) that they do not really
have. And so I do not think that sense-datum theorists
ought to regard (B) as a viable alternative.

(A) seems much more promising, because it allows,
what ought to be allowed, that the direction from which a
sound comes can be, and often is, one of its phenomenal
properties, on a par with its pitch (if any), timbre, and
loudness. And to allow this is to grant that just as the (phenomenal) visual field is three-dimensional, so too is the

(phenomenal) aural field.[54] This seems to be the best way for the sense-datum theorist to try to accommodate, within his theory, the fact that we are usually able to tell, by hearing alone, the direction from which a sound is coming.

But unfortunately for the sense-datum theorist, the idea of such a three-dimensional manifold of aural sense-data is not a legitimate one. For suppose the idea is legitimate; suppose, that is, that the direction from which a (phenomenal) sound comes is a purely auditory matter, that it is just another aspect of the perceiver's auditory sense-datum. If so, then it ought to be logically possible for someone to hear the direction from which a certain single sound (a bird-call, for example) is coming, and yet for him not to know in what direction he must point (or walk) if he is to point (or walk) in the direction from which the sound is coming, not to know in what direction he must look if he is to look in that direction, to be unable to say (in terms of things that can be seen, touched, smelled, etc.) from which direction the sound is coming—and so on for all related abilities. And this situation ought to be possible even if the person's vision, ability to speak, ability to point (or walk), and so on, are perfectly intact. This situation ought to be possible because, according to the view expressed in (A), the perceiver's knowing in what direction he must point, his knowing in what direction he must look (or walk), and the rest, would all be only contingently connected with his having the right kind of auditory sense-datum; and we are just imagining an occasion on which

[54] I think he need not insist that items in the phenomenal aural field, like those in the phenomenal visual field, have determinate locations—that is, that they are experienced both as coming from a certain direction *and* as being just so far away. He is free to say that aural sense-data have the spatial characteristic of coming-from-a-certain-direction, but that we merely infer, on the basis of their loudness and of the kind of thing that we think or know caused them, how far away they are. It is, in any case, only the alleged characteristic of coming-from-a-certain-direction that concerns me here.

these contingent connections happen to be broken. But in fact this situation is not logically possible. It is not possible because to say that a person hears the direction from which the (phenomenal) sound is coming is to say that the sound seems to him to be coming from such and such a direction, or to say that he thinks he knows from what direction the sound is coming, or something of the sort. But it cannot even *seem* to him that the sound is coming from a certain direction, and he cannot even *think* he knows the direction from which the sound is coming, if he has no idea in what direction he must point if he is to point in that direction, if he has no idea where to look if he is to look in that direction, and so on; because direction (in space) can only be specified, can only be thought of, in terms, ultimately, of what can be seen, touched, pointed to, and so on. To be sure, one sound can be specified as coming, or seeming to come, from a direction that is, say, twenty degrees to the right of the direction from which another sound comes (or came); but how does one think of "twenty degrees to the right" apart from all reference to what can be seen, touched, pointed at, and so on? So if all connections with other sense modalities are swept away, it cannot seem to someone, he cannot think he knows, on the basis alone of his hearing it, that a sound is coming from such-and-such a direction. With all those connections severed, there is nothing left to seem, nothing left to think. So what the sense-datum theorist makes out to be merely contingent connections are in fact necessary ones. I conclude, therefore, that the very idea of a three-dimensional manifold of aural sense-data is an incoherent one.[55] If this is correct,

[55] P. F. Strawson argues for what is essentially the same point, although he expresses it differently, in *Individuals* (London: Methuen & Co. Ltd., 1959), pp. 64-66. In thinking about the problems connected with hearing the direction from which sounds come, I have profited from reading B. O'Shaughnessy's "The Location of Sound," *Mind*, 66 (1957), 471-90, and R.M.P. Malpas' "The Location of Sound" in R. J. Butler (ed.), *Analytical Philosophy: Second Series* (Oxford: Basil Blackwell, 1965), pp. 131-44.

then alternative (A) is not open to the sense-datum theorist. Since (B) is also closed to him, he seems to have no satisfactory way of accommodating within his theory this very common aural phenomenon.

Our theory of perception, on the other hand, is easily able to cope with it. In normal cases, on our theory, a sound's sounding to someone as though it is coming from a certain direction is for it to cause him to acquire, in a certain specifiable way, the perceptual belief that the sound is coming from that direction. It holds further that his having that belief is just a matter of his being disposed to act in some such ways as these: if he wants to point (or walk) to the source of the sound, he points (or walks) in such-and-such a direction; if he wants to face the source of the sound, he moves his body in such-and-such a way; if he wants to look toward the source of the sound, he moves his body in a certain way; if he wants to specify in words where the sound is coming from, he says such-and-such; and so on. According to our theory, then, a sound's sounding to someone as though it is coming from a certain direction *is* (identical with) his being disposed, as the result of the sound waves affecting his ears, to act in those sorts of ways. That sound signals should have this effect on an experienced hearer is in no way mysterious. I conclude, therefore, that our ability to tell, by hearing alone, the direction from which a sound is coming, is no source of even the slightest embarrassment for our theory. In this respect, our theory has an advantage over certain others—for example, over sense-datum theories.

Incidentally, some experiments have been performed whose results accord beautifully with our behavioral account of what it is to hear the direction from which a sound is coming. If our account is correct, we should expect that just as people are able to adapt visually to distorting prisms of various kinds, they ought also to be able to adapt aurally to devices that make a sound signal sound as if it were coming from a different direction from the one it actually is

coming from. And they can.[56] Richard Held used a device
called a pseudophone that has the aural effect of shifting
the axis of the wearer's ears a small angle around the vertical axis of his head: the apparent direction from which
a sound is coming naturally shifts the same number of degrees. It was found that with continued wearing of the device, a person aurally adapts to the changed stimulus input, provided he can move about freely. There is evidence
that no such adaptation will occur if the wearer makes no
active movements. This is precisely what we would expect on our theory. Thus consider the following simple
example. Figures IV (a) and IV(b)[57] represent a perceiver
at A facing in the direction of B: the sound source is not
visible to the perceiver. Fig. IV(a) is the normal case: the
sound source, located at B, emits a steady signal, and if the
person at A wishes to walk towards the source of the sound,
he walks straight ahead, towards B. This response is rewarded, since the sound source remains steadily in front of
him. In Fig. IV(b), the perceiver dons the pseudophone
which rotates his aural axis a few degrees clockwise, as indicated in the drawing. The sound source, you will notice,
is no longer placed at B: it has been moved the same number of degrees clockwise. If the person again wants to walk
towards the sound emitted by the (hidden) source, he still,
of course, walks towards B, since the sound sounds to him
as though it were coming from straight ahead; but now his
response is not rewarded, for the sound keeps shifting off
to his right as he walks instead of remaining steadily in
front of him in the desired way. Obviously the perceiver
must learn new responses that are appropriate to the

[56] See R. Held, "Shifts in binaural localization after prolonged exposure to atypical combinations of stimuli," *American Journal of
Psychology*, 68 (1955), 526-48; R. Held and S. J. Freedman, "Plasticity in human sensorimotor control," *Science*, Vol. 142, No. 3591
(October 25, 1963), 455-62; and R. Held, "Plasticity in sensory-motor
systems," *Scientific American*, Vol. 213, No. 5 (November 1965),
84-94.
[57] From Held, "Shifts in binaural localization after prolonged exposure to atypical combinations of stimuli," *op. cit.*, p. 537.

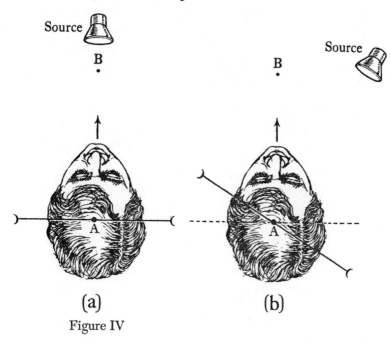

(a) **(b)**

Figure IV

changed conditions caused by the pseudophone. On our theory, we would predict that as more and more of his bodily responses are rewarded, the person would gradually become aurally adapted to the pseudophone, so that, for example, in a situation of the IV(b) type, the sound signal will sound to him as though it is coming (as it is) from a point several degrees to the right of B. And, as it turns out, our prediction is true.

Another kind of perception that eludes the explanatory grasp of sense-datum theories, but not of our theory, is the normal kinaesthetic perception we have of the positions and movements of various parts of our bodies, and of our whole bodies. As one sits or moves about, one ordinarily knows pretty well what position one's arms and legs are in (e.g., whether one's left leg is bent or straight), how one's hands are disposed (e.g., whether one's left hand is clenched or extended), what motions one's head is making (e.g., whether it is nodding or stationary), and so on. Sometimes—especially in unusual circumstances, or when the motion is violent, or when one's muscles are very tense—there are quite definite bodily sensations that indicate to one that the motion is occurring or that his body, or a certain part of it, is disposed in such-and-such a way. But usually there are no such sensations—and yet we know, without looking or feeling with our hands, what is going on. And this knowledge is properly deemed perceptual knowledge; we do not simply reason out how the various parts of our body must be disposed or must be moving at any given moment—we *feel* how they are disposed and how they are moving. There are nerves that send signals to the brain from our muscles, tendons, and joints, and if these signals are stopped—and especially if those from the joints are stopped—we are less able, or not able at all, to tell how the parts of our body are disposed and how they are moving, "just by the feel of it." And yet, as has already been remarked, these signals do not often produce bodily sensations. Indeed, in some cases, it is difficult to imagine what the appropriate bodily sensation might conceivably be. For example, we can generally tell, even without our eyes open, whether or not our body is vertical; but what would a "sensation of verticality" or a "sensation of being vertical" be like? If we add to these considerations the fact that it is only full-fledged bodily sensations that seem able to qualify as the appropriate kind of sense-data for this sort of perception—i.e., as bodily (or somatic or kinaesthetic) sense-data—we see that here is another kind of perception that lies quite beyond the scope of sense-datum theories.

On our theory of perception, by contrast, there is nothing inherently puzzling about the fact that we are usually able to tell, without looking or feeling with our hands, how the various parts of our body are disposed—even when we feel no special bodily sensations. Suppose, for example, that a seated person knows that his right leg is bent in a certain way, and that he knows it only because that's the way it "feels" to him, although he is not aware of any sensations in his leg. Within the framework of our theory of perception, what is happening in this case is that signals from the person's joints, muscles, and tendons are being received in his brain, with the result that he gets into whatever dispositional state it is that answers to his believing that his right leg is bent in that particular way. There is, of course, a great deal that is not known about the physiology of such processes, and as far as I know, psychologists have conducted very few experiments in this area. But the fact that signals from various parts of our body to our brain should cause us to have beliefs, inclinations to believe something, or suppressed inclinations to believe something, about the way our body and its parts are disposed, and that they can do so without causing any bodily sensations, does not pose any sort of conceptual or philosophical problem; it is completely intelligible.

IV

Colors: Our Perception of Them and Their Ontological Status

THE BROAD outlines of our theory of perception, some of its consequences, and some of the experimental evidence that lends it a measure of support have now been presented. A complete exposition of the theory in all its details, and a full defense of it against all possible objections, are tasks that will not be undertaken in this book; such an effort, I suspect, would take us into virtually every field of philosophy. One must limit the scope of one's investigations somewhere, and except for the two issues I shall be discussing in this final chapter, I propose to go no deeper into our theory at this time. My decision is prompted largely by considerations of prudence, or perhaps I should say of strategy. For if the theory is promising enough, or at any rate interesting enough, it ought to elicit comments and criticisms, and these would give one an indication of which particular questions about our theory, among all the possible ones that might be raised, it would be most promising to pursue.

If I were to widen the limits I have just imposed on the range of our present investigations, one of the first things I would surely try to do is offer a satisfactory dispositional analysis of perceptual beliefs, inclinations to believe, and suppressed inclinations to believe. This would obviously be work of prodigious difficulty, embroiling us in many issues that have little directly to do, furthermore, with sense perception itself. So I shall not weaken in my determination to exclude that issue from our agenda; accordingly, I shall simply assume that some adequate account can be given of perceptual beliefs, and the rest, in terms of the perceiver's dispositions to behave in a certain variety of ways. This is no doubt a huge assumption, but it is one that I nevertheless make.

There is a related, subsidiary issue, however, that I think I must say something about. Whether one accepts a dispositional analysis of perceptual states or not, he will not find it difficult to think of many actions, or modes of behavior, that could plausibly figure in such an analysis of a perceptual belief about a complex physical object—for example, of the belief that there is a table, or a chair, directly in front of the perceiver. But the situation seems to be different when we turn to perceptual beliefs about relatively simple properties—for example, to the belief that the thing before the perceiver is brown, or red. Here one is hard put to imagine what the appropriate actions or behavior could possibly be. And this is acutely embarrassing for our theory; because if there really are no actions such that a perceiver's being disposed to perform them constitutes his perceptual awareness of simple properties (e.g., color), then our theory can find no room for one's awareness of those properties and is for that very reason in trouble of the most serious kind. So the first of the two things I want to do in this chapter is to indicate what sort of account our theory can give of our perception of simple properties.

The second chore I have here set for myself is rather different. It is that of exploring the implications of our theory with respect to the question of how much perceptual knowledge it allows us to have of the world that we perceive. Causal theories of perception, among which ours must evidently be counted, are generally supposed to have disastrous epistemological consequences; so it would behoove us to lay to rest, if we can, whatever doubts about our theory may arise on that score.

A. COLOR PERCEPTION

I turn at once to the first of these two tasks. The difficulty, or apparent difficulty, for our theory here does not, I think, arise in connection with the so-called primary qualities—for example, with shape and size. It is quite easy to think of a great many actions that a defender of our theory might plausibly appeal to in specifying what constitutes, say, a perceptual belief that a certain line is straight or that a table is four feet long. Indeed, I have already mentioned five relevant kinds of acts (or modes of behavior) for the case of a line's looking straight to someone (see p. 153f.). It is rather the so-called secondary properties that seem to embarrass our theory, and so I shall concentrate my attention on them in what follows. Since we have been dealing primarily with vision in this book, I choose color as my example of a secondary property.

What is it, then, on our theory, for something, x, to look red to a perceiver, Q? On the assumption that we are dealing with a First Case, it is for Q to causally-receive, in a certain way, the perceptual belief that x is red. And for Q to be in this state is for him to be disposed to act, or behave, in a certain class of ways with respect to x. But what ways?

To begin negatively, we may note that one kind of action that it will not do to include in our class is this: If Q wants to point to something red, he points (or might point) to x. This will not do, because it is possible that Q wants to point to something red, that Q is disposed to use x as his example in order to satisfy this desire, where his being so disposed is caused in the right way (according to our theory), and yet that x nevertheless does *not* look red to Q. This combination of circumstances might arise, for example, if x looks muddy brown to Q, who suffers from red-green color blindness, and Q knows that anything that looks muddy brown to him in normal conditions is actually red. Things would not be improved, either, by changing the formula as follows: If Q wants to point to something that *looks* red to him, he points (or might point) to x. This formula suffers from utter triviality; for although it is true enough that when something, x, looks red to someone, he is by virtue of that fact in such a dispositional state that if he wants to point to something that looks red to him, he points, or might point, to x, still it is of course totally uninformative to say so.

In the previous chapter, I mentioned one type of action that might conceivably belong in the class we are investigating—namely, certain linguistic actions. Thus, for example, it just could be the case that x's looking red to Q is in part actually constituted by Q's being so disposed that if he wanted to name the color of x (or the color that x looked to him to be), he would say that x is (or looks) red, or say something that implied this. I expressed what amounted to grave doubts about the appropriateness of including these linguistic acts in our class, and pointed out that even if they do belong in it, they cannot be counted among its more important or central members. These latter will certainly be non-linguistic actions or behavior.

There are, of course, many kinds of quite specific non-linguistic actions that depend crucially on color perception—such as rejecting an apple because it has a brown spot on it, selecting another apple because of its uniform and pleasing red color—and that might be characterized in a way that would make them suitable candidates for inclusion in our class. I think it is indeed possible to characterize actions of this sort in much more general ways than I have just done, with the result that two large subclasses of actions (or modes of behavior) will be formed that may, in fact, be considered to make up the core of our class.

The first of the two ways of describing them I have in mind creates a class of what I shall call *discriminatory actions*, or (more generally) modes of *discriminatory beha-*

vior.[1] I shall now give a brief indication—I shall not try to
spell out all the necessary details—of the sorts of behavior
I mean. I begin with the case where the relevant conditions of observation (e.g., lighting) are standard, or nearly
so, and where the perceiver, Q, has normal color vision.[2] In
these ideal circumstances, x's looking red to Q consists in
part, I want to say, in Q's being so disposed (as the result,
normally, of the kind of familiar causal process whose general nature we specified long ago)[3] that if x were surrounded
by nothing but similarly shaped, similarly textured, and
similarly sized objects whose color is that of ripe tomatoes,
British post boxes, pieces of Holmgren yarn number such-
and-such, and the like, and if he tried to point quickly at
x, he would experience a certain amount of difficulty in doing so—more difficulty than if x were surrounded rather
by similarly shaped, similarly textured, and similarly sized
objects whose color is that of live grass, cloudless skies, ripe
lemons, and so on. In other words, Q is so disposed—to describe his state less ponderously but also not quite legiti-
mately—that he would find it more difficult to distinguish
x from surrounding red things than to distinguish it from
surrounding non-red things.

So far I have characterized one example of what I called
the discriminatory behavior answering to x's looking red to
a person with normal color vision only for the ideal case
where the relevant conditions of observation are standard,
or nearly so. How is such a perceiver, Q, disposed to behave, discriminatorily, when the conditions of observation
are not standard, or nearly so? Using the same example as
before, the answer is that Q is so disposed that if, with no

---

[1] My discussion here is indebted to J.J.C. Smart's treatment of color.
See his *Philosophy and Scientific Realism* (New York: The Humanities
Press; London: Routledge & Kegan Paul, 1963), pp. 75-84.

[2] Smart shows (*ibid.*, pp. 76-77) how the notion of having normal
color vision can be defined without circularity—i.e., without appealing
to the concept of color.

[3] In the most common cases, x's looking red to Q will of course be
an effect of light rays' impinging on Q's retinas. But there are also
uncommon cases; for example, Q might be experiencing a red after-
image while he looks at x, thus making x look red to him.

change in the way x now looks to Q, x were surrounded
by nothing but similarly shaped, similarly textured, and
similarly sized objects whose color is that of ripe tomatoes,
British post boxes, fire engines, etc., and these surrounding objects were being seen by Q under standard conditions
of observation (or nearly standard ones), then if Q tried
to point quickly at x, he would experience a certain amount
of difficulty in doing so—more difficulty than if x were surrounded by similarly shaped, similarly textured, and similarly sized objects whose color is that of live grass, etc.,
and these surrounding objects were being seen by Q under
standard conditions of observation (or nearly standard
ones). What this elaborate web of words clothes (but
perhaps also unfortunately obscures) is the simple idea,
hard to dispute, that when the relevant conditions of observation are non-standard and something looks red to
someone, it looks the way red things look to him under
standard conditions.

I have used, as my example of discriminatory behavior,
the relative difficulty, or lack of it, that a perceiver, Q, with
normal color vision would experience in trying to point
quickly at x. But of course there are many more modes of
such behavior. Other examples would be the relative difficulty, or lack of it, that Q would experience in trying to
look directly at x, to reach out and touch x, to describe
in words where x is, and so on. All of these modes of behavior could be used in characterizing discriminatory behavior,
the first of the two subclasses that, as I claim, may be considered to make up the core of our class.

The second of my two subclasses consists of what I shall
call *matching actions*, or (more generally) modes of *matching behavior*. They may be characterized in the following
sort of way: given standard, or nearly standard, conditions of observation, if Q wanted something different from
x that matches the color of x, he would accept, as fulfilling
this requirement, things having the color of ripe apples,
British post boxes, fire engines, and so on, but would reject anything having the color of live grass, ripe lemons,

cloudless skies, and so on. (I shall not stop to formulate a characterization for non-standard conditions of observation, although this could easily be done.)

There are, of course, many refinements and qualifications that one might well introduce into these characterizations of discriminatory and matching behavior; but my main concern now is to give only the broadest statement of my position, since I believe that the details are relatively unimportant and that it is the general type of position presented here that will meet with the greatest resistance. My view, then, to put it summarily, is this: a thing, x, looks red to a perceiver, Q, with normal color vision if and only if Q sees x and (as the result, normally, of the familiar kind of causal process) Q is in such a perceptual state that he is disposed to exhibit modes of discriminatory and matching behavior, such as those that I have indicated, with respect to x and certain other objects.

I can think of no reason whatever why anyone, no matter what theory of perception he may espouse, should wish to deny that Q would indeed be in the complex dispositional state I have just described when, under the specified conditions, x looks red to Q. But although anyone ought to be willing to admit this much, those who reject our theory of perception would insist that the dispositional state is quite distinct from that state of Q whereby x looks red to Q; the latter state, they would say, is the cause of the (altogether different) former state. According to our theory, on the other hand, the dispositional state is at least a large and essential *constituent* of Q's perceptual state of x's looking red to Q. This difference between our theory and others is, of course, a crucial one that keeps cropping up at every stage of our investigation. The same controversy would arise, for example, in the case of primary qualities; Q's being disposed to move his body in the ways I mentioned earlier is one thing, my opponents would argue, while the line's looking straight to Q is quite another—whereas on our theory the former state is an essential part of the latter, perceptual state. Our antagonists accuse us of leaving something essential out of our account, while to us it seems that they are introducing additional and problem-creating states and entities (sense-data, for example) entirely unnecessarily. Obviously there is no short, easy way to resolve this extremely basic dispute; the question can be decided, I think, only by a careful weighing of the pros and cons of the respective theories as wholes.

If it should seem that our opponents enjoy a certain plausibility advantage over us here, the reason for this may be the following. When a person indulges in what I called discriminatory or matching behavior, we find it natural to think that he does so *because* things look to him to have such-and-such colors. Thus, for example, if someone finds it difficult (easy) to pick out a red rose from a red (white) background, we think that he responds in that way *because* the rose looks red to him and the background looks the same (a different) color. We suppose, in other words, that the rose's looking red to him is one thing, that his discriminatory behavior is another, and—owing to the appropriateness of the word 'because' in this context— that the perceptual state is a cause of the behavior. Now the plausibility gap might seem to arise because these perfectly natural suppositions are true on our opponents' theories of color perception, whereas it appears that we, with our quite different theory, must deny one or more of these evident truths. But the fact is that we can consistently subscribe to all that is true in the suppositions. On our theory, the perceptual state (of the rose's looking red to the perceiver) is certainly something different from any given item of discriminatory behavior on the part of the perceiver, for the latter is just a realization of the former. But what is more important, our theory allows us to hold that the perceiver exhibits a given bit of discriminatory (or matching) behavior *because* he is in a certain perceptual state—for example, that he finds it difficult to pick out the rose *because* the rose looks red to him (and the background looks the same color). Similarly, when a soluble substance actually dissolves, one can say that it dissolves *because* it is soluble—or, to use a more suitable example, when a person who is in an irritable mood actually behaves in an irritable manner, we may say that he does so *because* he is irritable. The irritable state (which everyone, I take it, would admit to be a dispositional one) may not be the, or even a, *cause* of the irritable behavior, but then it is no more certain that a perceiver's perceptual state of the rose's looking red to him is the, or even a, *cause* of his discriminatory or matching behavior. Thus it is a mere illusion that our theory suffers in comparison with others on this score.

One phenomenon of color perception that fits in nicely with our theory is that of color constancy—the fact that things look to be the color they are, not just under standard conditions of illumination, but also under an enormous variety of other conditions as well. Taylor describes it as follows:

> If we look at a red apple in a variety of situations we see it as red in every case, and the most obvious common-sense explanation of this uniformity is that it is reflecting light of exactly the same composition on each occasion. But a moment's consideration shows that this cannot be so. If it is placed on a sheet of white paper and illuminated only by the light from the blue sky, the apple reflects light of one composition; if the sky is overcast the reflected light is changed by the elimination of some of the blue rays; if it hangs on the trees the apple is illuminated by green light reflected by the leaves and transmitted through them, so that once again the reflected light has a different wave composition. In short, the composition of the light reflected by any object is not constant but undergoes an endless succession of transformations according to the contributions made to the incident light by colored objects in the environment.[4]

This phenomenon is not in the least surprising if our theory of color perception and our principles of perceptual condi-

---

[4] J. G. Taylor, *The Behavioral Basis of Perception*, p. 234f.

tioning are accepted; for if they are true, then we would expect that through experience (with its inevitable conditioning), which normally involves seeing colored objects under a great variety of different lighting conditions, we would eventually learn to make, spontaneously, the right discriminatory and matching responses with respect to their colors, which means, on our theory, that they would eventually come to look to have the colors they do have in all these different circumstances. And this, we know, is exactly what happens. It is not clear to me that other theories can so easily assimilate color constancy, but I shall not stop to inquire into the matter.

So far we have discussed only the case of perceivers with normal color vision: I turn now to the case of those who do not have normal color vision. Consider, for example, a perceiver, R, to whom red things (e.g., fire engines, British post boxes, ripe tomatoes) look green, and to whom green things (e.g., healthy grass, limes, most emeralds) look red. We cannot hold that when something, x, looks red to R, he is in such a dispositional state that, for example, if x were surrounded by nothing but similarly shaped, similarly textured, and similarly sized objects whose color is that of fire engines, R would find it difficult to discriminate x from them—for those things look green to R, and he would therefore have no trouble discriminating x from them. Nor, apparently, can we say that x's looking red to R is a matter of his being so disposed that, for example, if x were surrounded by nothing but similarly shaped, similarly textured, and similarly sized objects whose color is that of healthy grass, limes, or most emeralds, R would have difficulty discriminating x from them: no doubt this is true of R—but then it seems utterly mysterious that R's perceptual state, as so described, should be an awareness of *redness*, whereas if Q (who has normal color vision) were in a similarly described state, his state would be an awareness of *greenness*.

These considerations bring to the fore the following apparently powerful objection to our theory of color vision:

"Your theory leaves out the very essence of color perception—namely, the actual seen quality of a color, the *quale*
which we experience directly when we see a color and
which is unique for each color. That your theory leaves
this out may be seen by considering the following possibility. Imagine two people, Q (who has normal color vision)
and S (who does not), who are disposed to make all the
same discriminatory and matching responses in the same
circumstances. What Q experiences as red and calls 'red,'
S experiences as green, although he, too, calls it 'red.' In
the same way, imagine that *all* of S's color experiences are
different from Q's in a systematic way, but that S nevertheless applies the same color words to just the same things
that Q applies them to. This situation is unverifiable, but
at least it is conceivable. Yet on your theory, this situation
is not logically possible; for if Q and S are disposed in all
circumstances to make all the same relevant discriminatory
and matching responses, then on your theory what looks
red to Q must also look red to S, and so on for all the colors.
But we are supposing that colors *don't* look the same to
Q and S, that Q and S's color experiences are different.
Your theory can't take account of this crucial difference, and
so is radically deficient."

This objection to our theory can be countered with the
following argument. There are two possibilities. Either (a)
there is no way of talking about the *qualia* a person immediately experiences, unless one characterizes them in
terms of that person's (actual or potential) overt responses
—in which case the objection is incoherent. Or (b) one *can*
talk about such *qualia* without any essential reference to the
person's overt responses—in which case the objection is
coherent; but our theory can, contrary to what the objection claims, take account of the difference in the *qualia*
that Q and S directly experience as well as any other
theory can. I want to say something about each of these
two possibilities.

I shall begin with alternative (a). If we were to take
this line, we would contend that if the (actual and poten-

tial) overt discriminatory and matching responses of Q and
S are all the same, then colors do—*necessarily*—look the
same to them, and it is nonsense to suggest that they might
not. This claim could be defended along Wittgensteinian
lines. That is to say, we could argue that if anyone—including S—should honestly match the color of a piece of cloth
with the color of such things as blood, ripe apples, fire engines, British post boxes, and the like, and honestly distinguish it from the colors of lemons, grass, cloudless skies,
and the like, then that piece of cloth necessarily looks red
to him. That is how the words 'looks red' are used. The nature of the *quale* of his "inner experience" as he looks at
the red cloth cannot be talked about except as something
that is expressed (or expressible) in relevant overt behavior—in his discriminatory and matching behavior. Since
this behavior is identical for Q and S, the *quale* of their
color experience of red (and the other colors) is, and must
be, the same, in so far as we can talk about it at all. So
it is nonsense to suggest that the piece of cloth may really
look *green* to S.

If the position just sketched is correct, the objection
against our theory collapses, since it is incoherent. Obviously, a complete justification of this view would be an
enormous and difficult undertaking; but fortunately, there
is no need for us to attempt it. Our purposes are served
when it is simply noted that *if* the view is correct, then the
objection to our theory falls to the ground.

Turning now to alternative (b), let us assume that the
view is not correct, and that the state of affairs described in
the objection is logically unexceptionable. In this case, I
want to argue that our theory is as able as other theories
to take account of the difference in the *qualia* experienced
by Q and S. As an example of a theory other than ours, let
us take a sense-datum theory. It would hold that the difference between the color *qualia* experienced by Q and S
consists in the fact that Q has a *red* sense-datum when looking at red things under standard conditions of observation,
whereas S has a *green* sense-datum under those conditions

—and so on for the other colors. But what does it mean to say that S has a green sense-datum, despite the fact that he is looking at something red under standard conditions? What it means, evidently, is that if Q, or some other person with normal color vision, were to have a sense-datum just like S's, he would think that what he sees looks green to him. But it is open to our theory to take an exactly analogous position. Red things, we are supposing, look green to S. This means that when confronted with a red thing under standard conditions of observation, S gets into a certain perceptual state which, on our theory, is a dispositional one: we say that S is disposed to make certain discriminatory and matching responses. He is disposed, for example, to match the color he sees with the color of such things as fire engines, British post boxes, and the like, all of which look green to him (although he calls them 'red'). But what does it mean to say that S is in such a perceptual state that the red thing looks *green* to him? What it means, evidently, is that if Q, or some other person with normal color vision, were to get into the same perceptual state, he would not be disposed to make the same discriminatory and matching responses that S is disposed to make—for example, he would be disposed to match the color he sees not with that of such things as fire engines and British post boxes, but rather with that of such things as live grass and ripe limes. I conclude, then, that our theory can find room for the bizarre situation described in the objection in a way exactly parallel to the way that other theories find room for it.

This defense of our theory might be disputed in the following way: "Look here, you have made an illegitimate move in describing what state Q (or some other person with normal color vision) would be in if he were to be in the same perceptual state that S is in. On your theory, perceptual states are all essentially dispositional ones. So if Q is to be in the same perceptual state as S, he must be disposed to do the same things that S is disposed to do in virtue of being in that state—for example, he must be disposed to match the color he sees with that of fire engines and British post boxes. But then this entails, on your theory, that what Q sees looks *red* to him, not green, as it does to S. And this just points up once again the inadequacy of your theory; for despite the fact that Q and S are disposed to make all the same discriminatory and matching responses, what looks red to Q looks green to S—a state of affairs that your theory is unable to find room for."

I shall now try to answer this objection. S's perceptual state in virtue of which something that is actually red (call it x) looks green to him may, like anything else, be characterized in a number of different ways. One of them is:

(1) a state of x's looking green to him.

On our theory, another way is:

(2) a state of his being disposed, as the result of a certain sort of causal process, and when "conditions of observation" are normal, to match the apparent color of x with that of things that are objectively red and to discriminate the apparent color of x from that of things that are objectively non-red.[5]

To imagine that Q is in this same perceptual state is to imagine that x looks green to him, or, as I shall put it, that he is in state (1). In Q's case, however, his perceptual state does not yield to a characterization of sort (2), but rather to the following:

(3) a state of his being disposed, as the result of a certain sort of causal process, and when "conditions of observation" are normal, to match the apparent color of x with that of things that are objectively green and to discriminate the apparent color of x from that of things that are objectively non-green.

Our theory of perception holds that state (1) is identical with ($=$) state (3) *only in the case of a person whose*

[5] This is, of course, merely a convenient, but strictly illegitimate, abbreviation of a correct, but unwieldy, characterization: the latter would be couched in the sorts of phrases indicated earlier.

color vision with respect to green is normal; it does not hold
that state (1) = state (3) for absolutely everyone. Similarly, the theory would hold that state (1) = state (2) only
in the case of perceivers whose color vision for green and
red is abnormal in the extraordinary way that S's is. So the
objection is wrong when it says that on our theory, if Q is
to be in the same perceptual state that S is in, he must be
in state (2).

Someone who espouses the objection might wonder
how it can be that state (1) = state (3) for Q, while state
(1) = state (2) for S. This kind of doubt stems from the
twofold conviction that state (2) $\neq$ state (3), and that state
(1) cannot be identical with two *different* states. But how
can anyone be absolutely certain that state (2) $\neq$ state (3),
since no one knows what adequate criteria are for the identity of personal states? I shall argue later that a plausible
case can be made for holding that state (2) = state (3); but
what I want to urge now is that even if we concede that
state (2) $\neq$ state (3), our theory is still on firm ground.
There is nothing illegitimate, or even odd, in maintaining
that sometimes state (1) = state (2) (in our example, this
is so in the case of S), and that sometimes state (1) = state
(3) (in our example, this is so in the case of Q), even if
state (2) $\neq$ state (3). Precisely this sort of thing occurs fre-
quently; thus, for example, it would not be surprising if
S's having a circular green after-image were identical
with his brain's being in a certain state, while Q's having
a circular green after-image was identical with his brain's
being in a quite different state. The example would be even
clearer if we imagine S to be a robot constructed of nothing
but steel, transistors, switches, wires, and so on. I don't
think there is any more to this point, really, than the bare
truism that changing circumstances can make a difference
to the characterizations, or descriptions, that truly apply
to a thing (state, process, or whatever); and this truism is
most glaringly true when we are dealing with the states
of something as fantastically complex as a human being.

Notice that our theory of shape perception is in exactly

the same boat, in this regard, as our theory of color perception. According to our theory, the perceptual state of a line's looking straight to a perceiver, Q = his state of being disposed to make what I called straight-responses, or $R(s)$ responses. However, if relevant conditions should change—e.g., if Q should become visually adapted to the sort of distorting spectacles described on p. 157f.—then many of his $R(s)$ responses would be different under what is perhaps their most basic description (see n. 28, p. 160f.). In other words, our theory holds that before he puts on the glasses, Q's perceptual state of a line's looking straight to him = a certain dispositional state, but that after he becomes visually adapted to the glasses, this same perceptual state = what it is not at all implausible to think of as a *different* dispositional state.

In discussing this example of shape perception (n. 28, p. 160f.), I said that although under one description of certain responses (viz., (W_2)), Q's post-adaptation dispositional state (answering to its looking to him as though a line is straight) is different from his corresponding normal, or pre-glasses, dispositional state, nevertheless under another description (viz., (W_1)), the two dispositional states are identical. I think the same is true in our example of color perception. As now described, state (2) $\neq$ state (3). This fact was thought to be the source of some embarrassment to our theory of color perception, although I have argued that it is no such thing. But now I want to urge that there is another description under which state (2) = state (3), namely:

(2-½) a state of his being disposed, as the result of a certain sort of causal process, and when "conditions of observation" are normal, to match the apparent color of x with that of things that would cause him to be in the same (relevant) kind of brain state that he is now in and to discriminate the apparent color of x from that of things that would cause him to be in a different (relevant) kind of brain state from that he is now in.

Because of the differences between Q (who has normal color vision) and S (who does not), state (2-½) is also describable as state (3) in the case of Q, and as state (2) in the case of S.

I said earlier that someone who propounds the objection we are now considering is motivated to do so by the two-fold conviction that state (2) $\neq$ state (3), and that state (1) cannot be identical with two *different* states. I take it that I have now undermined this motivation. I claimed that clearly acceptable criteria for state-identity are not available at present, but argued that even if state (2) indeed $\neq$ state (3), there is no reason why state (1) cannot in some cases $=$ state (2) and in other cases $=$ state (3). And finally, I urged that it is not necessary to concede, without a fight, that state (2) $\neq$ state (3), since there is at least one description under which state (2) $=$ state (3). I hope that this argument has removed whatever plausibility the objection may have had, by showing that it rests on too-superficial a conception of what it is for two people to "be in the same state."

This completes my defense of our theory against the larger objection raised earlier (p. 205f.). I answered it by presenting two mutually exclusive alternatives (namely, (a) and (b), p. 206), and arguing that whichever of them is true, our theory is not in the least damaged by the objection. Here, then, is the way I think we ought to characterize a person, R, who does not have normal color vision, when something, x, looks red to him: R sees x and (as the result, normally, of the familiar kind of causal process) R is in a perceptual state such that, if a person with normal color vision were in that state, he would be disposed to exhibit modes of discriminatory and matching behavior, such as those that I have indicated in discussing perceivers with normal color vision, with respect to x and certain other objects.

Notice that there is a very significant difference in our theory between the perceptual states that constitute our awareness of the so-called secondary qualities (e.g., color,

in the case of vision) and those that constitute our awareness of the so-called primary qualities (e.g., shape and
size). As we have just seen, perceptual states for colors are
dispositions to make certain discriminatory and matching
responses—that is, to discriminate the particular (apparent)
color now being seen from other colors and to match the
(apparent) color now being seen with other instances of it.
Our perceptual awareness of colors, then, is primarily an
intra-visual affair; that is to say, it does not seem to require
in any very essential way that one be disposed to use parts
of his body other than his eyes—for example, to move his
arms or his trunk in special ways. The (visual) perceptual
states for primary qualities such as shape, on the other
hand, definitely do require that the perceiver be disposed
to move various parts of his body in specific ways, as one
can readily see by examining the list (a)-(e) on p. 153f.
Our visual perception of primary qualities, then, if our
theory is correct, involves the conditioning of the whole
body of the perceiver in a way that our visual perception
of color does not.[6]

This aspect of our theory would seem to imply that it
ought to be more difficult to acquire the visual ability to detect the primary qualities of things than it is to acquire
the visual ability to detect their colors, since the former
ability demands that the perceiver have learned how he
must move various parts of his body when he receives a
certain kind of visual stimulation if he is to achieve certain desired results, whereas the latter ability does not demand anything as elaborate as that. There is actually
some evidence that tends to confirm this consequence of
our theory. M. von Senden, in his interesting book *Space
and Sight*,[7] discusses a great many cases of people who
were born blind and were subsequently given sight by sur-
gical operations of one kind or another. These people

[6] This point is connected with things that Jonathan Bennett says in
his illuminating article "Substance, Reality, and Primary Qualities,"
American Philosophical Quarterly, 2 (1965), 1-17.

[7] London: Methuen & Co. Ltd., 1960.

invariably learned to recognize the colors of things very quickly. In marked contrast to this, the visual recognition of shapes always required a long, sometimes painful, process of learning—and often the patient never succeeded in his attempts to perceive shapes visually.

> We cannot . . . point to a single instance in which the patient is said to have been baffled by colours when learning to see; though there are many who never succeeded in apprehending shapes.[8]

Newly sighted patients are usually able to tell almost at once (although from the evidence cited by von Senden I am not able to determine exactly how much visual experience is required for this) that objects with different shapes that are presented only visually do have different shapes—but not what specific shapes they are. Here is what happened to one patient on the fifth day of trials:

> He is shown a sphere and a cube, both of the same coloured wood and of similar cross-section. On looking at them together he realizes that the two are distinct, but does not know which is round and which cornered.[9]

It is only after weeks, or months, of training that patients can learn to recognize, by vision alone, the shapes of things. On our theory, this long period is required because the patients must learn a great many conditioned responses; they must learn indefinitely many things of the form: Given such-and-such visual stimulation, if I want to do such-and-such, I must move my body (or parts of my body) in such-and-such ways. In other words, they must learn to get into those very complicated dispositional states, such as those described in (a)-(e) on p. 153f., which, on our theory, constitute a visual perceiver's awareness of the primary qualities of things (e.g., their shape). And this is bound to take time and effort.

As far as I know, experiments using newly sighted people

[8] von Senden, *op. cit.*, p. 155.
[9] von Senden, *op. cit.*, p. 114.

have not been conducted by anyone who had any sort of behavioral theory of perception such as ours specifically in mind—that is, by anyone who might have wanted to test the consequences of that kind of theory. The available evidence, at any rate, does not tell us at all definitively whether or not the story I have just told, in the name of our theory, about what is involved in learning to see the primary qualities of things, is true. The nearest approach to helpful evidence for this purpose is presented by R. L. Gregory and J. G. Wallace in their moving account of the case of S. B.,[10] who lost effective sight in both eyes in infancy and regained it fifty years later as the result of receiving corneal grafts. It was found that the shapes he was best able to recognize visually were those for which he had tactual responses prepared, as it were, from his sightless days. For example, at their first interview with S. B., held some 48 days after his first operation, Gregory and Wallace discovered that S. B. could recognize visually any letter of the alphabet printed in upper case, but none printed in lower case. The reason for this difference:

> He had learned capital letters by touch, these being inscribed on blocks and taught at the blind school. Lower case letters were not taught.[11]

Again, when S. B. drew pictures of a motor bus, he could not draw the radiator hood, and in fact omitted it altogether from his drawings, even as late as a year after regaining his sight. The radiator, of course,

> would not have been known by touch, as the front of a bus is a position of danger to a blind man.[12]

This evidence does not conclusively prove that our theory's account of what has to be learned in order to achieve visual perception of shape is the correct one, but it

[10] R. L. Gregory and J. G. Wallace, *Recovery from Early Blindness: a Case Study* (Experimental Psychology Society Monograph No. 2, 1963).

[11] Gregory and Wallace, *op. cit.*, p. 17.

[12] *Ibid.*, p. 31.

suggests that there may well be some truth in it. Our theory, at least, is ready with a plausible explanation of why visual perception of shape is more difficult to learn than visual perception of color—an explanation, furthermore, that follows at once from the basic principles of our theory, and does not require the importation of ad hoc hypotheses. And this seems to be a great deal more than other theories of perception can boast—for example, sense-datum theories.

This concludes the first of the two tasks I set for myself in this chapter; it is time now to set to work on the second.

B. DIRECT REALISM

The second chore, it will be remembered (from p. 197f.) is that of determining what the epistemological consequences of our theory are. It is important to settle this matter if we can. I say this because it seems to me that apart from being able to accommodate, easily and naturally, all the different kinds of perceptual phenomena that there are, the two main virtues a philosophical theory of perception can possess are, first, being able to cope satisfactorily with the mind-body problem, and second, having satisfactory epistemological consequences. Our theory has the first of these two virtues, since it holds (to oversimplify a bit) that perceiving something consists, ultimately, in being disposed, as the result of a certain kind of causal process, to behave in certain ways; and a purely physical being could evidently have dispositions of that sort. If our theory is accepted, then, the mind-body problem simply does not arise, anyway as far as sense perception is concerned, since our theory does not require the introduction of non-physical states or entities into our happy physicalistic world-view. But this first virtue would count for little if our theory lacked the second—if, for example, it led to a total scepticism about the existence and nature of "the external world," as causal theories like ours are sometimes thought to do. It behooves us, then, to enquire a bit into this matter, so that we may be in a better position to judge the merits of our theory.

I shall assume in the following discussion that what is called *direct realism* is the most desirable sort of perceptual theory from an epistemological point of view. But what is direct realism, exactly? The term is a philosophical one, and gets its sense, I strongly suspect, only by contrast to what it rules out. That is to say, I think there is a use for the term 'direct realism' only after another philosophical theory of perception has already arisen—I mean representational realism. Once this theory is in the air, there has to be logical room for a theory whose salient feature is that it denies what representational realism asserts; and the term 'direct realism' is coined to designate this position. Direct realism denies, then, that in perceiving something, x, one is always aware of something y that is wholly distinct from x, and is aware of it, furthermore, in a more basic or immediate way than one is aware of x itself. The y, of course, is a sense-datum in many modern versions of representational realism, and the more fundamental mode of awareness that we allegedly have of it is often called sensing.

The upshot of our lengthy attack on sense-datum theories of perception in Chapter I was that there are no a priori forces that compel one to embrace any form of sense-datum theory, including representational realism, and hence no such forces that prevent one from espousing direct realism. For example, I dealt there with the traditional argument from the physiology (or the causation) of sense perception, which purports to show that anyone who admits (as everyone must) that perceptual states are caused in the way science tells us they are must accept some form of sense-datum theory. I maintained, against that argument, that a direct realist could consistently admit all the facts concerning the causation of sense perception; the fact that our perceptual states are caused does not rule out the possibility that in sense perception we are directly confronted with perfectly objective things, events, processes, states of affairs, or whatever.

At this point, it should be obvious that our theory of perception, in particular, is entirely capable of being a version of direct realism. It is also true, to be sure, that our theory is capable of being a version of *representational* realism, since we can find room for the representational realist's fundamental distinction within our theory. But the point to stress is that we are not forced by any a priori considerations to allow his distinction in all cases of perception. We are perfectly free to insist that in ordinary cases of sense perception, there are no sense-data or other intermediaries of which we are aware in some basic sense, and that we are just simply aware of whatever it is we see (hear, feel, and so on). We can claim that in normal sense perception, the perceptual states of our theory—viz., the causal-reception of perceptual beliefs, inclinations to believe, and suppressed inclinations to believe—all have as their object (what they are about) the thing, property, event, state of affairs, or whatever, that is being perceived —so that that thing, property, event, or state of affairs is the only "object of awareness."

Our theory of perception, therefore, is clearly construable as being a direct realist theory. And, since direct realism has manifest epistemological, as well as metaphysical, advantages over representational realism, we have good reason to exercise our option to so construe our theory. Moreover, as we saw in Chapter I, there are no good reasons against exercising the direct realist option. In these circumstances, the only reasonable thing for us to do, as advocates of our special theory of perception, is to boldly declare it a direct realist theory.

But the mere declaration that we are direct realists does not, of course, get us quite out of the epistemological woods, for sceptical doubts still abound: are perceivers in fact usually, or ever, "directly aware" of real physical objects, events, states of affairs, and the like? And if they are, can they know that they are? Our theory of perception is certainly open to such sceptical doubts. For example, in my attack on the sense-datum theorist's argument from the short causal chain, I conceded that a person can be put into the same inner state (I mean a state of awareness) by the action of light rays being reflected from external objects and by the direct electrical stimulation of his optic nerves or brain. I said that if his state is caused in the former way, then a direct realist is entitled to hold that the person is (directly) aware of the relevant objective state of affairs, or to see something; but that if his state is caused in the latter way, then even a direct realist will have to concede that the person is suffering a hallucination, or that he has a sense-datum, or something of the sort. The doubt that faces us is this: even if one grants to us direct realists that when a person's "state of perceptual awareness" has the right kind of cause, it is then a *direct* awareness of some real object, event, or whatever, still how can anyone ever be certain that what seems to him to be his (genuine) perceptual states are in fact caused in the right way and not in the wrong way? When he thinks he is "directly aware" of a real object, event, or whatever, how can he be sure that he is not rather lying on a laboratory table where an experimenter (or worse) is stimulating his brain with electrodes?

But although our direct realist theory is indeed open to such doubts, so of course is every other philosophical theory of perception as well. It is therefore not at all incumbent upon me, *qua defender of our special theory of perception*, to resolve these doubts, for that is a perfectly general problem in theory of knowledge. If I were forced to say something on the subject, however, I would adopt what I take to be the traditional line, as follows.

I do not see how it can be denied that the laboratory hypothesis is a logically possible one. It is also logically possible that a wicked demon, or that God, is stimulating all of our brains so as to make us think, falsely, that we are perceiving a real physical world, and that he (or He) has always done this, throughout the whole history of the human race. Each of these logically possible hypotheses can be elaborated in different ways so that either (a) there are describable circumstances which would count as the victims' discovering that the hypothesis is true, or (b) there are no such describable circumstances. We may excuse ourselves at once from any consideration of hypotheses of type (b)—if, indeed, they can be called hypotheses at all. For even if we are not quite sure what pejorative label befits them (empirically meaningless, vacuous, or whatever), we nevertheless *know* that they are illegitimate. Or, if this is too strong, at least each of us may say of himself: "If I am the person, or one of the persons, who, according to the hypothesis, is being deceived, then if the hypothesis is of type (b), it is illegitimate *for me*; I cannot be expected to take any account of it whatsoever." And this is quite strong enough, since it is only this case that is of concern to us—the case, namely, where the person raising the doubts about his own perceptual states is himself the victim, or one of the victims, of the hypothesized deception.

If, on the other hand, the hypotheses are of type (a), then our simple reply is that we have no reason to think them true and every reason to think them false. And surely we are right in this. At the present moment, for example, I have no reason to think that, despite all appearances—of myself sitting at the typewriter, the sun shining through my study window, the old familiar objects surrounding me, and so on—I am really lying inert in a laboratory with electrodes stimulating my brain. When I think of the staggering complexity of the stimuli that those electrodes would have to be pouring into my brain, I find the hypothesis utterly incredible. The hypothesis that my present perceptual states are being caused by the objects that I think I am perceiving, on the other hand, is the most plausible, the simplest—in fact, the best in every way. If I cannot be sure of *its* truth, I cannot be sure of anything. I am entirely warranted, then, in accepting it, and rejecting the other logical possibilities: to do anything else would be, to say the least, irrational.

The foregoing standard defense against doubts is one that any philosopher, no matter what his theory of perception is, may invoke. If it is a sound defense, then it entitles us, as *direct realists*, to hold that in most of their waking lives, people are (directly) aware of the objects, events, states of affairs, and so on, that they seem to be seeing (feeling, hearing, etc.).

C. PRIMARY AND SECONDARY QUALITIES

I want next to consider the following objection posed by sense-datum theorists against all direct realisms, and hence against our theory: if our sense organs and nervous systems were differently constructed, things would doubtless not look (sound, feel, etc.) the same to us. This is supposed to persuade us that we do not perceive the real properties of things, on the ground that the properties things appear to us to have are due in large part to the way our sensory apparatus happens to be constructed.[13]

The direct realist, however, need not be dismayed by the objection. It is open to him to reply that different kinds of sense organs and nervous systems reveal different ranges of qualities, but that all the qualities are equally real or objective. We human beings happen to have eyes, connected to optic nerves and brains; hence the colors and shapes of things are revealed to us by our sense of sight. If there were creatures with antennae sensitive to radio waves connected by wires to a weird brain, no doubt everything would appear radically different to them; but this consideration would not force one to say that human beings are aware merely of visual sense-data and that the antenna-ed creatures would be aware merely of radio sense-data. We could all be aware—directly, too—of objects in the external world; it's just that we human beings would detect one set of (real) qualities with our receiving apparatus, and the antenna-ed creatures would detect a different set with theirs.

This line of defense, I say, is open to us as direct realists; but I think we ought to spurn it, since it obscures an im-

---

[13] I alluded to this point at the beginning of my discussion of the sense-datum theorist's argument from the physiology (or causation) of sense perception (cf. p. 44), but did not pursue it.

portant difference between the ontological status of primary
and secondary qualities. The difference I mean is not happily expressed by saying that primary qualities (e.g., shape
and size) are in things, while secondary qualities (e.g.,
color) are not in things.[14] It is not clear to me that a claim
such as "Redness is not in blood, fire engines, and British
post boxes" can be asserting anything other than that blood,
fire engines, and British post boxes are not red—and this
strikes me as manifestly false. However, the issues involved
here are complex, and I do not wish to get embroiled in
them. Nor do I need to, for I think I can characterize the
distinction I want to draw between the "ontological sta-
tuses" of primary and secondary qualities in a different way
that will skirt them.

I want to try to show that the primary qualities of things
(I shall use shape as my example) are more fundamental
to them than their secondary qualities (I shall use color as
my example) in the following sense: the way peoples' perceptual apparatus happens to be constructed determines
to a much greater degree what colors things are said to be
than it does what shapes things are said to be. Colors are
in fact largely dependent on the nature of our natural visual equipment, while shapes are not at all dependent on
the nature of our natural perceptual equipment.[15]

First, let us consider colors. It is undeniable that a relatively small difference between the visual systems of two
people is enough, by itself, to make things look to have
certain colors to one and to have radically different colors
to the other. We have living proof of this in every color-
blind person; for relatively minor deviations of his visual
apparatus from the normal condition are enough to make
some things look to have radically different colors to him
from those they appear to have to people with perfect
color vision. On our theory of color perception this means

[14] See J. W. Roxbee Cox, "Are perceptible qualities *'in'* things?"
Analysis, 23 (1962-63), 97-103.

[15] In the discussion that follows, I am heavily indebted to Jonathan
Bennett's article "Substance, Reality, and Primary Qualities," *op. cit.*

that the color-blind man, in dealing with colors, will sometimes be disposed to make different matching and discriminatory responses from those that people with normal color vision are disposed to make. This will occasionally involve him in familiar kinds of trouble and confusion; but on the whole he gets along well enough in most of life's activities. (Think of how well we get on when wearing colored glasses). One can easily imagine that color-blindness might become the normal human condition, in which case we would make certain adjustments and changes—for example, some paintings that now hang in museums would probably be moved to the storage room or thrown out altogether, criteria for Grade A fruit of certain kinds might have to be changed—but our lives would go on pretty much as they do now. And the colors that things would then be said to be would almost certainly be different from what they are now said to be—ripe apples, for example, might be called grey, and ripe lemons green.

The foregoing remarks should help to give content to my claim that colors are dependent on the way our natural visual systems happen to be constructed. If these systems should be different in certain not very radical ways—for example, if we should all be what is now called color-blind— then the colors that things would be said to possess (or to be) would be different. This indicates that the colors things are said to *be* is very closely tied to the colors they *look* to be to a certain favored group—those with normal color vision. The reason for this is to be found, I think, in a tenet of our theory, mentioned earlier (p. 212f.), namely, that the perception of color is basically an intra-visual affair. Since that kind of perception is, in its essential nature, hermetically sealed, as it were, from other aspects of a perceiver's behavior—since it does not, for example, have any very essential connections with how the perceiver moves his body, but is a matter merely of the discriminatory and matching responses, with respect to color, that he is disposed to make—we are satisfied to let those kinds of responses on the part of a favored group count as the main criterion of what colors things are said actually to have. It is this relative isolation of color perception that explains, too, why people with deficiencies of color vision are able to get along generally as well as they do; it is only certain of their (color) discriminatory and matching responses that are deviant, and these do not, in essence, involve any deviance in the numberless other kinds of behavior that they regularly engage in.

The visual perception of shape is quite another matter, however. There is not the slightest temptation to allow the shapes that things look to have to some favored group (those with normal shape vision, perhaps?) to count as the main criterion of the shapes those things actually do have. And this is partially explained by that other tenet of our theory whereby visual perception of shape is precisely not hermetically sealed, in its essence, from a great many different kinds of bodily movements. Suppose that some small change were to be made permanently in all our visual systems that resulted in an alteration in our visual perception of shape—things that used to look circular, let us say, now look square, and vice versa. If this were to happen, we most certainly would not say that the things that look square (circular) to all of us, or to some favored group of us, now *are* square (circular); and it would definitely not be the case that after a few minor changes and adjustments, our lives would go on much as before.

Consider the sort of thing that could be expected to happen after this change in our eyes, or brain, or whatever, had been effected. A typical perceiver, Q, looks at a figure drawn on a blackboard; before the change it would have looked square to him, but now it looks circular. Because it looks circular, he thinks (for he is, as we may imagine, unaware of what has happened to him) that if he puts one leg of a pair of compasses on the center of the figure and the other somewhere on the figure itself, and rotates the instrument, the second leg will trace around the line that is drawn on the blackboard. But he finds, of course, that this does not happen; at four places spaced at equal intervals, the line he draws with the compasses diverges from the figure already drawn on the blackboard. The line he draws, to his amazement, looks like a perfect square to him, despite the fact that he did not feel the pair of compasses to be opening and closing as he rotated it. Or suppose he tries to trace around the figure with his forefinger; although his impulse is to describe a continuously curving line (since the thing looks circular to him), he finds that at four places he has to make a sharp change in direction in order to adhere to the line. And so on and on. All of his actions directed toward the figure on the blackboard —and toward every other figure as well, that is, toward almost everything, since almost everything has a shape— are thrown into confusion.

How would we have to fix up this imaginary situation in order to make shape have the same sort of status as color, relative to the nature of peoples' perceptual systems? Well, one important difference between color and shape is that color is (at least normally) apprehended by sight alone, whereas shape is apprehended both by sight and what can, I suppose, be called a combination of touch and the kinaesthetic sense. So instead of imagining a permanent change being made in just our visual systems, we must imagine that suitable permanent changes are made in all three senses—so that, for example, things that used to look and feel circular (square) now look and feel square (circular). Would such changes induce us to say that things which looked and felt square (circular) to some favored group really are square (circular)? And would most of our behavior flow smoothly on, much as before?

By no means. First of all, it is necessary to see how fantastically complicated the above-mentioned changes would have to be. For example, suppose that Q is again faced with a figure that looks circular to him (whereas before all the changes to his perceptual systems, it would have looked square to him), and that he tries again to trace around the figure with a pair of compasses. If we are to suppose that the imagined changes to his tactual/kinaesthetic system will result in his succeeding in this effort, then we ought to notice how very complicated and subtle those changes would have to be. If the second leg of the compass is to trace the figure drawn on the blackboard, then the pair of compasses must, during the entire operation, be constantly opening and closing. Presumably it must be Q himself who causes this to happen. So we have to imagine (a) that Q is applying some very deft finger-work to those compasses, and (b) that he is totally unaware, kinaesthetically, of the fact that he is doing it; otherwise the compasses would evidently *feel* as though they were opening and closing, and hence it would not feel to Q as though the figure were circular, contrary to our present hypothesis.[16] This is an extremely delicate and subtle change indeed in Q's kinaesthetic nature; for it is one that keeps him from feeling just this one very special kind of finger movement, not all his finger movements—for we are not imagining that Q's fingers have gone completely numb on him.

This change in our kinaesthetic make-up is of course just one of a staggeringly large number that would have to be effected if things that now look and feel circular (square) to us are to look and feel square (circular) to us. Indeed, so many highly specific—or, as we might say, ad hoc— changes would have to be made that there is even serious doubt that any coherent description or list of them could possibly be given. But let us ignore this difficulty, and grant that the suggestion is an intelligible one. Would this be enough to make us treat shapes the way we treat colors? No, there would still be formidable reasons against taking that course. Consider, for example, Q with his pair of compasses. Suppose that there is a cross bar attached to one of the legs, and that the bar is marked off into numbered divisions, much like an ordinary straight ruler. As he swings

---

[16] To be sure, we might imagine that he is aware of exerting that complex, ever-changing pattern of pressures on the legs of the compasses, and that he looks upon this as being necessary in order to prevent it from opening and closing—but then it is difficult to know where he might think the force he would be counteracting comes from.

the instrument, and the legs of the compasses open and close, the number on the bar that appears by the second leg (i.e., the one to which the bar is not attached), of course keeps constantly changing. Let us imagine that Q sees the pair of compasses as well as the figure they are describing on the blackboard.

Our grasp of this imagined situation now begins to weaken, and we shall find quite soon that we lose our grip on it altogether. For are we to imagine that Q sees the legs of the compasses opening and closing or not? If he does, then no sense can be made of the idea (which is already contained in our picture of the situation) that the figure described by the moving leg looks *circular* to him. So it must not look to Q as though the legs of the compasses are opening and closing as he rotates the instrument. But it is exceedingly difficult to fit this into our picture in any coherent way. For how are we to conceive of the change that his visual system would have to undergo in order that just this highly determinate physical fact should escape his visual notice? And even if that problem should be solved, what about those different numbers on the cross bar that appear by the second leg of the compasses? Is Q able to see them or not? If we imagine that he is not able, we have to introduce yet another extraordinary—and obviously completely ad hoc—change into Q's visual system. And if we imagine that he is able to see them, what are we to suppose that he is to make of them? He will have to invent some quite ingenious hypothesis to account for the fact that the numbers keep changing, despite the fact (as he falsely thinks it to be) that the legs of the compasses are stationary with respect to each other.

We have discussed but one very trivial case (that of Q and the pair of compasses), and we have seen that the complications that would have to be introduced into our picture of it, if shape were to be accorded the same sort of "ontological status" that is accorded to color, are staggering, even when we grant (what seems highly dubious) that the picture, when so complicated, is a coherent one at all. And when we think of the numberless other kinds of cases that would also have to be dealt with if the thought experiment were to be successfully carried through, we realize at once that the complications and difficulties would multiply so quickly that all hope would very soon be lost of our being able to cope with them.

I conclude from this that if all human beings' perceptual systems were to be changed so as to alter our perception of shape, we would not, and could not, maintain that things that then looked and felt square (circular, and so on) to us really were square (circular, and so on). On the contrary, there would be an enormous number of "punishing" experiences whenever we tried to move our bodies or to manipulate objects; and the result would be that we would eventually adapt to the new conditions—thanks to perceptual conditioning—so that in time things would look and feel to have the shapes they really do have. Or, if for some reason we could not ever adapt to the new conditions in this most favorable of ways, at least we would maintain that the actual shapes of things were different from the shapes they looked and felt to have; for the hypothesis that there was some deficiency in our perception of shape would be incalculably simpler than the hypothesis that our perception of shape was faultless (i.e., that the shape a thing looked and felt to have was the one it really had)—for as we have seen, this latter hypothesis would require the support, in order for it to be consistently maintained, of countless additional and ad hoc hypotheses.

Color is altogether different in this respect from shape. If a change should be made in all human beings' visual systems so that things now looked to have different colors from the ones they had before the change, there would be no point in persisting in the view that our color vision was now defective. No doubt that is what we would all think at first; but soon it would become evident that the change was to be permanent, and eventually the memory of the colors that things used to have (before the change) would fade out from the minds of humans—and then it would be idle to keep on with that thought. It would be idle because there would be no "punishing" experiences as we went about our daily business to warn us that there was a disparity between the apparent colors of things and their real colors. There would doubtless be a few mildly punishing experiences immediately after the change was effected, owing to the persistence of memory, but even these would tend to disappear gradually. This paucity, and eventual total lack, of punishing experiences means that there would be no motive, or certainly no very compelling motive, to adapt to the changed conditions—no motive, that is, to learn to respond differently to color stimuli so that things will again look to have the colors they really do have. Indeed, in these circumstances the very notion of adapting, in this sense, to the change begins to look like an illegitimate one, if the main line of reasoning we have been pursuing is sound. It is illegitimate because it presupposes a distinction between the colors things really do have and the colors they look to have to all of mankind, or at least to all of mankind having what is called normal color vision—and if what we have been saying is correct, then there simply is no such distinction.

In these past few pages I have been trying to establish an important difference between the "ontological status" of primary qualities (exemplified by shape) and that of secondary qualities (exemplified by color). The primary qualities that a thing has, I have argued, are not at all dependent on the structure of our human perceptual apparatus, while its secondary qualities definitely are so dependent. This means, of course, that the primary qualities of things are fundamental to their intrinsic natures in a way that their secondary qualities are not. The difference can be expressed, perhaps somewhat too metaphorically, as follows: the primary qualities that an object appears, perceptually, to have (that is, looks to have, feels to have, etc.) accurately reveal the nature of the object itself, while the secondary qualities it appears, perceptually, to have, do not, for they are determined just as much by the nature of the perceiver as they are by the nature of the object itself.

In this book, I have tried to expound and defend a theory of perception: it is a behavioral theory, a direct realist theory, and a causal theory. It seems to me to have all the virtues that one looks for in a philosophical theory of perception. First, it provides a very general conceptual framework within which various different perceptual phenomena, including some esoteric ones discovered only in the laboratories of experimental psychologists, can be accommodated easily and naturally. Second, in virtue of being a behavioral theory, no mind-body problem exists for it. And third, in virtue of being a direct realist theory, it allows us to escape the radical kind of scepticism that certain other theories—notably sense-datum theories—saddle us with. If my reasoning in the last few pages of this chapter was correct, one could say that any direct realist theory ought to be a restricted one—a direct realism of primary qualities, not a direct realism of secondary qualities, as we might put it, perhaps not altogether happily. A good way *not* to put this difference, certainly, is to say that primary qualities exist "out there" in the physical world, while secondary qualities exist "in the mind" (i.e., in another "place"); for then one will fall victim to the following spurious line:

> . . . If you will trust your senses, is it not plain all sensible qualities coexist, or to them appear as being in the same place? Do they ever represent a motion or figure as being divested of all other visible and tangible qualities?[17]

And then the perfectly reasonable position we have arrived at will look incoherent. But however the matter may best be expressed, our theory is easily construed as being a di-

[17] Berkeley, *Three Dialogues between Hylas and Philonous*, First Dialogue.

rect realism of the restricted sort; indeed, as we saw, the difference between the kinds of behavior that on our theory are relevant to the perception of primary qualities (such as shape), on the one hand, and those that are relevant to the perception of secondary qualities (such as color), on the other, helps to make intelligible the very difference between primary and secondary qualities that calls for the restricted form of direct realism. In conclusion, I might be tempted to say that the fact that our theory is a causal one is another of its virtues—but I do not know what a theory that is not a causal one would be.

A Short Bibliography

Some important philosophical books on perception

D. M. Armstrong. *Perception and the Physical World* (London: Routledge & Kegan Paul; New York: The Humanities Press, 1961), 196 pp.

————. *A Materialist Theory of the Mind* (London: Routledge & Kegan Paul; New York: The Humanities Press, 1968), 372 pp.

J. L. Austin. *Sense and Sensibilia* (Oxford: at the Clarendon Press, 1962), 144 pp.

A. J. Ayer. *The Foundations of Empirical Knowledge* (London: Macmillan & Co. Ltd., 1953), 276 pp.

R. M. Chisholm. *Perceiving: A Philosophical Study* (Ithaca, New York: Cornell University Press, 1957), 203 pp.

R. J. Hirst. *The Problems of Perception* (London: George Allen & Unwin, Ltd., 1959), 330 pp.

H. H. Price. *Perception* (London: Methuen & Co. Ltd., 1932), 332 pp.

Anthologies of important philosophical articles

R. J. Hirst (ed.). *Perception and the External World* (New York: The Macmillan Company; London: Collier-Macmillan Limited, 1965), 310 pp.

R. J. Swartz (ed.). *Perceiving, Sensing, and Knowing* (Garden City, New York: Doubleday & Company, Inc., Anchor Books, 1965), 538 pp.

Books on psychology of perception

W. Epstein. *Varieties of Perceptual Learning* (New York: McGraw-Hill Book Company, 1967), 323 pp.

R. L. Gregory and J. G. Wallace. *Recovery from Early Blindness: A Case Study* (Experimental Psychology Society Monograph No. 2, 1963), 46 pp.

J. E. Hochberg. *Perception* (Englewood Cliffs, New Jersey: Prentice-Hall, Inc., 1964), 118 pp.

I. Rock. *The Nature of Perceptual Adaptation* (New York, London: Basic Books, Inc., Publishers, 1966), 289 pp.

M. von Senden. *Space and Sight* (London: Methuen & Co. Ltd., 1960), 348 pp.

C. M. Solley and G. Murphy. *Development of the Perceptual World* (New York: Basic Books, Inc., 1960), 353 pp.

J. G. Taylor. *The Behavioral Basis of Perception* (New Haven and London: Yale University Press, 1962), 379 pp.

Anthologies of important psychology papers

D. C. Beardslee and M. Wertheimer (eds.). *Readings in Perception* (Princeton, New Jersey: D. Van Nostrand Company, Inc., 1958), 751 pp.

H. W. Leibowitz (ed.), *Visual Perception* (New York: The Macmillan Company; London: Collier-Macmillan Limited, 1965), 177 pp.

P. Tibbetts (ed.), *Perception* (Chicago: Quadrangle Books, 1969), 406 pp.

M. D. Vernon (ed.), *Experiments in Visual Perception* (Penguin Books, 1966), 443 pp.

S. Wapner and H. Werner (eds.), *The Body Percept* (New York: Random House, 1965), 112 pp.

NOTE

There is a useful review of recent philosophical work on perception and an excellent bibliography in P. K. Machamer's "Recent Work on Perception," *American Philosophical Quarterly,* 7 (1970), 1-22.

Index of Proper Names

Subject Index

Agnosia, visual, 186
Ames room, 149
Analysis, 113n, 124
Awareness, direct, 21-23, 45f; direct vs. indirect, 10, 14

belief, and perception, 67-70, causal-reception of, 73f; conscious vs. nonconscious, 70f; nature of, 66, 71; perceptual, 70, 90f
    inclination to have, 92; *organic unity among*, 103; *richness of*, 88; *suppressed inclination to have*, 93; *thin*, 110-12
'belief about,' stringent vs. liberal conception of, 79-81
brain, computer model of, 98f

causation of sense-perception, argument from, 43-59
color, 228f
color constancy, 204f
color, perception of, 121-23, 197-216
    and discriminatory behavior, 199-201; *and language*, 175-80, 184f; and matching behavior, 201f
color *quale*, 206-208
conditioning, perceptual, first principle of, 141; second principle of, 144

differential certainty, argument from, 20-28
direct realism, 4, 12, 18f, 37f, 40, 42, 48, 54-58, 62, 216-21
double vision, 31f, 41f

external world, scepticism about, 219f

Gibson effect, 165n, 166

hallucinations, 83; argument from, 13-20; central cases of, 15
house/white dot example, 25-27
hunter/pheasant example, 78-81

illusion, 28-42; bent stick, 84; moon, 69f
incorrigibility, 21-23
inference, conscious, 96; unconscious, 97-99

light rays, 123
like causes/like effects, principle of, 55-57
looking, 85-112
looks, First Cases of, 86-91, 94-96; Middle Cases of, 91f, 94-96; Last Cases of, 92f, 94-96
'looks,' phenomenal sense of, 86

perception, "efference readiness" theory of, 168f; inference in, 96-112; kinaesthetic, 193-95; and language, 170-86; and motion, 152-70;
    theory of, 4, 7f, 59-63, 230f *criteria for the goodness of*, 60f; *philosophical vs. psychological*, 168; *relevance of empirical facts to*, 132f, 150-52, 159-62, 163f, 167-70, 191-93;
    and valuation, 132-52
perceptual relativity, argument from, 28-42
phenomenalism, 27, 30, 34, 63

DATE DUE
